T0301566

The Political Economy of Sustainable Development

For
Leonie

The Political Economy of Sustainable Development

Policy Instruments and Market Mechanisms

Timothy Cadman

Institute for Ethics, Governance and Law, Griffith University, Australia

Lauren Eastwood

Plattsburgh State University of New York, USA

Federico López-Casero Michaelis

Institute for Global Environmental Strategies (IGES), Japan

Tek Narayan Maraseni

University of Southern Queensland, Australia

Jamie Pittock

Australian National University, Australia

Tapan Sarker

Griffith Business School and Griffith Asia Institute, Australia

Edward Elgar
PUBLISHING

Cheltenham, UK • Northampton, MA, USA

Published by
Edward Elgar Publishing Limited
The Lypiatts
15 Lansdown Road
Cheltenham
Glos GL50 2JA
UK

Edward Elgar Publishing, Inc.
William Pratt House
9 Dewey Court
Northampton
Massachusetts 01060
USA

A catalogue record for this book is available from the British Library

Library of Congress Control Number: 2015945463

This book is available electronically in the **Elgar**online
Social and Political Science subject collection
DOI 10.4337/9781783474844

ISBN 978 1 78347 483 7 (cased)
ISBN 978 1 78347 484 4 (eBook)

Typeset by Columns Design XML Ltd, Reading
Printed and bound in Great Britain by TJ International Ltd, Padstow

Contents

Authors

Timothy Cadman BA (Hons) MA (Cantab) PhD (Tasmania) is a Research Fellow in the Institute for Ethics, Governance and Law at Griffith University, Queensland, Australia. He is also a Research Fellow in the international Earth Systems Governance Project and an Adjunct Lecturer and Member of the Australian Centre for Sustainable Business and Development at the University of Southern Queensland. He specialises in the governance of sustainable development, climate change, natural resource management including forestry, and responsible investment.

Lauren Eastwood BA (Rollins College) MA, PhD (Syracuse) is an Associate Professor at the State University of New York College, Plattsburgh. Her primary areas of research involve civil society engagement in policy-making processes related to environmental issues, including the United Nations Framework Convention on Climate Change and the Convention on Biological Diversity. She has also been conducting research on civic engagement in, and resistance to, policies related to natural gas extraction and infrastructure. She was a Social Science Research Council Abe Fellow from 2009–2011.

Federico López-Casero Michaelis MA (Augsburg) PhD (Tokyo) is the Team Manager of the Biodiversity and Ecosystem Services Task at the Institute for Global Environmental Strategies, Hayama, Japan. He conducts strategic research on environmental policies for sustainable development in the Asia-Pacific Region with a focus on natural resource management and ecosystem services. He specialises in socio-ecological production landscapes, governance in the forest sector, biodiversity offsets, the verified legal and sustainable timber trade, and climate change mitigation and adaptation.

Tek Narayan Maraseni BSc (Tribhuwan) MSc (Asian Institute of Technology, Thailand) PhD (University of Southern Queensland) has over 20 years' work experience in the areas of climate change adaptation, mitigation, and greenhouse gas emissions accounting/modelling research in different countries including Nepal, Thailand and Australia and China. He has produced over 100 publications, including two books, in the last ten years. His research work has been recognised through several national and international awards, grants and fellowships.

Jamie Pittock BSc (Hons) (Monash) PhD (ANU) is an Associate Professor in the Fenner School of Environment and Society at The Australian National University, Canberra, Australia. He is also Director of International Programs for the UNESCO Chair in Water Economics and Transboundary Water Governance. He specialises in research on governance of the conflicts and positive synergies among the institutions for biodiversity, climate change, energy, food and water.

Tapan Sarker BSc (Hons) MA (Keio) PhD (ANU) is Discipline Leader of Sustainable Enterprise at Griffith University Business School. From 2011 to 2013, he was a Visiting Professor in International Management at the World Bank Program at Keio University in Japan. He is currently a Visiting Professor at Rajalakshmi School of Business, Chennai, India. Dr Sarker's main research interests include business strategy for sustainability, international political economy of resources, corporate social responsibility and governance, business ethics, and public sector management.

Abbreviations

ABARES	Australian Bureau of Agricultural and Resource Economics and Sciences
ABC	Australian Broadcasting Corporation
ABS	access and benefit sharing
ACT	Australian Capital Territory
APEC	Asia Pacific Economic Cooperation
APP	Asia Pulp and Paper
AR	Assessment Report
ASI	Accreditation Services International
BCH	Biosafety Clearinghouse
BCSD	Business Council for Sustainable Development
BINGO	business and industry non-governmental organisation
BOM	Biodiversity Offset Mechanism
BRIC	Brazil, Russia, India, China
C&I	criteria and indicators
CB	certification bodies
CBD	Convention on Biological Diversity
CBDR	common but differentiated responsibilities
CCD	Convention to Combat Desertification
CDM	Clean Development Mechanism
CDM EB	CDM executive board
CDP	Carbon Disclosure Project
CER	Certified Emissions Reduction
CF	Carbon Fund
C&I	criteria and indicators
CI	Conservation International
COP	Conference of Parties
CRS	Creditor Reporting System
CSA	Canadian Standard Association
CSO	civil society organisation
DBSA	Development Bank of Southern Africa
DDS	due diligence system
DFI	Development Finance Institution
DNA	Designated National Authority

DP	Delivery Partner
EIA	environmental impact assessment
EIT	economy in transition
EMS	environmental management system
ENGO	environmental non-governmental organisation
EPI	environmental policy integration
ES	ecosystem services
ETS	emissions trading scheme
EU	European Union
EUTR	EU Timber Regulation
FAO	Food and Agriculture Organisation
FAS	focal area set-asides
FCPF	Forest Carbon Partnership Facility
FERN	Forests and the European Union Resource Network
FFCS	Finnish Forest Certification System
FIP	Forest Investment Program
FLEG	Forest Law, Enforcement and Governance
FLEGT	Forest Law Enforcement, Governance and Trade
FNE	France Nature Environnement
FPIC	free, prior and informed consent
FPP	Forest Peoples Programme
FSC	Forest Stewardship Council
FTA	free trade agreement
GCF	Green Climate Fund
GDP	gross domestic product
GEF	Global Environment Facility
GEG	global environmental governance
GHG	greenhouse gas
GHI	gross happiness index
GSP	Global Sustainability Panel
HCV	high conservation value
IA-CEPA	Indonesia-Australia Comprehensive Economic Partnership Agreement
IET	International Emissions Trading
IFL	intact forest landscape
IGES	Institute for Global Environmental Strategies
IGI	International Generic Indicator
IGO	intergovernmental organisation
IIED	International Institute for Environment and Development
INDC	Intended Nationally Determined Contribution
INGO	international non-governmental organisation
IP	intellectual property

IPBES	Intergovernmental Platform on Biodiversity and Ecosystem Services
IPCC	Intergovernmental Panel on Climate Change
IPF	Intergovernmental Panel on Forests
IPO	Indigenous peoples' organisation
ISO	International Organization for Standardization
ITL	International Transaction Log
ITTA	International Tropical Forest Timber Agreement
ITTO	International Tropical Timber Organisation
IUCN	International Union for Conservation of Nature
JI	Joint Implementation
JUSCANZ	Japan, US, Canada, Australia, New Zealand
KP	Kyoto Protocol
LDCF	Least Developed Countries Fund
LDM	loss and damage mechanism
LEED	Leadership in Energy and Environmental Design
LMO	living modified organism
LULUCF	Land use, Land-use Change and Forestry
MAP	Modular Approach Programme
MDG	Millennium Development Goals
MEA	multilateral environmental agreement
MOP	Meeting of Parties
MRV	monitoring, reporting and verification
MW	megawatts
NAMA	Nationally Appropriate Mitigation Action
NAPA	national adaptation programmes of action
NGO	non-governmental organisations
NLB	non-legally binding instrument
NORAD	Norwegian Agency for Development
NPBV	net present biodiversity value
NPD	National Programme Document
OECD	Organisation for Economic Co-operation and Development
OP	offset production
OPEC	Organisation of the Petroleum Exporting Countries
P&C	principles and criteria
PC&I	principles, criteria and indicators
PCF	Prototype Carbon Fund
PEFC	Programme for the Endorsement of Forest Certification
PEFCC	PEFC Council
PES	Payments for Ecosystem Services
PNG	Papua New Guinea
PNGFIA	Papua New Guinea Forest Industry Association

Ramsar	Ramsar Convention on Wetlands of International Importance
REDD	reducing emissions from deforestation and forest degradation
REDD+	Reducing emissions from deforestation and forest degradation and the role of conservation, sustainable management of forests and enhancement of forest carbon stocks in developing countries (Post COP 15)
RF	Readiness Fund
RFBPS	Royal Forest and Bird Protection Society
RINGO	research and independent non-governmental organisation
R-PP	Readiness Preparation Proposal
SAGE	Strategic Advisory Group on the Environment
SBSTTA	Subsidiary Body on Scientific, Technical, and Technological Advice
SCCF	Special Climate Change Fund
SD	sustainable development
SDG	Sustainable Development Goals
SFI	Sustainable Forestry Initiative
SFM	sustainable forest management
SGS	Société Générale de Surveillance
SMF	sustainable management of forests
SUNAT	Peruvian National Customs Superintendency
TEEB	The Economics of Ecosystems and Biodiversity
TEK	traditional ecological knowledge
TFAP	Tropical Forest Action Plan
TLAS	Timber Legality Assurance Scheme
UNCED	United Nations Conference on Environment and Development
UNDP	United Nations Development Programme
UNEP	United Nations Environment Programme
UNFCCC	United Nations Framework Convention on Climate Change
UNFF	United Nations Forum on Forests
UNODC	United Nations Office on Drug and Crime
US	United States
USGBC	United States Green Building Council
VCO	Voluntary Carbon Offset
VLC	verification of legal compliance
VLO	verification of legal origin
VPA	Voluntary Partnership Agreement
WBCSD	World Business Council for Sustainable Development
WCD	World Commission on Dams

WCO   World Customs Organisation
WG 8(j)   Working Group on Article 8(j)
WGPA   Ad Hoc Open-ended Working Group on Protected Areas
WRM   World Rainforest Movement
WSSD   World Summit on Sustainable Development
WTO   World Trade Organization
WWF   World Wildlife Fund
YOUNGO   youth non-governmental organisation

Preface

There are defining moments in our lives when our understanding of 'the way things are' changes forever. I grew up in a small English village, and in many ways it was an idyllic place to live. Our house was a short walk from the school, the school a short walk from the church, and the church a short walk from the playing fields. A large amount of my time was spent walking between these places. I scarcely paid any attention to the increasing levels of traffic pouring over the tiny medieval bridge, on this, the only route to London.

But I vividly remember coming home one day in 1974 to find that all the trees along the lane had been cut down. Huge machines, now working far off in the distance, had cut a swathe through the woodlands as far as I could see. I ran to my friend's house, and we slipped through his back fence to gaze on the destruction with a combination of awe and outrage. Where were we going to play? The big copper beech that stood at the end of the garden had been saved, but it was perched somewhat precariously on the edge of a deep cutting that marked the passing of the bulldozers. Even when it was explained to me that those forests had been cleared to make way for a new motorway that would make our village safer, I did not really understand. The experience left me shocked by the way in which humans could destroy the world around them. Surely there had to be a better way?

After graduating from college several years later I migrated to Tasmania, determined to make a new life in a place that was still wild and free, unlike old Europe. On arrival, I found out that where I was to live had been scheduled for logging. And so began a twenty-year campaign involving many people from Australia and around the world to protect Kooparoona Niara (the Great Western Tiers) – and to develop other sources of income for the local community in addition to forestry. The 'Tiers' are now World Heritage, and the basis for a thriving tourism industry. Yet they remain under threat, as the federal and state governments argue over whether they should be logged, or not.

I have since moved to the 'mainland' with a PhD from the University of Tasmania, to find work as a newly minted academic. Bellingen seemed like a welcoming and progressive-thinking community that inspired me with its commitment to sustainability. But as I write, the forests at the top of my street are being cut down. Chainsaws are screaming, machinery is grinding its way up and down the steep slopes, and log trucks are driving past my house. New subdivisions are being planned in what is left of the forest below. A track has been cut through the bush that crosses several creek lines, and mud and silt from the land clearing is making its way onto neighbouring properties. At the same time, a new motorway is carving its way through the wetlands of Shortcut Road, gravel trucks are pouring through the centre of our town, and our shire council and citizens seem completely powerless to do anything. Is there no escape from what humanity is doing to our environment?

I believe and hope there is. For me, the 1992 Rio de Janeiro 'Earth Summit' provided an answer to that question. It was a rare moment, when countries from around the world came together to find a common solution to our collective impact on the planet. I support both the idea, and practice, of sustainable development. Working as I do in developing countries and polluted cities, the necessity of improving people's daily lives is obvious. But I am acutely aware that this cannot be at the expense of the environment. Sustainable development offers humanity and the many other species that inhabit this globe an alternative to the profit-maximising, planet-destroying model of late twentieth-century capitalism. It provides an opportunity to produce and consume goods and services in a new way that takes the environment and society, as well as the economy, into consideration. Capitalism has evolved.

But 'SusDev' is not without its contradictions and there is no easy way forward. This book looks at some of the most celebrated – and at times problematic – efforts to harness market forces for good. My colleagues and I acknowledge and give thanks to the many practitioners, advocates and experts who gave so freely of their time in the course of our research. They have helped shine a light on this exciting and challenging endeavour to make the world a better place for future generations. Any mistakes are entirely our own.

Timothy Cadman
Bellingen,
New South Wales,
AMDG

Acknowledgements

A great deal of thanks is offered to those who contributed to the making of this book. The conceptual and structural approach adopted is in part fulfilment of a three-year research fellowship with Griffith University, *Improving the quality of global environmental governance and sustainable development*. It has also been an unfolding journey of discovery that would not have taken place without my fellow travelling co-authors. I am indebted to Tapan Sarker, who works a flight of stairs away from me in the Macrossin Building at Nathan Campus, for suggesting that we should write a book together. But, as those of us in the academy know, one floor can be millions of light years away, and so I am grateful to the forces of the universe for bringing us together. Tapan provided the materials on the sources and means of the delivery of finance for sustainable development in this book. I also acknowledge my dear friend and closest collaborator, Tek Maraseni, with whom I have worked on many governance and emissions trading-related publications and projects. Tek is responsible for the statistical analysis and validation of the responses to the surveys associated with each of the case studies. My thanks go to my esteemed colleague Jamie Pittock and my study buddy Lauren Eastwood for making the interview materials and related commentary available for publication. I would also like to give an extra plaudit to Lauren for her excellent material on the CBD, and for jumping in at the last minute to give the text a pre-copy onceover with her eagle eye. I am extremely grateful to Federico López-Casero, another intrepid sustainability policy researcher, governance expert and friend, for making a lot of his personal time available to prepare the eloquent materials on FLEGT, PES and BOM. My appreciation goes also to Marnie Ryan and Ellie Cheney, who provided me with invaluable research assistance on more recent developments in FSC and PEFC. I could not go any further without giving due recognition to my very best friend, partner and (now) research colleague, Beth Gibbings, for her 'forensic' analysis of the criminal wheelings and dealings in the world of illegal logging. My thanks go also to the team at Edward Elgar, especially Alex Pettifer, who has been so supportive over the rather long gestation period for this work (we first discussed publishing possibilities at the 2012 Earth System Governance Conference in Lund), and to Victoria Nichols, for her helpful tips on dealing with EE protocols. To Hilary Cadman and Sam Bravery of Cadman Editing Services, your help was invaluable. Finally, as ever, I give homage to the trees that gave their lives for the (hard copy) version of this book; may they not have died in vain.

Introduction: the political economy of sustainable development

BACKGROUND

Sustainable development, defined as 'development that meets the needs of the present without compromising the ability of future generations to meet their own needs' is at the heart of global efforts to respond to the dual imperatives of environmental protection and economic development (UN 1987: 16). At the 1992 United Nations Conference on Environment and Development (UNCED, or the Rio de Janeiro 'Earth' Summit) sustainable development was formally adopted as the intergovernmental policy response to solving global environmental problems, embodied in the document *Agenda 21* (UN 1993).

Sustainable development was an attempt to acknowledge the 'limits to growth' first argued by the Club of Rome in 1972, while at the same time reconciling the need for economic development with environmental protection (Jacobs 2012: 4–5). This reconciling approach was taken one step further post-Rio, with the emergence of the 'triple bottom line' business philosophy, which linked the ideas of people, planet and profit, with society, the environment and the economy, and became a new form of business activity reporting, that took more than profit (single bottom line accounting) into consideration (Hindle 2008: 193–4). Perhaps the most serious competitor, 'green growth', emerged in the second half of the 2000s. This discourse appears to be more of an attempt to regain market and policy traction than a serious attempt to subvert the original intent of UNCED. Although it accepts the necessity of growth, it should perhaps be seen as a next generation effort to 'green up' the economy in the face of ongoing business-as-usual practices (Jacobs 2012: 5–6). Nevertheless, sustainable development remains at the heart of the UNCED legacy. How it is expressed, as the case studies in this book demonstrate, varies considerably over time, and context. The goals of sustainable development also remain somewhat elusive, both in terms of definition and implementation.

The most relevant constituting agreements to arise out of Rio were the conventions on biological diversity (1992), climate change (1994), desertification (1996) and the non-legally binding *Statement of Forest Principles* (1992) (UN 1993). These have generated enabling policy instruments, including market-based mechanisms. After more than two decades, beyond the language of 'SusDev', specific sub-discourses have arisen within each initiative (in the case of the *Forest Principles* for example, sustainable forest management, or SFM). Policy commitments are implemented through a range of programmes, related governance arrangements and on-the-ground projects. The international community has also created other initiatives since the Earth Summit. The Millennium Development Goals (MDGs) aimed at tackling broader issues of poverty eradication, education, equality and health by the year 2015, included ensuring sustainable development (goal 7). Currently, a series of sustainable development goals (SDGs) are under negotiation, aimed at taking the sustainability-related aspects of the MDGs beyond 2015.

Responding to the issues identified at Rio and beyond poses considerable organisational challenges, and has created what has been referred to in recent years as a 'regime complex' (Victor and Keohane 2010). A wide range of institutions that share a number of commonalities coexist, but at times these can function within a series of 'silos' (Stiglitz 2003: 62–3). Discrete – even competitive – programmes have resulted in a considerable degree of 'static' across silos. In the case of climate change management, while the various initiatives under the UN Framework Convention on Climate Change (UNFCCC) are relatively well integrated, historically there has been a lack of coordination with the other Rio conventions. It has been suggested that the lack of effective interaction with other policy arenas – notably biological diversity – has led to 'trading off degradation of some ecosystems to achieve particular climate change adaptation and mitigation objectives' (Pittock 2013: 144). Governance scholars have called for more research into the institutional design and quality of the policy instruments in question (Zurn and Koenig-Archibugi 2006). This book is a response to this call, and investigates a number of major policy instruments and selected mechanisms (largely market-based) that have arisen in the wake of UNCED.

CASE STUDIES

In the wake of globalisation and the 'downsizing' of the public service as a consequence of neo-liberal political ideology, business and civil society, as well as government agencies, often implement sustainable development initiatives at the national level. Jurisdictions have increasingly shifted away from regulation solely under the control of *government* to methods of *governance* characterised by increased levels of non-state participation. This has resulted in a melange of public, private and civic service delivery, often based on 'soft' law approaches. These include voluntary standards and certification programmes, to be contrasted with traditional 'command/ control' regulatory models of state-based authority.

In the case of sustainable development, a range of types has been identified, including voluntary agreements, environmental management systems, 'eco-labels' and market-based instruments (Jordan et al. 2005). *Agenda 21* referred specifically to 'economic and market-oriented approaches' (UN 1993: 70) in the context of climate change (Chapter 9, 'Protection of the atmosphere'), forest management (Chapter 11, 'Combatting deforestation') and biodiversity (Chapter 15, 'Conservation of biological diversity). This book focuses on these three central elements of *Agenda 21* through a variety of case studies:

(1) Protection of the atmosphere: two approaches under UNFCCC aimed at *reducing greenhouse gas emissions*, the Clean Development Mechanism (**CDM**) – the fate of which is uncertain, as it was tied to the Kyoto Protocol (KP, which has now expired); and an emerging mechanism, anticipating the 2015 'post-Kyoto' climate negotiations, 'Reducing emissions from deforestation and forest degradation and the role of conservation, sustainable management of forests and enhancement of forest carbon stocks in developing countries' (**REDD+**);

(2) Combatting deforestation: *Forest certification*, exemplified by two rival schemes, the non-governmental organisation (NGO)-driven Forest Stewardship Council (**FSC**) and the industry-led Programme for the Endorsement of Forest Certification schemes (**PEFC**)–'eco-labelling' programmes for 'good' wood; and a European (EU) *legality verification* initiative to encourage timber-producing and processing countries to comply with EU-consuming countries' forestry regulations and procurement policies known as Forest Law Enforcement, Governance and Trade (**FLEGT**);

(3) Conservation of biological diversity: two *financial incentives mechanisms* originating within the UN Convention on Biological Diversity (CBD) to encourage the conservation of biological diversity, Payments for Ecosystem Services (**PES**) and biodiversity offset mechanisms (**BOM**).

The 'sustainability complex' is used here to refer to the policy-related discourses, agreements, institutional arrangements, policy instruments, mechanisms and programmes of sustainable development. This complex is depicted in Figure 0.1 below.

CENTRAL RESEARCH QUESTIONS AND PARAMETERS FOR ASSESSMENT

In order to examine these initiatives, the book adopts a perspective informed by political economy. Here, a broad interpretation is used, to encompass the social, economic and environmental interests and issues that impact, both positively and negatively, on the case studies investigated. These interests are both state-based and territorial, such as national governments, and non-state and non-territorial, such as transnational corporations and civil society organisations. The issues surrounding sustainable development include geo-politics, money and governance. The intention of the book is to better understand the various types of policy instruments, mechanisms and specific programmes employed. It investigates the governance quality of the institutional arrangements employed to deliver the desired policy outcomes, and evaluates the nature of the interactions between the different interests involved in the case studies selected.

Against this backdrop, the book asks two main questions. First, *what is right and wrong with the policy instruments for sustainable development?* Second, *what is the best model to advance sustainable development in the programmes identified?* These questions are important, because they will assist stakeholders, the policy community and the general public to determine the governance capacity of market-based approaches to solve contemporary environmental, social and economic problems – and thereby contribute to sustainable development. 'Stakeholders' should be broadly understood, as the term relates to those who create, manage and implement such programmes, as well as those who may be either positively or negatively impacted by such programmes. Each of the programmes identified has its own unique strengths and weaknesses, and careful analysis of these endeavours, including participating stakeholders' perspectives, will assist in identifying the effectiveness of the mechanisms investigated.

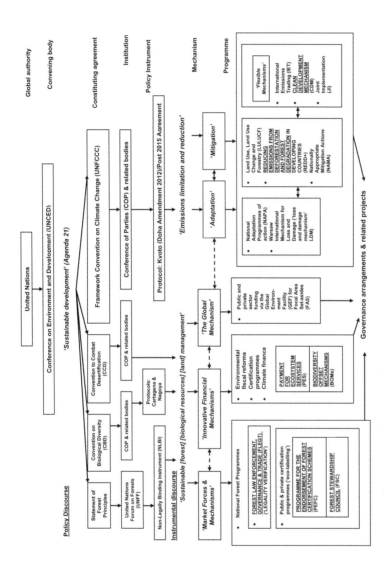

Figure 0.1 The sustainability complex

Note: Italicised text indicates actual terms from constituting agreements. Programmes in block capitals (underlined) are the case studies in the book.

In response to the book's central questions, each of these initiatives is investigated using three parameters: the *sources and means of delivery of finance*; the *'North/South divide' and state and non-state actors*; and the *governance quality of sustainable development*. Using the case studies, the book demonstrates how these parameters are crucial for the success – or failure – of approaches for promoting human development and achieving environmental sustainability.

Sources and Means of Delivery of Finance

The availability and efficacy of internal and external means of financing are central to sustainable development. There are primarily two important sources and means of delivery of finance that can promote sustainable development: market-based instruments and external means at the international level.

Market-based instruments (e.g. economic instruments) can encourage behavioural change among consumers and polluters of environmental resources, while also raising revenue for environmental protection efforts (Panayotou 2013). There is also a degree of fiduciary investment, but the degree of engagement between policymakers and investors is limited (Haigh 2013: 111). At the state level, some sovereign wealth funds contribute, as is the case with Norway. A key internal source of finance is taxation, which can also play an important role in enhancing fiscal sustainability by redistributing the revenue to advance social, economic and environmental development outcomes (Sarker 2013: 85). This is particularly true for developed and advanced economies as they continuously try to broaden tax bases as a means of reducing budget deficits through promoting fiscal discipline. Alternatively, developing and least developed countries often suffer from a narrow tax base, and have limited ability to finance programmes and strategies that can promote sustainable development outcomes. In the case of resource-rich developing countries in particular, restoring fiscal sustainability means that such countries need to better utilise their natural resource endowments, and use the rents derived from the use of resources for social and economic development (Kazi and Sarker 2012). However, such countries often face the dilemma of a natural resource curse, and also suffer due to lower economic growth and welfare relative to resource-poor countries (Auty 2002). Resource-rich developing economies face challenges that could undermine their future development, including sustaining macroeconomic stability, a rapidly growing population and increased corruption (The World Bank 2011). For instance, many resource-rich developing countries in Africa, such as Angola and Nigeria, are experiencing regressive growth and significant poverty despite the vast resource rents available (Kazi and Sarker 2012). Selecting the right instruments to finance sustainable development outcomes remains a key challenge for developing countries as they often fail to meet the institutional and human resource requirements.

The second important source of finance is at the international level, where there are some external means to finance SDGs. These include country-specific foreign aid (such as overseas development assistance) and other forms of financial assistance (including soft loans via international financial institutions such as The World Bank, Asian Development Bank and the African Development Bank). The underlying principle driving overseas aid is that those who can do so have an obligation to help those who are in extreme need (Riddell 2007). This assumption is also maintained by a belief that the capacity-building provided actually helps those in need, and consequently creates a self-sustaining environment that can enhance sustainable development by meeting or fulfilling the MDGs (IMF 2015). Other examples of external funding include bilateral or country-specific assistance (e.g. the Indonesia-Australia Comprehensive Economic Partnership Agreement, IA-CEPA) and multilateral funding initiatives such as REDD+. A surge in external funding in all aspects of sustainable development (with the major focus on poverty and development) emerged after the United Nations World Summit on Sustainable Development (WSSD) in Johannesburg in 2002. Many UN organisations and donor agencies (partner countries) are contributing to finance projects that aim to enhance SDGs. The Global Environment Facility (GEF), for instance, has provided funds for more than 300 initiatives, with an emphasis on developing country forest management and conservation (Global Environment Facility 2010).

Focusing on improving the investment climate for sustainable development, and achieving long-term economic growth rather than short-term gains, will benefit future generations; that is, it will support intergenerational equity. The appropriate relationship between intergenerational equity, sources of finance, maintaining or enhancing capital, and sustainable development, is expressed in Figure 0.2.

However, in the aftermath of the global financial crisis in 2008, funding for sustainable development has been seen as a lower priority than restoring national economies. However, fiscal sustainability is a precondition to advancing social, economic and environmental development outcomes. The sources of funding for sustainable development, including private investment and sovereign wealth funds, as well as income taxation, need to be expanded, not contracted. Opportunities for

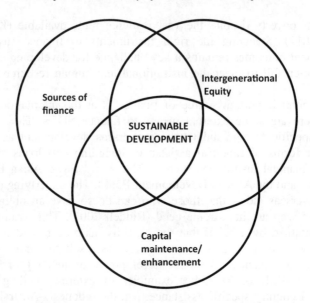

Figure 0.2   Financial system for sustainable development (Sarker 2013 adapted)

investment in sustainable development are currently hampered by incon-sistencies, uncertainties and instabilities in the global regime's financial architecture (Haigh 2013). At present, the proportion of domestic taxes in developed countries going to overseas aid remains at a low level, and collection is often poorly enforced. Taxation systems should also main-tain and develop rather than deplete capital for sustainability (Sarker 2013).

North/South Relations and State/Non-State Actors

Discussions at the Earth Summit over finance quickly led to conflict between developed and developing countries, and the creation of what have become entrenched geo-political groupings, lending popularity to the terms 'global North' and 'global South'.

The North, exemplified by the United States (US) and Europe, has historically been the developer of environmental technologies, and has been unwilling to share with, or transfer its products to, the South, expecting instead that these should be either purchased or simply delivered by Northern service delivery agencies and companies. The developing countries of the South, the largest grouping of which is collectively referred to as the 'G77', have fought strongly over the years to gain access to these technologies, while keeping control of the financial benefits arising from the exploitation of their own traditional and cultural knowledge. Towards the end of UNCED, a 'North/North' split arose between the US and the EU. The US opposed the idea of any kind of international regime to grant access to technology and benefit-sharing, while the EU was prepared to provide financial assistance – so long as the intellectual property (IP) that went along with the technologies being shared was protected under World Trade Organization (WTO) rules on IP (Birnie 2000: 366–8).

The conference was not able to reach consensus on developing an 'Earth Charter', nor did any conventions on land-based pollution or deforestation eventuate. The South was of the view that developed countries intended to challenge their national sovereignty by placing a responsibility for dealing with the costs of the North's historical environmental pollution onto the South (Birnie 2000: 366–8). These disputes remained unresolved, and were to play out subsequently in other post-Rio forums. The South continued to push for financial support for tackling environmental problems, but it wanted that support delivered via official development assistance, while the North generally pushed for private sector activities, which were to its financial benefit (Humphreys 2006: 102–9). This conflict has become increasingly nuanced over the years, particularly within the Climate Change Convention, where it has become formalised – institutionalised even – by identifying countries as either 'Annex I parties' (developed) or 'non-Annex I parties' (developing) countries. This effectively entrenched the 'common but differentiated responsibilities' (CBDR) approach, which exacerbated tensions around finance, market mechanisms and political ideologies. However, this divide has become a significant point of contention for major players from the global North in the lead-up to UNFCCC negotiations in Paris 2015, for example. A primary argument used by the global North in opposition to the KP negotiations was related to concerns about the antiquated nature of these categories given current economic transformations (and environmental impacts, such as atmospheric pollution) in some countries identified as representing the global South. The North continues to push for market-based approaches as a method for combatting climate change, while the South largely objects to capitalist – and explicitly, neo-liberal – approaches to combatting environmental degradation (Abreu Mejía 2010).

UNCED has now receded into the past, along with the 2002 Johannesburg WSSD (or 'Rio +10') and the 2012 'Rio+20' (Rio de Janeiro). A number of developing countries, notably Brazil, Russia, India and China – the so-called 'BRICs' – have advanced economically, and their developed/developing status has become blurred. This has led to a fragmentation of the Southern 'bloc' in more recent times. Countries such as India are challenging previous geo-political and geo-economic perceptions, and are undergoing massive economic growth. Indeed, the North/ South divide has itself been challenged as a Northern construction that is hampering progress towards understanding environmental degradation and represents a de-territorialising transnational phenomenon (Doyle and Chaturvedi 2010: 516–17). However the 'convergence' model of North/ South relations should not be overstressed. Inequality is still an impediment to collaboration and necessitates structural and procedural changes to the way in which negotiations take place (Parks and Roberts 2008: 621 and 644).

As sustainable development has evolved, so too has non-state participation in its structures and processes. Two interesting developments happened as a consequence of UNCED. Business interests and private foundations provided support for the conference. Public interests, notably NGOs, were involved in lead-up discussions, and played a part in some of the preparatory committee work. There were also many non-state observers present at the Rio conference who were there with the express purpose of lobbying government delegations (Birnie 2000: 360–68). This had the effect of increasing their status in the eyes of some states, even if they could not participate formally in negotiations in the same way parties (member states of the UN who have ratified agreements) do. This influence has gone so far as to result in parties including text in negotiated agreements at the explicit request of – and, in some cases, even formulated by – NGOs. But it should be said that while NGOs can *influence* the texts that come out of intergovernmental sustainable development processes, such influence does not necessarily translate into actual *impact* (Humphreys 2004: 60). It should also be stressed that in such intergovernmental negotiations, the term 'NGOs' covers a wide range of actors, all with their own sub-acronyms, including business and industry NGOs (BINGOs), environmental NGOs (ENGOs), research and independent NGOs (RINGOs), youth NGOs (YOUNGOs), as well as women, farmers, labour, municipalities and so forth, depending on how various bodies under the UN system demarcate and categorise civil society participation. Within each sector or category, there are often significant divisions between those who have very different objectives – fossil fuel industries versus the renewable energy sector within business, for example. It is also worth bearing in mind that non-state actors extend beyond these officially recognised NGOs to include civil society organisations (CSOs) and Indigenous peoples' organisations (IPOs), some of whom may be represented in the pre-determined UN-based categories for participation, and others who provide a broader base of stakeholder concerns for those who do engage under officially recognised categories. Even the definition of NGO in the UN system diverges with that adopted by the International Organization for Standardization (ISO): 'a non-profit association of citizens that operates independently of government or business structures and has non-commercial objectives related to environmental, consumer interest or sustainable development' (ISO TC 207 2003: 4).

But whatever the definition, the number of non-state actors has grown dramatically as a consequence of global environmental deliberations (Keck and Sikkink 1998: 10–12). This growth can be attributed to a change in economic influence from national to international venues of power, as well as on account of globalisation, the liberalisation of trade and the privatisation and deregulation agenda of many (most) governments themselves. All of these changes have increased the role of non-state sectors in the governance regimes that pertain to the political economy of sustainable development (Courville 2003: 271)

Governance Quality of Sustainable Development

With the rise of globalisation, and the shift away from government-led top down models, to governance involving multiple actors, several questions relating to the legitimacy of emerging institutional arrangements arise. Policies or programmes gain legitimacy on the basis of the validity of the structures and processes used to make them (input legitimacy), or if they deliver the goods (output legitimacy) – (Kersbergen and Waarden 2004: 156–8). On the input front, legitimacy has been linked to interest representation. It has been noted that 'regimes with a generally inclusive access and participation profile tend to be more effective than regimes with a more exclusive profile' (Wettestad 2001: 320). Regimes with limited participation seeking a 'quick fix' generally work well over the short term, but over the long term are less likely to have useful and positive outcomes, as stakeholders who may have either contributed to generating the problem and/or a solution to the problem have been excluded (Kölliker 2006: 208).

On a global level, the network-like nature of contemporary governance involves multiple actors, whose interactions can be more collaborative than traditional models (Haas 2004: 1). Environmental governance, understood as 'the coordination of interdependent social relations in the mitigation of environmental disruptions' represents one of the best examples of collaboration between civil society, private industry and the state (Mackendrick 2005: 22). Natural resource management specifically has been identified as one of the most useful focus areas to examine 'the increasing tendency for collaboration in many sectors where political and economic trade-offs also exist' (Overdevest 2004: 192).

Inclusiveness, equality and resources (also referred to as capabilities, or capacity-building in the literature), have been identified as the key elements of interest representation in global environmental governance (Cadman 2011: 17). Legitimacy is also closely linked to accountability and transparency (Bäckstrand 2006, Courville 2003). Accountability and transparency, interrelated concepts in much of the governance literature, have been connected under the broader rubric of organisational respons- ibility (Cadman 2011: 13–14). These can be seen as 'structural' com- ponents of participation in contemporary environmental governance.

Attention is also given to deliberation (decision-making) and implementation (Wettestad 2001). Collective decision-making has been identified as an important democratic component of legitimacy. Collect- ive decision-making assists in the creation of agreements that result in collectively binding action (Scharpf 1997: 153). Although traditional approaches to making decisions such as voting are seen as more efficient, contemporary governance is showing an increasing preference for more discursive approaches such as consensus (Coglianese 2001, Dryzek 1994, Susskind 1994, Janicke 1992).

Where agreement cannot be reached, the presence of dispute settle- ment mechanisms is also identified as a critical aspect of decision- making, and one that is not generally well done in intergovernmental processes (Susskind 1994, Cadman 2011). Democracy, reaching agree- ment and settling disputes have all been linked to the notion of 'deliberation as process' in contemporary governance (Cadman 2011: 4).

Implementation is more related to output legitimacy, whereas interest representation and organisational responsibility as well as decision- making are more related to the processes of governance, and con- sequently more input-orientated. Focusing on the structural and procedural inputs of governance without focusing on the ensuing outputs can have a negative impact on efficiency (Smismans 2004: 459–60). Governance scholars also therefore pay attention to the idea that legitim- acy is a product of the substantive outputs of the governance system and includes standards setting or the development of identifiable criteria. These outputs relate to the application and formulation of the governance system, and contribute to effectiveness on the basis of the quality of the outputs themselves (Kooiman 1993: 259–60). This is to be contrasted with the legitimacy derived from inputs, the implication being that success legitimates policies and related programmes: if the outputs do what they are supposed to, they are endowed with legitimacy by the general public – (Kersbergen and Waarden 2004: 156–8). However, there is a distinction to be made analytically between the *outputs* of a given policy programme and longer term *outcomes*. The implementation of agreements does not in itself guarantee success. Effectiveness is also related closely to behaviour change and problem-solving (Young 1999: 189). Durability, understood in terms of regime longevity, flexibility and adaptability is also essential (Wettestad 2001: 319, Cadman 2011: 15). These are the longer term outcomes required for success.

Evaluating Governance Quality

For the purposes of understanding the nature of the relationship between the various governance arrangements discussed above, a framework of principles, criteria and indicators (PC&I) relating to governance quality is presented here (Lammerts van Beuren and Blom 1997: 5–9).

Table 0.1   Principles, criteria and indicators for assessing governance quality

Principle	Criterion	Indicator
'Meaningful participation'	Interest representation	Inclusiveness
		Equality
		Resources
	Organisational responsibility	Accountability
		Transparency
'Productive deliberation'	Decision-making	Democracy
		Agreement
		Dispute settlement
	Implementation	Behavioural change
		Problem-solving
		Durability

Source: Cadman 2009: 104.

In this study, two criteria (or categories) contribute to the principle (or value) of meaningful participation, *interest representation* and *organisational responsibility*. It refers to the *structures* of governance. In the discussion above regarding quality of governance, interest representation was connected to three governance components, which function as indicators (parameters for assessment): *inclusiveness*, demonstrating who participates in the system of governance; *equality*, indicating the calibre of relationship the participants enjoy; and *resources*, referring to the financial, technical and/or institutional capacities for a participant to ensure that their interests are represented in the system of governance. Two indicators make up the second criterion, *organisational responsibility*, and which are often closely interlinked: *accountability,* relating to the degree to which the actions of participants (usually delegated representatives of specific organisations) can be called to account by other actors, and the wider public; and *transparency*, which relates to the openness or visibility of participants' activities.

The two criteria of *decision-making* and *implementation* make up productive deliberation. This principle is concerned with the *processes* of governance. Three indicators are linked to decision-making: *democracy*, i.e. the extent to which actors can exercise democratic choice; *agreement,* concerning the manner in which that choice is exercised (voting, or consensus and so forth); and *dispute settlement*, relating to the ability to seek redress or take action if conflicts arise or if agreements cannot be reached. Implementation consists of three indicators: *behaviour change*, concerning the extent to which implementing agreements leads to changed behaviour regarding the problem in question; *problem-solving*, which relates to the extent to which the problem itself is actually resolved; and *durability*, encompassing the ideas of adaptability, flexibility and longevity.

APPROACH AND METHODS OF EVALUATION

Each case study was evaluated against these three parameters, using source materials, interviews with participants and surveys. Source documents included texts from the case studies themselves, literature from state and non-state actors, and commentaries provided by academic scholars and researchers. Interviews were also conducted with some of the participants directly involved in the mechanisms.

This qualitative interview-based research was undertaken in light of the fact that knowledge of the best practices and also major impediments to success in environmental policy instruments and market mechanisms are poorly understood. Additionally, participants in policy-making regimes and scholars alike argue that these instruments are complex, require specialist knowledge, and concern sensitive and often highly politicised issues of intergovernmental relations. Through the application of the method of open-ended interviewing (Ritchie and Lewis 2003), a range of perspectives was sought from key actors involved in international institutions in the biodiversity and climate change sectors. Questions were designed to elicit comments from interviewees on the need, effectiveness and potential for enhanced integration of governance, including of relevant policy instruments and market mechanisms. Data were collected through conducting interviews with senior, English-speaking government, intergovernmental, and non-governmental individuals whose work is associated with multilateral environmental agreements. Intergovernmental interviewees included those from UN agencies and treaty secretariats. Non-governmental interviewees were drawn from organisations actively involved in global scale negotiations of UN-based policy and multilateral environment agreements. Current or former ministers or senior officials were interviewed from each of three blocks of countries, namely the EU, JUSCANZ (other Western developed nations, originally comprised of Japan, the US, Canada, Australia and New Zealand as an intended counterbalance to the EU bloc). Now JUSCANZ is often referred to as 'the Umbrella Group', as several other countries, including Liechtenstein, Switzerland, Norway and, in some cases, Israel, have joined the group with the original founding members, and G77 (developing countries).

Thirty-five in-depth interviews were undertaken between May 2011 to May 2012, using confidential and semi-structured (open-ended) techniques (Minichiello et al. 1995). The range of views expressed by the interviewees on environmental policy instruments and market mechanisms are integrated into subsequent chapters where relevant. Quotes from the interviewees can be identified in the following text by citations containing a descriptor (intergovernmental organisation official, non-government organisation representative, European nation official, [other] developed nation official, or developing country representative) and an interviewee number. Quotes from respondents have been modified slightly for readability and coherence, yet with the intention of retaining the respondents' meanings. The observations from these interviewees are incorporated throughout the text where relevant, and are contained in the comparative analysis and recommendations.

In addition to the qualitative research conducted, primary source data for this book were gathered through an online survey that was developed and deployed in early 2015 to evaluate the governance quality of each of the mechanisms. This survey was based on the framework presented in Table 0.1. See Table 0.2.

Table 0.2   Summary of survey questions

Question	Indicator
Do you think [the programme] is inclusive of your interests?	Inclusiveness
Do you think [the programme] treats all interests equally?	Equality
What level of resources does [the programme] provide for you to participate?	Resources
Do you think [the programme] is accountable?	Accountability
Do you think [the programme] is transparent?	Transparency
Do you consider [the programme] acts in a democratic manner?	Democracy
Do you consider the making of agreements in [the programme] to be effective?	Agreement
Do you consider the settling of disputes in [the programme] to be effective?	Dispute settlement
Do you think [the programme] will contribute to changing the behaviour it was created to address?	Behavioural change
Do you think [the programme] will help solve the problem it was created to address?	Problem-solving
Do you consider [the programme] will be durable?	Durability

Note: Explanatory text and introductory materials omitted.

Survey participants were recruited through internet searches of publicly available email addresses of those involved in each of the programmes. Respondents were also invited to identify whether they came from the 'Global North/Developed Country' and 'Global South/Developing Country', and consisted of members of the biodiversity, forest and climate related policy communities. They were also asked to identify as 'Environmental', 'Social', 'Economic', 'Government', 'Academic' and 'Other'. Those who responded were invited to make substantive comments relevant to each indicator. Participants were asked to select and rate the programmes with which they had experience, and rated their perceptions of the governance quality of the various programmes by means of a five-point Likert scale, using the terms 'very low', 'low', 'medium', 'high' and 'very high'. The survey was confidential, and ran for four weeks in early 2015.

Survey respondents came from 60 countries. The majority of countries provided only one or two respondents, while the US had the largest number (nine), followed by India and Germany (six) Indonesia, Nepal and Malawi (four), and Canada, China, Malaysia, Spain and the UK (three). A total of 107 individuals responded, dispersed across the different mechanisms on the basis of their knowledge of the mechanism in question. The largest number of responses was for FSC (93) and the lowest for PES (81). A total of 47 respondents were from the North (developed countries) and 60 from the South (developing countries), with varying numbers selecting the specific mechanisms with which they were familiar. It should be noted that numbers of respondents varied across sectors. The largest sectors were environment (42) and academic (35). The smallest sectors were government (16), 'other' (6), social (5) and economic (3). In these latter four instances, there was a considerable 'outlier effect' whereby smaller numbers may have biased results, and the scores from these sectors should consequently be interpreted with some caution. Forty-six respondents from all sectors and regions provided specific comments. The results of the survey are contained in the following chapters.

CHAPTER OUTLINES AND KEY FINDINGS

Chapters 1–4 follow a similar format. A brief history and descriptive background introduces the relevant policy arena. This is followed by the case studies. A historical overview outlines the origins, development and controversies of the mechanism in question. This leads to a discussion of the sources and means of delivery of finance, which precedes an evaluation of North/South–state/non-state relations and an assessment of quality of governance, making use of the quantitative results and qualitative commentary contained in the online survey. A concluding section provides a brief analysis of the studies selected.

Chapter 1 focuses on the UNFCCC, the CDM and REDD+. Chapter 2 contains two case studies and two policy responses that arose, it could be argued, in the absence of a forest convention: forest certification, exemplified by the FSC and the PEFC. Chapter 3 investigates the EU trade-related initiative aimed at combatting illegal logging, FLEGT. This initiative is perhaps the 'odd person out' in the study, as it is less a sustainable development initiative and more of a regulatory mechanism that uses the market to combat illegal logging. There are, however, strong conceptual linkages between illegality and sustainability, and it is the synergies and tensions between these, that makes FLEGT an interesting policy instrument. Chapter 4 investigates the CBD and two associated policy instruments: PES and BOM. Chapter 5 provides a comparative analysis of the empirical data collected from both the online survey and interviews. The Conclusion provides an overview of environmental policy and policy instruments, and speculates on the future prospects of market-based mechanisms as a means of achieving sustainable development. The volume ends with a series of recommendations identified from the key informant interviews, along with the commentary provided by interviewees themselves.

BIBLIOGRAPHY

Abreu Mejía, D. 2010, 'The evolution of the climate change regime: Beyond a north-south divide?', *International Catalan Institute for Peace, Working Paper*, (2010/6).
Auty, R. 2002, *Sustaining development in mineral economies: the resource curse thesis*, London: Routledge.
Bäckstrand, K. 2006, 'Multi-stakeholder partnerships for sustainable development: Rethinking legitimacy, accountability and effectiveness', *European Environment*, **16** (5) 290–306.
Birnie, P. 2000, 'The UN and the environment', in Roberts, A. and Kingsbury, B. (eds) *United Nations, Divided World: The UN's Roles in International Relations*, Oxford: Oxford University Press.
Cadman, T. 2009, *Quality, legitimacy and global governance: A comparative analysis of four forest institutions*, PhD thesis, University of Tasmania.
Cadman, T. 2011, *Quality and legitimacy of global governance: case lessons from forestry*, Basingstoke, London: Palgrave Macmillan.
Coglianese, C. 2001, *Is consensus an appropriate basis for regulatory policy?* Cambridge, MA: Harvard University Press.
Courville, S. 2003, 'Social accountability audits: Challenging or defending democratic governance?', *Law and Policy*, **25** (3) 269–97.
Doyle, T. and Chaturvedi, S. 2010, 'Climate territories: A global soul for the global south?', *Geopolitics*, **15** (3) 516–35.
Dryzek, J. S. 1994, *Discursive democracy: Politics, policy, and political science*, Cambridge: Cambridge University Press.
Global Environment Facility 2010, *The GEF incentive mechanism for forests a new REDD+ multilateral finance program*. Viewed 7 April 2015, https://www.thegef.org/gef/sites/thegef.org/files/publication/REDDEnglish.pdf.
Haas, P. M. 2004, 'Addressing the global governance deficit', *Global Environmental Politics*, **4** (4) 1–15.
Haigh, M. 2013, 'Stakeholders in climate policy instruments: What role for financial institutions?', in *Climate Change and Global Policy Regimes: Towards Institutional Legitimacy*, London: Palgrave Macmillan, 111.
Hindle, T. 2008, *Guide to management ideas and gurus*, Hoboken, NJ: John Wiley & Sons.
Humphreys, D. 2004, 'Redefining the issues: NGO influence on international forest negotiations', *Global Environmental Politics*, **4** (2) 51–74.
Humphreys, D. 2006, *Logjam: Deforestation and the crisis of global governance*, London: Earthscan.

IMF 2015, *Factsheet: The IMF and the millennium development goals.* Viewed 27 March 2015, http://www.imf.org/external/np/exr/facts/mdg.htm.

ISO TC 207 2003, 'Increasing the effectiveness of NGO participation in ISO TC 207', *N590 Rev/ISO/TC NGO TG N28.*

Jacobs, M. 2012, 'Green growth: Economic theory and political discourse', London, Inggris: Grantham Research Institute on Climate Change and the Environment, London School of Economics and Political Science (LSE). Viewed 15 April 2015, http://www.lse.ac.uk/GranthamInstitute/wp-content/uploads/2012/10/WP92-green-growth-economic-theory-political-discourse.pdf.

Janicke, M. 1992, 'Conditions for environmental policy success: An international comparison', *The Environmentalist,* **12** 47–58.

Jordan, A., Wurzel, R. K. W. and Zito, A. 2005, 'The rise of "New" policy instruments in comparative perspectives: Has governance eclipsed government?' *Political Studies,* **53** (3) 441–69.

Kazi, W. B. and Sarker, T. 2012, 'Fiscal sustainability and the natural resource curse in resource-rich african countries: A case study of Uganda', *Bulletin for International Taxation,* **66** (8) 1–12.

Keck, M. E. and Sikkink, K. 1998, *Activists beyond borders: Advocacy networks in international politics,* New York: Cornell University Press.

Kersbergen, K. v. and Waarden, F. v. 2004, '"Governance" as a bridge between disciplines: Cross-disciplinary inspiration regarding shifts in governance and problems of governability, accountability and legitimacy', *European Journal of Political Research,* **43** (2) 143–71.

Kölliker, A. 2006, *Conclusion 1: Governance and public goods theory,* Basingstoke, London: Palgrave Macmillan.

Kooiman, J. 1993, *Findings, speculations and recommendations in modern governance: New government society interactions,* London: Sage.

Lammerts van Beuren, E. M. and Blom, E. M. 1997, *Hierarchical framework for the formulation of sustainable forest management standards,* Leiden: The Tropenbos Foundation.

Mackendrick, N. A. 2005, 'The role of the state in voluntary environmental reform: A case study of public land', *Policy Sciences,* **38** (1) 21–44.

Minichiello, V., Aroni, R., Timewell, E. and Alexander, L. 1995, *In-depth interviewing: Principles, techniques, analysis,* Sydney: Addison Wesley Longman.

Overdevest, C. 2004, 'Codes of conduct and standard setting in the forest sector constructing markets for democracy?' *Relations Industrielles/Industrial Relations,* **59** (1) 172–97.

Panayotou, T. 2013, *Instruments of change: Motivating and financing sustainable development,* London: Routledge.

Parks, B. C. and Roberts, J. T. 2008, 'Inequality and the global climate regime: breaking the north-south impasse', *Cambridge Review of International Affairs,* **21** (4) 621–48.

Pittock, J. 2013, Climate change and sustainable water management, in Cadman, T. (ed.) *Climate change and global policy regimes: towards institutional legitimacy,* London: Palgrave Macmillan.

Riddell, R. C. 2007, *Does foreign aid really work?* Oxford: Oxford University Press.

Ritchie, J. and Lewis, J. 2003, *Qualitative research practice*, London: Sage Publications.

Sarker, T. 2013, 'Taxing for the future: an intergenerational perspective', *The Asian Century, Sustainable Growth and Climate Change*, Cheltenham: Edward Elgar, 85.

Scharpf, F. W. 1997, *Games real actors play: Actor-centered institutionalism in policy research*, Boulder, CO: Westview Press.

Smismans, S. 2004, *Law, legitimacy, and European governance: Functional participation in social regulation*, Oxford: Oxford University Press.

Stiglitz, J. E. 2003, 'Globalization and development', in Held, D. and Koenig-Archibugi, M. (eds) *Taming globalisation: Frontiers of governance*, Cambridge: Polity Press.

Susskind, L. 1994, *Environmental diplomacy: Negotiating more effective global agreements*, New York, Oxford: Oxford University Press.

The World Bank 2011, 'Uganda country brief', Washington: World Bank.

UN 1987, *Report of the World Commission on Environment and Development: Our common future*, New York: United Nations Publications Department of Public Information. Viewed 15 July 2015, http://www.un-documents.net/wced-ocf.htm.

UN 1993, *Agenda 21: Programme of action for sustainable development, Rio declaration on environment and development, statement of forest principles*, New York: United Nations Publications Department of Public Information.

Victor, D. G. and Keohane, R. O., 2010, *The Regime Complex for Climate Change*, Cambridge, MA: The Harvard Project on International Climate Agreements.

Wettestad, J. 2001, 'Designing effective environmental regimes: The conditional keys', *Global Governance*, **7** (3) 317–41.

Young, O. R. (ed.) 1999, *Hitting the mark: Why are some environmental agreements more effective than others? Environment* **20** 189–91.

Zurn, M. and Koenig-Archibugi, M. 2006, 'Conclusion II: Modes and dynamics of global governance', in Koenig-Archibugi, M. and Zurn, M. (eds) *New Modes of Governance in the International System: Exploring Publicness, Delegation and Inclusion*, Basingstoke, London: Palgrave Macmillan.

1. Protection of the atmosphere – CDM and REDD+

HISTORY AND DESCRIPTIVE BACKGROUND OF THE CLIMATE CONVENTION

Agenda 21 did not specifically refer to climate change, other than to acknowledge 'the 1992 United Nations Framework Convention on Climate Change and other international, including regional, instruments' (UN 1993: 76). While the need for a convention to address climate change was acknowledged at Rio, the UNFCCC was negotiated largely outside UNCED. The primary objective of UNFCCC is to 'prevent dangerous anthropogenic interference with the climate system' (UNFCCC 1992: 9). It entered into force in 1994, and was principally determined by the need to develop a technical solution to climate change, as well as the market ideology of neo-liberalism, which led to the creation of the 'flexible mechanisms' of the 1997 KP: the CDM, joint implementation (JI) and International Emissions Trading (IET). The first (and only) supra-national emissions trading scheme (ETS) was established in 2005. The first phase of the ETS until 2007 was based on reducing emissions through a focus on internal EU sources in the power and heat sectors, oil refineries, etc. Starting in 2008, ETS participants were also able to purchase carbon credits from JI and CDM projects (Bäckstrand and Lövbrand 2007: 130). This linkage allowed for the 'offsetting' of emissions via the creation of investment projects in developing countries, which could then sell their 'carbon credits' into the compliance-based market established under KP, and be bought by greenhouse gas (GHG) emitting industries within the EU (Cadman 2013b: 1–2).

The Convention and the policy responses to climate change it develops through the annual Conference of Parties (COP) are informed by the advice provided by the Intergovernmental Panel on Climate Change (IPCC), a body that reviews the state of the science of climate change. It was established in 1991, before the Earth Summit, and made a considerable contribution to the climate discussions at UNCED. The IPCC essentially peer reviews previously peer-reviewed publications, under the philosophy that it is policy descriptive rather than policy prescriptive, and it is the policy community that must ultimately determine the responses that need to be developed. Originally the IPCC had a strong emphasis on preventing (or mitigating) the increase in mean global temperatures by the reduction of GHGs into the atmosphere by humans. But between COP 7 in Marakesh to COP 12 in Nairobi (2001–2006) it gradually shifted focus and began to include research into adjusting (or adapting) to climate change, as negotiators began to accept the reality on the ground. As a consequence, the climate negotiations themselves, as well as the IPCC, began to move away from a purely technical discussion to a social discourse around environmental factors (Cadman 2013b: 2–3).

In 2014, the IPCC released a Fifth Assessment Report (AR) summarising the various outputs of its working groups and taskforces, and the findings of two specific reports that were first issued in 2011 (Pachauri 2014). There is now compelling evidence that human society, as a whole, must create pathways for future development that are based on low-carbon technologies. Since the Fourth AR in 2007, the certainty that the warming trend in global temperatures since the 1950s is a result of human activity has increased from 90 per cent to 95 per cent – a statistically significant change in certainty. The degree and rate of change in temperature since the mid-twentieth century, it is argued, are unparalleled in human history. What previously took thousands of years has now been achieved in under a century. These impacts have been observed in increased oceanic and atmospheric temperatures, resulting in the rising of sea levels and creating extremes in climate variability. Disruptions to planetary cycles of water, for example, have led to reductions in ice and snow, which in turn have contributed to the rise in sea levels identified. The heat of the upper ocean has also increased, leading to an expansion (and hence rise) of sea levels, but this increase in oceanic temperature is also working its way down to depths of 700 metres – and more. This has potentially major consequences for marine life as well as fisheries. There are already examples of fish species moving to new areas due to changes in existing habitats, which are being impacted by temperature rises (notably coral reefs). Extreme temperature and precipitation events, accompanied by marked variability, are also on the rise, particularly in the Asia region. Similar impacts are also being detected in terrestrial species. Fruit previously cultivated at low altitudes is now being grown at higher altitudes. Modelling indicates that extreme temperatures, which previously occurred once every 20 years may become biannual events, leading to predictions that both the intensity and frequency of events will increase, along with more extreme precipitation (Pachauri 2014).

The relationship between science and society has taken on greater significance with the ending of the first commitment period of the Convention and the expiry of the KP in 2013. 'Pure' science has given way to the necessity of finding ways to enact (and fund) societal change in the face of a changing global climate. The need for large funds to address climate issues and drive changes in behaviours has become more urgent with each COP. The constant rise in the economic activity of segments of the global population who have been incorporated into the global economy remain the key drivers behind fossil fuel combustion, which is the largest source of CO_2 emissions from energy production and transportation. Without policy action to curb production and emissions, fossil fuel usage will continue to increase. Industrial growth is a significant contributing factor through the use of energy to extract materials and process them (upstream/downstream atmospheric pollution). Land use, especially for agriculture and forestry, is also responsible for a significant proportion of emissions – currently around 24 per cent. Reducing emissions from all these areas of human activity is essential (Pachauri 2014).

KP's market-based approach to problem-solving resulted in developing countries claiming that developed countries were simply trying to buy their way out of historical responsibilities, and at the same time, turning carbon into a tradable commodity from which they could profit. These claims did not prevent the KP mechanisms from being implemented, but in the wake of the end of the KP commitment period, these perceptions have come to the forefront of negotiations. This has impacted considerably on the shape and proposed future of one of the most well-developed mechanisms under negotiation, REDD+, which seeks to reduce global GHG emissions by reducing deforestation and forest degradation in developing countries through payments in exchange for reduced impact – or avoided – logging (Cadman 2013a: 3–4).

A lack of certainty is therefore affecting discussions on the type of instruments to replace the KP models. Under KP the countries with the greatest emissions levels agreed to reduce the GHGs by 5 per cent below the levels of the reference year (1990), the most well known of which is carbon dioxide (CO_2). The present round of negotiations have been challenged to achieve a far more formidable target of 18 per cent (UNFCCC 2014b). This would indeed be ambitious and essential to combat global warming, but it seems unlikely to be reached, given that under the original KP, current GHGs rose to 50 per cent above 1990 levels. The trading in emissions has also failed to deliver a genuine market, and at present carbon is an almost worthless commodity. The markets as such that exist are heavily criticised by anti neo-liberal countries who reject this approach, and have been lobbying within the negotiations for payments for ecosystems services instead, with this charge being led by Latin America (Cadman 2014).

In view of the push for payments, it is not surprising that funding climate change responses make up a considerable proportion of the discussions, as well as the institutional apparatus of the Convention. Finance covers mitigation and adaptation, technology transfer as well as existing ongoing commitments. A range of actors contributes to climate finance, from the private sector, to multilateral development- and bilateral banks and donor countries. Most initiatives are implemented via recognised UN agencies and NGOs at the national level especially adaptation, which is a real and present necessity for small island states and other vulnerable countries. This is guided by the Cancun Adaptation Framework and via national adaptation plans as well as national adaptation programmes of action. There are other mitigation-related elements in addition to the flexible mechanisms, notably country-level Nationally Appropriate Mitigation Actions (NAMAs) and national reporting around land use, land-use change and forestry (LULUCF). LULUCF addresses terrestrial land-use changes. Tradable carbon can be generated from reductions in carbon emissions as a result of positive changes in land-use activities. These become 'assigned amount units' eligible to enter the emissions-trading market as 'emissions reduction units', which in turn can be used in JI projects. Annex 2 countries within the broader Annex 1 grouping can establish projects in economies in transition (EIT) – former Soviet Union countries and emerging economies in Eastern Europe and elsewhere. These projects can be developed nationally and effectively be self-managed ('Track 1'), or internationally ('Track 2'), under the auspices of the JI Supervisory Committee. A global emissions-trading scheme has not yet eventuated, and remains confined to regional schemes such as the ETS of the EU, or on a state or sub-national level. It is possible that an IET could come out of one of the negotiating streams in the climate talks – the so-called 'new market-based mechanisms' discussions (UNFCCC 2014a).

The nature and type of funding climate action over the next commitment period has also aroused much debate, and change. The GEF (a UN-accredited agency of the World Bank) has been largely responsible for managing climate-related funds, as well as broader funds related to sustainable development generally since Rio. It receives contributions from developing countries and allocates and oversees their use in developing countries. Specific in-country or international implementing agencies manage on-the-ground activities in priority countries (in the case of climate change, those are the most vulnerable developing countries). These can be aid agencies, such as Norway's Norwegian Agency for Development Cooperation (NORAD) (active in Indonesia on REDD+). UN agencies, such as the United Nations Development Programme (UNDP), the Food and Agriculture Organisation (FAO) and the United Nations Environment Programme (UNEP) work with local partners (usually government ministries) and NGOs, which run the projects. GEF has managed several rounds of funding over the years, and billions of dollars have been expended, largely under the CBD, but also UNFCCC. The GEF is responsible for oversight and management of the Special Climate Change Fund (SCCF), the Least Developed Countries Fund (LDCF), and a range of other small funds that relate to climate change. It also played a role in the Adaptation Fund in its early institutional development. At COP 16 in Cancun (2010) Parties determined that the Convention needs its own fund, and the Green Climate Fund (GCF) was established. This has posed something of an existential threat to GEF's activities in the climate policy arena, and it has been suggested that the SCCF and LDCF should be managed by GCF, as the 'mega fund' for climate finance (Cadman 2014).

Nevertheless the allure of carbon credit trading as a mechanism to raise funds for climate mitigation and other sustainable development is incredibly powerful and drives a lot of experimentation with new mechanisms. For example, EU national official 4 said:

> We have initiated what we call 'the sustainable trade initiative' and they, of course, look at certifying commodities and making sure that farmers get a price premium for sustainable coco or sustainable palm oil or whatever.

> But they also are now looking into the possibility, together with World Wildlife Fund (WWF) – they call it carbon bundling. They look at the carbon that is stored in the fields while taking all the measures needed to have sustainable coco or sustainable palm oil.

> And the carbon so far has been neglected and their question is, can we measure it and if we can measure it, can we market it? Thus providing another priced premium. But if you take that kind of thinking, you can take it one step further because there will be a biodiversity premium as well, and if you can capture that as well as the carbon, then you are finally closing in on what you might call 'sustainable land management'.

Similarly, developed country national official 3 concluded:

> What would help most of all is climate financing, in my view, because it will provide, it is *already* providing, quite a lot of money that will leverage the sort of development that can deliver a vision of the green economy that makes it successful and that people want to be part of. I think the fundamental point

[is] that you can't any longer hope to develop now and fix things out later. The only way that I think we can make a fundamental change in the application is to make money available for green projects: projects which create economic activity, but economic activity that supports environmental concerns.

Financing the required technological changes has resulted in often acrimonious discussions between 'Non-annex' (or developing) countries, who are recipients of finance and technology, and 'Annex 1' (or developed) countries, who are the donors (technically, those who signed up to reduction targets, and who also provide funds within Annex 1 group, are referred to as 'Annex 2' or Annex B countries). Under the 2011 Durban Platform for Enhanced Action, developed and developing countries were expected to generate their own 'intended nationally determined contribution' (INDC) towards reducing GHG, and their activities have been separated into various thematic areas (mitigation, adaptation, finance, technology development and transfer, transparency of action and support, and capacity-building). There is little support for a rerun of the Kyoto model, and the negotiations have focused on a 'protocol, another legal instrument or an agreed outcome with legal force under the Convention applicable to all parties'(UNFCCC 2012b). The previous 'two-track' model of developed/ developing country pledges is giving way to a 'one track' approach to reduction commitments. How this affects the long-established UN dictum of CBDR – that is, developed countries give the most, and developing countries give what they can – is unclear. These factors made for fraught discussions about emissions trading at COP 20 in Lima 2014, and COP 21 in Paris, the supposed concluding point for negotiations around the institutional arrangements for the next commitment period to 2020 (Cadman 2014). The announcement in November 2014 that the US would reduce its emissions by 26–28 per cent of its 2005 levels, and that China would increase the level of non-fossil fuels in primary energy consumption to 20 per cent by 2030 were encouraging (Office of the Secretary 2014). In the command-and-control economy of China, this is realisable. But the US, a non-signatory to Kyoto, has a history of unimplemented commitments in the climate change policy arena, as well as a hostile Republican Party currently in control of Congress, which branded the agreement a 'one-sided deal' (Voldovici and Lauder 2014).

CDM

The negotiations leading to the creation of the KP at COP 3 in 1997 represents the first time that developed countries were prepared to accept responsibility for historical GHG emissions, agreeing to cap emissions by means of legally binding targets. The principal aim of the CDM is to assist recognised GHG-emitting entities (such as industry) in developed countries to meet nationally quantified emission reductions obligations in an economically efficient manner, while simultaneously enabling developing countries to benefit from the transfer of technology as well as sustainable development (Maraseni 2013: 96). There were over 7000 projects by 2013, and the amount of credits issued equated to 1.2 billion tonnes of carbon (UNFCCC 2012a).

There are two types of carbon markets, the regulated, or compliance market, centred on the CDM, and the voluntary offset market. Carbon credits relate to emission-based allowance as well as project-based offsets. Carbon offsets are a sub-set that allows targets for emissions reduction that need to be met in one jurisdiction to be addressed through the purchase of reductions elsewhere, through project-based climate mitigation activities. The compliance market exists solely as a consequence of KP, with the voluntary carbon offset (VCO) market, largely driven by NGOs and private sector-driven schemes, occurring as a spin-off (Lovell 2010: 353).

While they are regulated differently, they are interlinked due to their common origin. They are often also retailed together, with 'failed' or delayed compliance offsets being sold on the voluntary market. This raises to key governance challenges, namely whether they generate robust and credible offsets that actually reduce atmospheric emissions and how to communicate with, and reassure, consumers that they do indeed do this (Lovell 2010: 354). The CDM is made up of an Executive Board (CDM EB) and related CDM-methodology and accreditation panels and small-scale working groups. Corporations and NGOs participate in these bodies. The process for issuing carbon credits is complex and lengthy, with various stages relating to project design, method approval, validation, registration and verification, and ultimately the issue of a Certified Emissions Reduction (CER). The process usually lasts about 500 days, and concerns have been raised over the overly bureaucratic nature of the process. The buying and selling of credits requires legal documentation, but once registered through the CDM EB, carbon finance is channelled through the private sector or the various World Bank carbon funds, which then finance the projects as they are implemented in the developing countries. Host countries and purchasers of credits must be in a Kyoto signatory country. Host nations must provide a Designated National Authority (DNA) to certify that the project contributes to sustainable development (part of the UNFCCC treaty requirements). Once operational, the credits (CERs) are listed on the International Transaction Log

(ITL) and may then be used by Annex I governments to reduce their emissions levels in compliance with their commitments under the Protocol. The ITL is intended to provide transparency of CERs within the compliance-based market (Lovell 2010). These accountability provisions, along with the requirements for validation, review and verification, have led some scholars to view it as a leading example of what public–private partnerships can provide (Bäckstrand 2008: 96–100).

Given its development in the post-Rio policy environment, it is not surprising that the CDM has been identified as a 'second generation' environmental policy instrument, typified by its voluntary, market-based approach. It embodies neo-liberal ideologies and is heavily influenced by the elites of industrial capital in developed countries. However, given its origins it is also subjected to a degree of NGO influence, and exhibits many of the network-like arrangements that make up contemporary global environmental governance. However, the degree to which non-state interests are reflected in policy practice is moot, due largely to a focus on the 'flexibility' aspects of the mechanism, rather than poverty reduction. The emphasis on markets and the technocratic verification requirements make it more the domain of state-centric, managerial and scientific elites than civil society (Bäckstrand and Lövbrand 2006).

However, the ability to which the CDM can both reduce GHG emissions and deliver sustainable development has been questioned. This led to calls for a reform of a broad range of structures and processes around implementation. While it has indeed facilitated technology transfer, included developing countries in emissions-trading mechanisms and enabled the private sector to develop innovative cost-effective emissions reductions projects, this does not necessarily equate to sustainability. It has been both theoretically and practically difficult for it to do so. While there is general agreement that it has led to the transfer of funds to pay for emissions reductions, its focus on project-based reductions rather than larger programmes of technological transformation of developing countries, has not lowered transaction costs nor created wider benefits. At COP 15 (2009) the CDM was instructed to develop more broadly applicable and standardised baselines for projects, and to ensure that these projects were more closely aligned with reducing emissions via NAMAs (Bumpus and Cole 2010: 541–2).

In addition there have been some economic inefficiencies around how CDM projects have been funded. The majority of investors in CDM projects are from the EU and the UK, which has effectively reduced competition. In addition, encouraging developing countries to create their own 'unilateral' projects without developed country investment and then sell the credits proved ineffective. Transaction costs were extremely high, due to lack of external investments, requiring internal funding; since payments only occurred at the end of the project, a considerable amount of costs had to be carried before remuneration. In addition, very little technology transfer occurred, and consequently the level of sustainable development was also limited. The 'additionality' requirement for all projects to be able to demonstrate that their activity genuinely added to emissions reduction, which would not otherwise have happened, also added further complexity to an already complex system, even if it added integrity (Maraseni 2013: 99–102).

There were also some unintended consequences associated with a number of policy settings. The emphasis on developing country projects ultimately led to equity issues, whereby a few countries ended up dominating the mechanism. Approximately 67 per cent of projects were established in three of the four 'BRIC' countries. China dominated the scheme with over one-third of projects (36 per cent), while India took up nearly a quarter (23 per cent). Smaller countries, desperately in need of technology transfer and investment, missed out. There was also one much-publicised example where companies in China inappropriately profited from the 'greenhouse potency' of hydroflourocarbons (HFC-23) used for refrigerants, and nitrous oxide (N_2O), a by-product of nylon manufacture. These gases had vastly more impact than CO_2, and companies found they could generate more income from selling these as CERs, than both the products they were manufacturing, and the technologies that could be installed to avoid their production. One tonne of avoided HFC-23 could be sold for almost 1200 credits. Before this loophole was closed, almost 5 billion euros went to Chinese manufacturers, while it was estimated that abate cost of producing the pollutants in the first place would most likely have been less than 100 million euros. In addition to such perverse incentives, China's emissions have grown more than 120 per cent since 2000. Consequently, the credibility of the CDM as a mechanism for reducing emissions has been challenged, despite the large number of projects and the actual tonnage of carbon offset (Maraseni 2013: 103–7).

The CDM has also been criticised for part-financing climate change mitigation projects that have negative impacts on the environment and people. This is evident in the CDM's subsidisation of hydropower projects at the expense of freshwater ecosystems and potential perverse impacts of sequestration through plantations on biodiversity conservation. The CBD Secretariat warned: 'The neglect and/or omission of social, environmental and economic considerations can lead to conflicts which could undermine the overall success of carbon mitigation projects, and long-term biodiversity conservation' (CBD 2003: 277). Many developing nations have adopted targets for hydropower development in their national climate change strategies (Pittock 2011: 25). CER certificates are granted to hydropower projects in developing countries registered by the CDM, providing additional income for such projects. Only projects that exceed a power density ratio of more than 4 mega watts (MW) generation capacity per square metre of land inundated in the development can be registered (CDM EB 2009: 18). This is intended to minimise the area of flooded land and the resulting social and environmental impacts. Some environmental degradation may be attenuated by smaller reservoirs, but barriers to fish migration and other severe ecological impacts are not (de Leaniz 2008: 83, Nilsson et al. 2005: 609). As of March 2012 there were 2194 active hydropower projects, amounting to around a quarter of all CDM projects. Most were sited in Brazil, China, India and Vietnam (International Rivers n.d., CDM 2015b). EU companies purchase most CDM hydropower CERs. For credits accepted into the EU ETS, the EU requires hydropower projects with a capacity greater than 20 MW to demonstrate adherence to the applicable criteria and guidelines of the World Commission on Dams (WCD) (European Union 2008: 2). This is a consequence of a considerable level of advocacy to limit social and environmental impacts of dam building (Orr 2001). Yet, of the 675 registered and proposed CDM hydropower projects assessed in a 2010 study, only 35 cited the WCD guidelines in their project-definition documents (Pittock 2010). CDM projects are also meant to demonstrate economic 'additionality,' in other words, that they are only financially viable with the income provided by CERs as well as genuinely contributing to emissions reductions that would not otherwise have occurred (Shrestha and Timilsina 2002, Lecocq and Ambrosi 2007, Tanwar 2007). Of large hydropower projects registered under the CDM in November 2007, 35 per cent were completed before project registration, 89 per cent were expected to be completed within a year, and 96 per cent within two years, which raises questions as to their additionality (Haya 2007: 6, Pottinger 2008).

The Ramsar Convention adopted a resolution encouraging its contracting parties to use all:

> Available information, including information provided by the [WCD], in association with relevant guidance adopted by Ramsar Convention ... in order to ensure that wetlands and their values and functions are fully taken into account in decision-making on large dams. (World Commission on Dams 2002: 10)

The CBD introduced elements of the WCD report into its programme of work, and directed parties to 'use, where appropriate, all available information on dams in order to ensure that biodiversity considerations are fully taken into account in decision-making on large dams' (CBD 2000: paragraph 4). It also encouraged them to 'apply environmental impact assessments on water-development projects' (CBD 2004: 29). By contrast, CDM guidelines and the approved methodology for hydropower projects merely require that environmental impact assessments are 'undertaken in accordance with the procedures as required by the host Party' (CDM EB 2008: 19). This demonstrates that the CDM is providing incentives for hydropower projects without rigorous checks such that they that may seriously impact upon biodiversity and wetlands, in conflict with the resolutions of international biodiversity agreements.

The future of the CDM continues to be uncertain. In 2012 an expert review determined that the mechanism was 'imperilled', citing the collapse of the carbon price by 70 per cent in that year alone. The experts blamed the weak mitigation targets in discussion in the climate talks, and the failure of national governments to take up the opportunity of developing CDM projects and of not linking mitigation projects governments were developing to the CDM. This led to policymakers questioning its value, which had in turn driven private sector investors away. The authors of the report were concerned that, while many policymakers might not mourn the CDM's passing and 'new generation' instruments were under development, they were not yet ready, and the world could be left with no global mechanism at all. This was despite the robust assessment and verification methodologies, and the success of the CDM in generating over USD 215 billion in investments over its life (CDM Policy Dialogue 2012: 3). The authors made a dire prediction:

> If nations permit the CDM market to disintegrate, the political consensus for truly global carbon markets may evaporate along with much of the world's developing country carbon market capacity. Developing countries and the private sector are unlikely to see sufficient benefits to justify aggressive emissions mitigation steps in those nations. The collapse of the CDM, in short, could seriously set back international climate cooperation, with potentially devastating consequences for all. (CDM Policy Dialogue 2012: 3)

One of the problems that have confronted the CDM has been the declining value of carbon markets. It has been estimated that the European market required a value of around 30 euros to drive sustainable investment levels. But mistakes there (notably the issuing of free credits) had depressed prices. In 2008 the carbon price was at 28 euros, but by 2013 it had plummeted to less than 4 euros (Ares 2014: 2). The extent to which this can be laid at the feet of the CDM is questionable, but it does appear to be the case that uncertainty over the price and prospects for carbon markets has challenged its viability in the future. As the KP commitment period has now expired, there is not necessarily a reason to keep the mechanism, although the CDM EB is continuing to meet and promote ongoing activities, including the development of methodology for aviation industry to measure its emissions, engage in reduction activities and 'earn saleable credits' (CDM 2015a).

Sources and Means of Delivery of Finance

Although one of the objectives of a CDM is to assist in sustainable development and to reduce poverty in developing countries, concerns regarding the efficient delivery of benefits to pro-poor have long been raised, mostly in terms of the effectiveness of minimising climate change risks. To address such concerns, a major challenge for CDM planners is how to prioritise projects that provide both sustainable development and pro-poor benefits (Crowe 2013: 58). It is reasonable to suggest that it is easier to address CDM objectives on reducing GHG emissions in developed countries rather than to allocate the benefits among developing communities on a market-based approach, where other externalities may result in market failures. At the same time, those communities encounter hand-to-mouth problems, and must overcome disasters influenced by extreme climatic variability. In this perplexing context and within the concept of 'climate as a public good', equitable delivery of finance holds significant meaning in alleviating poverty.

Allocating CDM benefits with a market-based approach strongly demands that investment and new technology cope, for example, with extreme increases in the price of energy (Mohammadi et al. 2013: 210), and where normal CDM policies should have upgraded high-priced carbon credits to ensure extra pro-poor benefits. Given the fact that poor people are more vulnerable due to their socioeconomic constraints, climate change may thus impose additional burdens on them. Therefore, prioritising quality governance through developing local partnerships not only consolidates such demands but also develops aptitude in managing resources at the local level. Due to the prominence of the agricultural contribution in employment and livelihood in these communities, CDM projects have to invigorate the objective of sustainability into 'win–win' strategies (Torvanger et al. 2013: 471), generating non-farm employment, and ultimately offsetting market-based production. Therefore, in this CDM-poverty nexus, additional incentives, along with investments in technology and regular carbon benefits, are required in combatting climate change.

There have been a number of studies on CDM projects, including pro-poor mechanisms allocating benefits to poor people in Africa. Karani and Gantsho (2007: 203) analysed the interactions of Development Finance Institutions (DFIs) with existing CDM projects. Employing a bottom-up approach, the study investigated the projects that focused on building local capacity by working experts in Cameroon, Ghana, Mali, Mozambique and Zambia. The results revealed that the existing projects had acted as catalysts for the development of a carbon market even though high transaction costs were major barriers for CDM implementation. A fragile carbon market cannot develop homogeneity in resource allocation. A similar situation of inequality related to CDM benefits in Africa results from South Africa's larger share in the Development Bank of Southern Africa (DBSA) loan portfolio than other African country members. Therefore, further investment in a DBSA mechanism, in this case, can concentrate any allocated loan benefit in South Africa, and may thus enhance the disparity among developing communities of Africa in the longer term.

CDM has direct and indirect links with agriculture and its market instruments. Agriculture as the mainstay of developing economies provides the main opportunity for pro-poor growth as it provides employment opportunities to increase the livelihoods of poor people. Thus, CDM projects have an important role in turning subsistence farming into agribusiness systems. Using a systematic review and meta-analysis, Resanond et al. (2011: 80) analysed the role of a company's competitiveness enhancement in Thai agribusiness, and illustrated that companies make key decisions to move towards better technology with efficient operational performance when this also generates non-farm employment. For instance, Sirohi highlights an urgent need for mechanisms in Indian CDM projects to improve infrastructure, and to generate non-farm employment that supplements agricultural income (Sirohi 2007: 91). Thai CDMs have to focus on technology and innovations in addition to the macroeconomic infrastructure created by the government to improve its agricultural productivity and reduce escalating poverty (Resanond et al. 2011: 80). Slow market innovation (Karani and Gantsho 2007: 226), on the other hand, leads to institutions' administrative constraints in improving CDM-benefits to achieve pro-poor growth. Thus, to create natural inflows of resources in agribusiness, administrative efficiency has to be improved in the Thai agricultural system.

A comparative enquiry of CDM projects in China, India, Saudi Arabia, UAE and Qatar in Mohammadi et al. (2013: 211) identifies China and India as first in the way of implementation of CDM-objectives. In contrast, Saudi Arabia and UAE come first and second respectively when investigating economic criteria of investing in CDM improvements. The study recommends implementing high-priced carbon credits, which could play a meaningful role in post-2012 energy policies where a political decision could change the situation. Politically unstable countries have a lesser chance to consolidate the policies towards better outcomes of CDM projects. In this case, Torvanger et al. (2013: 473) suggest a two-track CDM mechanism of sustainable development (SD) and offset production (OP). Such a mechanism helps to break political deadlock, and allows the inclusion of SD benefits in the price system itself, and sanctions both sustainable development and OP objectives to be simultaneously achieved.

Newell (2009: 425) argues that the quality of CDM outcomes depends on the type of governance, particularly in developing countries where political decisions are generally inconsistent. The political-economic context, a vital element of CDM governance, outlines a spectrum of carbon mechanism. By broadening the capacity of CDM projects, reasonable mechanisms can be developed to include the justifiable use of local resources. Thus, the quality outcomes of CDM projects depend significantly on how the planners understand the broader nexus of political conflicts, institutional aptitudes and globalisation. In this regard, a balanced composite of SD and OP, referred to in Torvanger et al. (2013: 477), has to be maintained in order to achieve good governance, and to broaden the prospect of market-based incentives on a global level.

Efficient delivery of finance through CDM projects has been questioned in many respects, including the equitable allocation of resources. There are some examples of CDM projects that demonstrate equitable revenue sharing. Crowe (2013: 58) analysed 114 CDM projects in order to develop indicators on reducing poverty and promoting pro-poor growth. The study used two approaches: a description and assessment approach of seven pro-poor indicators, and a stakeholder-participation approach. The study identified 67 respondents as carbon market participants in five job types, and found that only one of the analysed projects, RE-biomass in India, had positive ratings for all seven indicators, where one of those indicators is equitable revenue-sharing. The participants indicated that there is good market potential for an explicitly labelled pro-poor CDM add-on standard to deliver on. This means that while regular CDM projects are only moderately successful at delivering pro-poor benefits, CDM projects with premium add-on standards may accomplish more comprehensive results through finance.

With respect to investment, there is an ongoing argument related to which should come first, adaptation or mitigation, or both simultaneously. Delivering benefits is determined by which objective is prioritised to minimise climate change impacts. From a socioeconomic perspective, as opposed to mitigation, adaptation seems to have many more dimensions. To overcome this argument, Haites (2011: 967) has suggested that a country should have a balanced approach of financing to mitigation and adaptation, and the most efficient way to finance mitigation measures is for governments to adopt policies that address GHG emissions and other market failures. Similarly, an analysis of the Organization of the Petroleum Exporting Countries (OPEC) database in Mohammadi et al. (2013: 236) recommends investing in technology advancement to combat several-fold energy price increases that could serve to reduce GHG emissions in the long run. Hence, simultaneous investment in both mitigation and adaptation can better alleviate poverty in developing countries, and can bring the GHG emission into benchmarks targeted by developed countries.

As the objectives of CDM for developing countries and developed countries are different in terms of resource allocation and its use to maintain economic growth, implementation of an ideal tool is a must to refresh inflows of investment and technology. Industrialised countries, for instance, may prefer to reduce GHG emissions in the targeted time frames, whereas developing countries are expected to continue their development. Thus CDM needs to be framed along these two trails. Torvanger et al. (2013: 478) developed an approach for CDM-countries and formulated a mechanism to harmonise SD benefits and offset GHG productions. Sirohi (2007: 104) suggested a different approach to achieve a 'win–win' strategy for rural poverty alleviation in India. He suggested designing a system for rain-fed farms as a major CDM project to accelerate agricultural growth, and motivate pro-poor growth in non-farm employment that supplements agricultural incomes. Such micro-level strategies should be equipped with macroeconomic infrastructure created by the government.

According to Resanond et al. (2011: 82), a major challenge of CDM implementation is the local and international approvals structure, leading to fault assessment and misinterpretation of carbon market because of uncertainty in CDM processing. Local approvals come along with socioeconomic attributes of local communities whereas international approvals are determined by global sociopolitical elements. Sometimes these approvals move in different directions as the stakeholders have developed different interests with regard to climate change and sustainability. To overcome this challenge, a set of globally approved and accepted guidelines should be formulated. Decreasing the CDM processing time can offer opportunities for big national and multinational companies to improve their operational performance and GHG reduction

(Resanond et al. 2011: 84) though some country-specific strategies may need to supplement the mainstream.

Overall, empirical studies of CDM projects describe significant misgivings towards the efficient delivery of benefits to pro-poor growth in developing countries. However, these studies recommend different ways or solutions to achieve better results. For example, some studies (e.g. Crowe 2013, Sirohi 2007, Resanond et al. 2011) argue that regular CDM projects are only moderately successful at delivering pro-poor benefits, suggesting that a lack of efficient mechanisms has created big hurdles. Still fewer studies such as Karani and Gantsho (2007) and Mohammadi et al. (2013) have identified grey areas while analysing investment indicators such as overall economic criteria, such as recent CDM investments in Saudi Arabia and UAE. China and India have come to the forefront in implementing CDM projects. All of the studies show fragile aptitudes in political decision-making in developing countries to overcome the vicious poverty cycles. This is why there will need to be hard-hitting mechanisms to achieve pro-poor growth in order for developing countries to escape from poverty caused by already overstrained impacts of climate change.

REDD+

Nearly 20 per cent of global GHG emissions are a consequence of deforestation and forest degradation. Deforestation is a consequence of the conversion of natural forests to non-forest uses such as palm oil plantations and soybean production. It is dropping in some countries, but increasing in others. Degradation contributes no less than 20 per cent of carbon emissions from forests, and is a consequence of logging for timber and fuel wood. Logging increases access to resources, which in turn leads to further extraction. Forest fires also contribute to degradation. Logging and burning create a feedback loop of expanding degradation, and eventually, deforestation (de Oliveira et al. 2013: 9–10).

The idea of paying countries to reduce emissions from deforestation (first termed 'RED') has been linked to an MBA thesis written by Kevin Conrad. Conrad was one of the driving forces behind the Coalition of Rainforest Nations, representing the main regions with tropical forests, and who were successful in encouraging UNFCC to include payments for combatting deforestation into the climate negotiations around mitigating carbon emissions (de Oliveira et al. 2013: 8). The idea of planting trees as carbon 'sinks' was not new, dating back to the development of the flexible mechanisms under Kyoto, and the World Bank Prototype Carbon

Fund (PCF) (World Bank 2015). This led to a growing interest in 'afforestation' projects, which it was demonstrated had resulted in the establishment of monoculture 'carbon sinks' plantations established through the clearing and burning of ancient forests and rainforests – thereby defeating the purpose of the projects (Cadman 2000). This partially contributed to the breakdown of negotiations in COP 6 (2000) in The Hague, requiring a second, COP 6 'bis', in Bonn the same year to resolve the issue of how to include forests in mitigation activities (Carbonweb 2001: 2–3). This may have dampened interest in using forests for offsets notably in Europe, and by 2004 they appeared to have slipped off the climate agenda (de Oliveira et al. 2013: 9). But at COP 13 in Bali, 2007, Papua New Guinea and Costa Rica launched the concept of REDD, submitting a formal proposal for discussions (Chiroleu-Assouline et al. 2012: 2–3). As a consequence, the concept was elaborated around the issues of how to deliver financial payments, what reference levels would be required to determine emissions reductions, how monitoring, reporting and verification (MRV) should take place, and how to 'promote' Indigenous peoples' and local communities' participation. It was further recommended that any subsequent programme that was developed be broken down into three phases: national strategy development, capacity-building and demonstration activities; implementation of the policies and measures developed; and performance-based payments against agreed reference levels (Zarin et al. 2009: vii).

A series of institutional arrangements were developed in subsequent negotiations. Partner-based projects were encouraged, led by the Forest Carbon Partnership Facility (FCPF) of the World Bank, and UN-REDD, which provide financial and technical support. Other organisations with a supporting role include the Forest Investment Program (FIP – also World Bank), the GEF, the REDD+ Partnership (a countries-based alliance) and the UNFCCC itself, which effectively guided the nature and intent of REDD+ via the climate negotiations (Multipartner Trust Fund Office (MTFO) 2013).

The United Nations Collaborative Programme on Reducing Emissions from Deforestation and Forest Degradation in Developing Countries (REDD) was launched in September 2008 to assist capacity-building in developing countries to reduce emissions and develop related market mechanisms – (UN-REDD 2009: 11). The 'plus' in REDD+ was adopted after the COP 15 in Copenhagen in 2009 to include the sustainable management, conservation and enhancement of forests and forest carbon stocks. REDD+ allows 'avoided deforestation' to be included in market-based carbon trading mechanisms. It is linked to the KP and the KP-related CDM, and offers developed countries a means of meeting their emissions targets through reducing GHG emissions in developing countries (de Oliveira et al. 2013: 8–9).

The FCPF was formally launched in Bali in December 2007 and became operational in June 2008 (REDD Monitor 2008). The Facility grew out of internal discussions that started in 2006 at the World Bank, but situated in a broader context about carbon rights, notably Indigenous peoples' rights, which IPOs and NGOs feared could be weakened (The Forest Peoples Programme (FPP) 2008). These discussions, which involved a number of countries and organisations including environmental NGOs, highlighted the value of developing the Facility in partnership with a broad range of actors, to balance the interests of potential donors and buyers, recipients and sellers and other stakeholders. The FCPF provides a fresh source of financing for the sustainable use of forest resources and biodiversity conservation. Eventually, it is hoped that this will lead to a large-scale system of incentives for reducing emissions from deforestation and forest degradation in developing countries. The FCPF involves countries as recipients of funds, donors of funds and participants on committees. Donors are developed countries; recipients of funding are developing countries wishing to use forest resources sustainably and conserve biodiversity. All countries participating in the FCPF, either as donors or recipients of funding, are members of the Participants Assembly. The FCPF has two separate funding mechanisms: the Readiness Fund (RF), which provides eligible governments with public grants to support policy and institutional reforms aimed at preparing the country to implement REDD; and the Carbon Fund (CF), which will link countries that are ready to implement REDD with payments for the purchase of their avoided GHG emissions. These mechanisms each have their own trust fund, for which the World Bank acts as trustee. Donors are known as Donor Participants (if they contribute to the RF) or CF Participants (if they contribute to the CF); whereas developing countries participating in either fund are known as REDD Country Participants (Forest Carbon Partnership Facility 2010).

At 1 January 2013, 14 developed countries and the European Commission had donated to the RF, and a total of USD 259 million was pledged to the RF (Forest Carbon Partnership Facility 2012c). Using the FCPF's framework and processes for REDD+ Readiness, each participating country develops an understanding of what it means to become ready for REDD+. The main ways that countries do this are by developing reference scenarios, adopting a REDD+ strategy, designing monitoring systems and setting up REDD+ national management arrangements, in ways that are inclusive of the key national stakeholders (Forest Carbon Partnership Facility 2013b). Readiness funds could also be used to establish the foundations of good forest governance; for example, by providing secure tenure over forest land and resources, enforcing forest laws and empowering forest-dependent communities to participate in forest management (Davis et al. 2009). The FCPF RF relates to Phase 1, whereas the FCPF CF relates to Phase 2. Initially, the World Bank was the only delivery partner (DP) for the RF. However, a meeting of the Participants Committee in June 2011 approved two additional DPs: the Inter-American Development Bank and the UNDP. In October 2011, the UN FAO was approved as an additional DP. These additional DPs can provide REDD+ Readiness support services to distinct countries (Forest Carbon Partnership Facility 2013a).

The CF became operational in 2011, and piloted performance-based payments for verified emission reductions from REDD+ programmes in countries that have made considerable progress towards REDD+ Readiness. The goal was to provide incentives to reduce emissions while protecting forests, conserving biodiversity and enhancing the livelihoods of forest-dependent peoples and local communities (Forest Carbon Partnership Facility 2012a). The CF, which has a target size of USD 350 million, is a public–private partnership, and FCPF has acknowledged that 'the private sector is critical, not only to scale up funding for REDD+ but also to provide management capacity and experience with innovative financial instruments' (Forest Carbon Partnership Facility 2012d: 2). Programmes were required to be undertaken at a significant scale (for example, at the level of an administrative jurisdiction within a country or at the national level) to align with the proposed national REDD+ Strategy and management framework, and to be consistent with the emerging national REDD+ MRV system and national reference emission levels (Forest Carbon Partnership Facility 2012a: 33). By March 2013, the European Commission as well as seven other developed countries and three private entities had contributed to the CF (Forest Carbon Partnership Facility 2012c).

The intent of the UN-REDD Programme was to manage and simplify the distribution of financial resources for the implementation of initiatives to reduce deforestation and forest degradation at the national level (MTFO 2013). UN-REDD provides support to national-level 'REDD+ Readiness' initiatives, delivered through two principle methods: global support at the international and regional levels; and specific, targeted assistance in the development and implementation of country programmes (UN-REDD 2009: 11). An emphasis is placed on Joint Programmes between international and national-level agencies (FAO et al. 2008: 1). The intention is to encourage effectiveness and efficiency (United Nations Development Group n.d.). Where possible, there is also an expectation that funds will also be delivered through one programme, one lead agency, one budget and one office, under the UN's wider drive for efficiency, expressed in the 'delivering as one' concept (2015). As an institution, UN-REDD is a collaborative management arrangement between the UN bodies: the UNEP, the UNDP and the FAO (UN-REDD 2009: 11). The UN-REDD Framework Document and the Programme Strategy 2011–2015, approved in November 2010, has been responsible for guiding activities to date. In the context of national-level actions to mitigate and adapt to climate change mitigation and adaptation, UN-REDD's economic and social strategies are aimed at providing performance-based payments in exchange for sustainable forest management and changed land-use practices to reduce emissions (UN-REDD 2011b).

However concerns about the potential for perverse impacts from REDD remain. Additionally, there are concerns about the lack of attention under REDD frameworks (even REDD+ frameworks) for addressing ecosystem benefits. For instance, IGO official 3 says:

> You have things like REDD and REDD+. There's a lot of worry about those, actually undermining the whole approach, the way it is used and things like that in terms of sectorally-based carbon sequestration increasing through forestation and not doing damage to other aspects of biodiversity and disenfranchising local communities, Indigenous people. So, a lot of concern is flying around about that at the moment.

> All the right words are there, if you look at the UN-REDD Programme objectives and purpose and so on, but it hardly works on the ground and there's a lot of concerns from what I've heard that large amounts of money are being poured into preparation of REDD Readiness, REDD+ Planning and so on. And then implementation on the ground risks a large extra pot of money ending up in the hands of unsustainable forestry interests.

> For example, it [REDD+] certainly is an area that is causing some quite difficult challenges that we face. We have a situation where at least one party is fundamentally opposed politically at the moment. Any attention to evaluation of ecosystems, monetisation, economic values of services, REDD+, a whole lot of this concern rests on the grounds that this monetises ecosystems and particularly supports the private sector making profit. That's a bit extreme but it's a valid concern. Yet at the same time many of our parties are desperately putting top priority on getting better information about the importance of wetlands and the values through team-related work and so on, to help them get into the heads of the decision-makers, that they've got to understand the real implications of destroying ecosystems. They are making better-informed decisions on tradeoffs and hopefully informed by the value of what they might be destroying. So we have a real conflict of view between different parts of the world and countries on some of these issues at the moment.

As REDD+ is delivered largely at the national level, programmes are expected to engage effectively with UN agencies in country and demonstrate the country's contribution to reducing emissions and thereby mitigating climate change. Assistance from the relevant UN agencies in each country is available as 'targeted support' from the global support to the national REDD+ Action fund to assist in the development of strategies to achieve REDD+ Readiness. Country-level activities are also directed towards the creation of Readiness Preparation Proposals (R-PP), either through UN-REDD or FCPF under a 'harmonised' preparation process. All these activities, strategies and proposals are included in a National Programme Document (NPD). It is effectively the guidance manual that is used to describe and coordinate the nature and extent of UN agency financial and technical support, and the legal basis on which collaboration with governments occurs. The NPD, R-PP and a signed submission are provided to UN-REDD at the international level when requesting funds. All these activities and processes are guided by various documents and tools, as well as approaches to safeguards regarding such issues as stakeholder engagement and the participation of Indigenous peoples and forest-dependent communities (UN-REDD 2012: 7–15).

Despite the progress on implementing REDD+ pilots, the fate of Phase 3 (performance-based payments) is less certain. In the June 2014 Climate talks in Bonn there was a clear difference of opinion between donor countries and recipient countries over the use of market-based approaches. Developing countries sought to de-couple implementation funding of REDD+ from the trade in emissions, a position supported by a number of countries in both the Asia-Pacific region and Latin America, notably Indonesia, Brazil and Bolivia. This objection may be based on ideological grounds (revisiting the critique of 'carbon imperialism') or economic grounds, given the low market value of carbon. The US attempted to provide a reconciling position and indicated that it would support payments in a 'mixed economy' of market and non-market-based approaches, but was keen to link REDD+ to carbon markets. This was not positively received. This leads to the conclusion that lack of certainty around the future of carbon markets in the climate negotiations may well be contributing to underperforming markets. These disagreements created another point of contention leading up to COP 21 (Cadman 2014).

Sources and Means of Delivery of Finance

There are widespread concerns about reducing emissions from deforestation and forest degradation, and enhancing forest carbon stocks in developing countries (REDD+) in terms of market mechanisms, acting on global strategies in local communities and achieving SD. Market mechanisms are directly and indirectly involved in the delivery of pro-poor growth benefits through REDD+ in developing countries. One of the major objectives of REDD+ is to provide strong incentives through performance-based approaches to carbon right holders (Angelsen et al. 2009: 296), and thus reduce GHGs emissions in the long term. In this regard, governmental and institutional capacity to build interactive linkages between the national and local delivery systems determines the efficiency of the mechanism, and involves institutional reforms to move REDD into REDD+.

In the supply chain of market-based benefits, enhancements of private sector involvement and investments determine the success of efficient finance delivery, thus allowing extractive industries in the REDD+ supply chain to operate in effective ways (Bernard et al. 2012: v). At the same time, a public–private partnership as referred to in Darragh et al. (2014) could play a vital role in using compensation credits to secure financing for REDD+. Therefore, the design of projects requires attention to be paid in this area in order to have country-specific mechanisms and to create inclusive strategies for marginalised communities. This is also due to the fact that a REDD typology of global mitigation policies cannot transfer the overall qualities into REDD+ until (and unless) a locally relevant forest payment system is created and acted upon. In this regard, it is important to overcome institutional barriers and rectify fragmented structures of global governance architectures (Kanowski et al. 2011: 114), and to integrate the outcomes of the best REDD+ initiatives (Richards and Swan 2014: 14).

As was alluded to in the remarks of interviewees noted above, a great challenge to implementing REDD+ in a number of countries is related to overcoming forest tenure issues (Angelsen et al. 2012: 114). This includes legislative apparatuses that may not sufficiently address indigenous land tenure concerns. To assess market payments to the carbon holders, transparency in a forest tenure system is important. For this, illegal use of land and the exploitation of resources raise challenges to forest sector regulations. Other than this, the concept of a voluntary carbon market has long been raised in combination with result-based payments (Darragh et al. 2014: 27). A trade-off between agricultural policies and energy policies is another issue to be addressed by REDD+ in developing countries. As agriculture-based local communities continue traditional ways of farming for their livelihoods, it is a great challenge to switch into forest conservation for stocking carbon in sufficient ways. The chance of shifting land becomes more challenging in these communities as they have been facing the increasing impacts of climate change. Therefore, it is imperative to discuss delivery of finance through REDD+ in developing countries, and to seek good evidence of these market-based payments to pro-poor growth.

There have been a number of case studies on REDD+ in recent years. Darragh et al. (2014: 4) compare financing options in the EU, and give possible options for mobilising finance such as REDD+ compensation credits, sustainable supply chains, ring-fencing public finance, stimulating results-based payments for REDD+, coordinating EU results-based financing, member-state incentives and public–private partnership. It has offered a variety of options as the persistent economic weakness manifest across the EU has led to public finances being stressed, and thus putting pressure on public allocation for REDD+. The establishment of voluntary carbon markets can support public finances, although stakeholders identified a number of barriers. Technical issues associated with REDD+ (Darragh et al. 2014: 7) and inefficient stimulation in private investment are creating difficulties in EU countries, and are slowing institutional transformation from REDD to REDD+.

The private sector plays an important role in financing REDD+ and in developing a secondary carbon market. Bernard et al. (2012: xi) have analysed implementing safeguard information systems to foster the role of private sectors in Kenya, Japan and California by engaging them in the REDD+ supply chain. California's emerging cap-and-trade system very quickly created a compliance-based market for REDD+ credits. In addition, a bilateral offset mechanism in Japan which disseminated advanced low-carbon technologies, has created a conducive environment for an efficient secondary carbon market. However, Somorin et al. (2011: 399) argue that while investing in technological advancement, the success of the multiple aspects of REDD+ remains critical, as forest dwellers are likely to be severely impacted. As such, some African government respondents suggested that local participation is the only way to find better solutions, and to cope with the challenges of complexity, governance and decentralisation.

Political instability in developing countries continues to raise security concerns for private investment. A case study of the Amazon basin conducted by UNEP (2014: 113) refers to the case of Terra Global Capital in Cambodia, who, through incentive-based conservation contracts and co-management with communities, invested in the project with a political risk insurance contract from the Overseas Private Investment Corporation. UNEP argues that this demonstrates that, to ensure ecosystem services through REDD+ payoff, it is essential to focus on positive environmental external influences along with the marketing of biodiversity-friendly products (UNEP 2014: 113). In this regard, Rey and

Swan (2014: 56) have provided a country-led safeguard approach with national REDD+ guidelines, one of which states: 'while defining safeguard guidelines, a country should consider who will be involved and be responsible for collection, aggregation, review and a potential assessment of the information'. Similarly, channels for the dissemination of information play an important role in bridging global REDD guidelines and national strategies, and community participation in information sharing can resolve local disputes.

Government intervention is required to balance ecosystem payments and the cost of implementing REDD+ at a national level. A study in Brazil-Amazon by Mann et al. (2012: 279) has raised an issue around policy intervention in agricultural conversion, and suggests a preference towards a municipality-level tax in land conversion. According to the report, the local level tax provides two benefits: (1) generating additional annual funding through the uniform tax, and (2) keeping a check on haphazard conversion of land creating unfriendly environmental outcomes. However, different types of critical issues are experienced in Kenya (Bernard et al. 2012: 5). Finding extractive industries that will convert land to achieve sustainable outcomes is difficult while providing REDD+ credits to them. In this case, Corbera and Schroeder (2011: 96) have suggested improving local governance, whereby government should design a land-use plan by conducting in-depth examinations of how policies and actions unfold in local contexts through existing commercial networks, extension services, and both legal and illegal markets for natural resources.

Overall proficiency of REDD+ projects is ultimately determined by how efficiently the projects are delivering to achieve the pro-poor growth benefits in developing countries. Thus the methodology of delivery and strategy of regulation requires careful examination. The Institute for Global Environmental Strategies – IGES (2014: 4) has reviewed the efficiencies of eight REDD+ projects, mostly based in Brazil, in terms of their architecture and jurisdictional approaches. The report depicts that certified REDD+ projects have only transacted about half of the carbon offsets that the projects are able to trade, therefore it suggests that 'the UNFCCC negotiations must lead towards targets for deep emissions cuts to generate the levels of funding required for REDD+ to be significant as an instrument for climate change mitigation'. Hence, there is an urgent need for the development of a basis set of standards that each country can adapt to their own contexts to ensure that the safeguards are appreciated and addressed.

Every REDD+ project is examined in terms of equal and equitable delivery of benefits in actual contexts. The lack of properly defined roles of stakeholders, including means to disseminate the benefits, creates disputes among communities. For example, Bolivian communities face difficulty as two ministries compete for attention, where the forest is administered by the ministry of rural development and climate change is administered by the ministry of environment; both are responsible for allocating resources (Angelsen et al. 2009: 294). In this sense, it is unclear who is going to receive the benefits. Hence, REDD+ projects have to specifically identify the beneficiaries, especially in forest-dependent communities. A good example of this is a Tanzanian project (Angelsen et al. 2009: 39) which distributes benefits equally to communities by classifying the groups of beneficiaries. The same solution is seen in a Vietnamese REDD+ project, where the cross-sectoral coordination has been prioritised. However, the way of classifying the beneficiaries depends on the policy which governments have in place. For example, market liberals (Angelsen et al. 2012: 37) favour market mechanisms and prioritise improvement in the forest products to reduce the poverty in developing countries, and forest users choose forest conservation if the compensation they receive is higher than their potential earnings from alternative forest uses.

In many cases, the land tenure system has become a great challenge in financing REDD+. Severe tenure insecurity, for example, is faced by smallholders whereas large landholders have been enjoying forest rent in Indonesia (Angelsen et al. 2009: 33). In this scenario, a better option is to involve local communities as in a Cameroon REDD+ project (Angelsen et al. 2009: 37) where a benefit-sharing portfolio of 50–40–10 (50 per cent to national administration, 40 per cent to communal office and 10 per cent to communities living around the logging area) is managed by the forest users. However, the benefit-share portfolio depends on institutional structures, perceptions of local communities and socioeconomic constructs. Therefore, countries have different approaches in designing the benefit-sharing portfolio. Moreover, policies with national and international negotiations (Corbera and Schroeder 2011: 96) lead to the broader framework in designing the portfolio, though in-depth examination of how policies change while manifesting at the local level is essential to avoid community disputes.

REDD+ regulation also needs to be considered in delivering benefits for pro-poor growth. Diversity of institutions is a great challenge (Kanowski et al. 2011: 114), and brings inefficient outcomes. Fragmented structures of national and international governance have diverse impacts on the consolidation of the guidelines of REDD+ regulations. The information systems on the other hand also play a vital role in formulating national guidelines. 'Who will be involved and be responsible for collection, aggregation, review and a potential assessment of the information' (Rey and Swan 2014: 56) should be included in the guidelines prepared. Some steps are suggested by Richards and Swan (2014: 12) regarding methodology and step-by-step guidance such as: preparatory studies, drivers analysis, interventions analysis, safeguards analysis, monitoring plan and reporting and socialising results. Thompson et al. (2011: 108) present a different argument and suggest that REDD+ regulations should be observed as environmental governance. According to the report,

> the best way is to carefully consider how participation of affected communities is facilitated in the REDD+ process, both to ensure that the voice of a wide range of affected people might be heard in this process, and to make a significant effort to make participation as unconstrained as possible, so as to hear the real concerns and needs of these communities as these programs and projects move forward.

In another version in compliance markets for REDD+ by USAID (2013: 16), materialising demand and supply are observed closely to foster result-based mechanisms of REDD+ countries, highlighting that emission reductions and removals from REDD+ need to be tradable and eligible for use to meet future emission reduction commitments. The study (p. 54) suggested that between 2016 and 2020 demand could significantly exceed the estimated credit insurance, and a lack of strong demand until after 2020 could cause financial harm to governments, local communities, civil society and the private sector already engaging in REDD+ activities. Through this crisis, the countries whose growth and development primarily depends on agriculture will bear the brunt of challenges resulting from the new market dynamics (La Vina et al. 2014: 12). To tackle the situation, national and sub-national policies have to concentrate on the issue of land-use change in developing countries, and have to regulate the supply to meet the demand till 2020.

Developing a uniform set of REDD+ guidelines is necessary to achieve checks and balances in national and local decision-making. An increased risk of national and local political interests threatens the project's proficiency. Hence, a set of global guidelines can contribute to resolve national and international disputes. In addition, this can also offer opportunities for the private sector to develop better understandings of the potential market of carbon credits (Bernard et al. 2012: vi), providing greater collaboration between the public and private sectors and ultimately assessing, articulating and classifying the beneficiaries. A well-planned public–private network will help to coordinate different resource-allocating institutions, and increase the efficiency of the delivery of finance as there will be less chance of duplication of beneficiaries. This 'local-flavoured' strategy should be aimed at rural communities, and designed to accelerate agricultural growth in the rain-fed regions of developing countries. It could be a genuine solution that would enable a test of the REDD+ at the local level before enabling broad policy reforms.

Finally, there is an urgent need for an efficient REDD+ mechanism to mobilise finance to improve incentives for SD in developing countries. Public finances should be free of persistent economic weakness. To achieve consistency in policy development, some of the options referred to in Darragh et al. (2014: 9 and 10) such as compensation credits, ring-fencing finances and member-state incentives, can ensure how and when the benefits could be delivered to local communities. Institutional regulation should be developed on the basis of social-REDD+ experiences and local knowledge. In this way, the overall goals of REDD+ can be achieved through the incentivising of sustainable supply chains and overcoming market failures. Thus, an efficient mechanism of delivering finance through REDD+ projects can be achieved and a reduction in abject poverty in developing countries can be realised.

NORTH/SOUTH RELATIONS AND STATE AND NON-STATE ACTORS

Given the historical relations in the climate talks between developing and developed countries, it would be easy to conclude that these geo-political divisions have become entrenched. The literature argues that the North/South divide has contributed to an almost complete 'ossification' of the regime (Depledge 2006: 9–15). Other scholars have made similar observations, characterising the regime's governance as constituting a pattern of arrested development (Young 2010). Inequality has been identified as a central impediment to collaboration within the climate regime, and epitomised by the impasse between North and South, and which therefore necessitates changes to the structural barriers which developing countries face in climate negotiations (Parks and Roberts 2008: 621 and 644). The construction of the climate problematic as one which requires economic neo-liberal responses, it has been argued, is essentially a Northern construction of the problematic, foisted on the South, and is hampering progress towards understanding climate change as a de-territorialising, transnational phenomenon. Countries such as India, which is heavily reliant on economic growth, tend to vacillate between accepting this discourse while also trying to engage with alternative geo-political and geo-economic conceptions (Doyle and Chaturvedi 2010: 516–17).

It is not surprising to see some changes in the geo-political and stakeholder dynamics, given the age of the Convention. These changes have been placed into three distinct phases. The first is portrayed as consisting of a formalised North/South divide through the designation of Convention participants as being either Annex I, i.e. developed countries, or non-Annex I parties. The second is better understood as a North/North struggle between various alliances either in support of – or reluctant to ratify – the KP and implement market mechanisms; and a period of increasing North/South cooperation around Kyoto implementation, but also commensurate with a fragmentation of South, culminating in the Copenhagen Accord of 2010, which created a separation between those developing countries which were expected to support mitigation measures ('will' in the text), and least developed countries as well as small island states, who were not obliged to do so ('may' in the text) (Abreu Mejía 2010: 9–39). Phase 1 commenced with negotiations around the climate regime formation, including the creation of the IPCC, and culminated in the 1994 Framework Convention on Climate Change. In this phase the North/South divide was formalised and institutionalised through the designation of countries as being either Annex I (developed) or 'non-Annex I parties' (i.e. developing countries) and the consequential CBDR dictum of international diplomacy (Abreu Mejía 2010: 14–18). Phase 2 has been interpreted as commencing with the Berlin Mandate in 1995 and the ratification of the KP. This period was marked by the heavy influence exerted by the neo-liberal market order (Abreu Mejía 2010: 20–6). The third stage can be seen as ongoing, but effectively commenced with the first dialogue in Montreal in 2005, around what arrangements should be put in place once the KP commitment period ended in 2012. Initially, this period generated a good degree of cooperation among parties to the Convention, reaching a high point in 2007 with the 'Bali Road Map', which included a 'shared vision', as well as renewed commitment to taking action on both mitigating and adapting to climate change. In addition, parties agreed to transfer technologies to enhance 'green' development, and provide financial resources to assist all the points agreed. Discussions became fraught, however, around the expectation that all countries, developed and developing, should implement programmes to mitigate climate change (Abreu Mejía 2010: 26–9). This was to become particularly pronounced at negotiations at Copenhagen in 2010, and at this point it is possible to identify the emergence of what has been referred to as 'a fragmentation process in the South', combined with an increasing closeness between the US and large developing countries (Abreu Mejía 2010: 3). This was a consequence of the last-minute attempt to rescue discussions through the release of the

Copenhagen Accord, which for the first time divided non-Annex I parties (i.e. developing countries) between those who were expected to implement mitigation actions and least developed countries and small island states, who were not obliged to do so (Abreu Mejía 2010: 27).

Some heavy criticisms have been levelled against the CDM. These have both an ethical and practical basis. On the ethical side the CDM has been characterised as re-introducing methods of re-colonialisation and control by the North over the South, notably through the use of afforestation projects, created as carbon 'sinks'. This has engendered an imperialist dimension to global environmental governance leading to an 'empire of carbon management and control' (Paterson and Stripple 2007: 163). On the practical side it has been argued that the division between Non-annex and Annex countries (those with responsibility to reduce emissions) was based on a world order that ceased to be relevant very quickly after the collapse of the Soviet Union). China and India also had no reduction commitments under KP. This is particularly relevant given their quasi-developed status. This effectively placed most of the blame and most of the costs on developed countries (Okereke 2010: 467). At the same time, developing countries did not have to take ownership of their own historic responsibility for rising global emissions. The focus on mitigation inherent in the CDM (and the developed country agenda this represents) also resulted in a lack of action around adaptation and capacity-building in areas other than mitigation generally (Okereke 2010: 468–70).

NGOs have documented a number of poorly managed CDM projects in developing countries over the years, and a sub-sector has emerged that tracks such projects. One of the first of these, SinksWatch, arose after the inclusion of forests in the offsets market, as a consequence of COP 6 bis in Bonn, 2000. It began tracking one of the earliest projects seeking CDM accreditation, Plantar in Brazil. This project, one of the early World Bank PCFs, drew the attention of NGOs as the company had also had its afforestation activities FSC-certified. The company was attempting to have its iron-smelting activities offset by establishing monoculture eucalypt plantations for the production of charcoal, rather than using coal (SinksWatch 2003). The case was pursued by another monitoring NGO, CDMWatch (CDMWatch 2002). It claimed in an online report that Plantar had plans to establish the plantation before the creation of the CDM, thereby calling its 'additionality' into question (Person 2002). NGOs continued to express their opposition to the project, which was registered as a CDM project in 2007, despite claims that local Indigenous communities had not been consulted, and that the auditor's concerns had not be adequately addressed (Carbon Market Watch n.d.). A number of NGOs from both the North and South wrote to the CDM EB objecting to

the project on the grounds that 'large-scale, chemical-intensive plantations of fast-growing eucalyptus trees and their subsequent burning can in
no way be considered a mechanism for climate justice' (World Rainforest
Movement (WRM) 2010). Carbon Market Watch (previously CDM Watch)
has continued to document problematic CDM projects in developing countries, including pollution generated by a coal-fired power station in India,
contaminated groundwater arising from a waste incinerator in China, and
the falsification of consultation documents associated with a hydroelectric
scheme in Honduras (Carbon Market Watch 2013: 3–9).

The CDM appears to have taken a long time to respond substantively
to NGO objections, only agreeing to rules to ensure that 'local stakeholders have a say' in projects in July 2014 (CDM 2014). This was part
of a broader process of investigation into CDM procedures, including those
associated with deregistration of CDM projects, and addressing the problem of 'double counting' of projects under national emissions reduction
schemes (CDM 2014). However, it should be noted that the method of
complaining to CDM remains complex, and is subject to a mandatory
process of submission of pro-forma documents to the EB (CDM 2015c).

In REDD+ the stakeholder dynamics differ somewhat. The North/
South power balance, it has been claimed, has been somewhat reversed,
as REDD+ 'facilitates a co-incidence of developed and developing
country self-interest' (Cadman and Maraseni 2012: 166). National-level
involvement in REDD+ is on the basis of developing country status.
Developed countries provide funds, and developing countries receive
them, without the intermediation of companies seeking to develop
industrial projects. But for non-state actors, the situation is less clear-cut.

The REDD+ programme was somewhat controversial from the outset,
because Indigenous peoples were not included in the initial consultations
(Griffiths 2008). It has even been the subject of some detailed analysis
and criticism from academics questioning its 'white' (i.e. Northern) bias:

> The core concept behind REDD+ is its implicit contention that only countries
> with non-white populations and governments are guilty of producing emis-
> sions of $CO2$ when they undertake forestry … it is 'white' countries that do
> far more logging annually than non-white countries (60% of total timber
> forest production in all countries in 2004 came from countries like Canada,
> Norway, Sweden, Finland, Germany, FAO 2005). Moreover, it is the white
> countries – mostly in the northern hemisphere – whose timber harvesting (i.e.
> logging) is showing a strong rising trend. At the same time it is the countries
> most fiercely targeted by the German and Australian government and their
> academics promoting application of REDD+ to SE Asia, especially in
> Malaysia and Indonesia, whose timber harvesting has actually dropped since
> 1995 for reasons wholly independent of REDD. Both these countries have

diverted timber acreage to oil palm trees, in Indonesia's case oil palm trees in 2010 occupied 5 million hectares, up from only 1.2 million ha in 1995. However Australia's REDDists claim the increase was mostly due to deforestation. (Curtin 2012: 3)

Concerns have also been raised by NGOs regarding UN-REDD and FCPF activities. In 2013 Indigenous peoples withdrew from UN-REDD activities in Panama, citing as it had not offered any 'guarantees for respecting indigenous rights [nor for] the full and effective participation of the Indigenous Peoples of Panama in all phases and in the implementation' (Lang 2013). While UN-REDD in principle has procedures for consultation of non-state actors, the observation has been that (as of 2013), there was 'no detailed guidance available in terms of what would happen if there is insufficient effort put into applying these principles' (Martin 2013: 51). FCPF has received similar criticisms. In 2010, NGOs complained about the lack of consultation over activities in Indonesia (Lang 2010). In the same year Greenpeace published a report critical of Papua New Guinea's involvement based on its poor forest governance arrangements (Greenpeace Australia Pacific 2010). The World Bank has claimed that it has put mechanisms in place to ensure civil society participation (Martin and Elges 2013: 56). These have been challenged, however. One NGO was of the view that 'the lack of binding requirements seriously undermines public accountability of the FCPF to civil society and potentially affected communities. There are few mandatory requirements … which generally use optional terms like "should", "could", "may"' (Dooley et al. 2011: 41).

Given the multiple nation states and varying legal frameworks under which it operates, CSOs and IPOs undertook a concerted effort to secure the inclusion of environmental and social justice mechanisms (referred to as safeguards) at COP 15 in Copenhagen in 2009 (Eastwood 2013: 51–3, Global Witness 2009). At COP 16 in Cancun, 2010, the outcome document called for 'transparent and effective national forest governance structures' as well as 'the full and effective participation of relevant stakeholders, in particular indigenous peoples and local communities' in relation to REDD+ activities (Decision 1/CP.16, Appendix I, 2. (b) (UNFCCC 2011: 26)). This caused the World Bank to review its current policies, and FCPF responded in kind, but was heavily by criticised by NGOs for creating 'a dense set of guidelines that appear to water down existing policies and obfuscate minimum standards' (Dooley et al. 2011: 7). UN-REDD responded by developing a process of 'participatory governance assessment' of country activities in consultation with stakeholders (UN-REDD 2011a). But the issue of safeguards was raised again in COP

17 in Durban, and both FCPF and UN-REDD responded by developing safeguards systems for country-level projects (UN-REDD n.d., Forest Carbon Partnership Facility 2012b). The effectiveness of these was again questioned by NGOs, who extended their concerns to the broader issue of the institutional integrity of REDD+ finance, and the activities of the funds at the national level (Martin 2013, Martin and Elges 2013). Of particular concern was the issue of ensuring the free, prior and informed consent (FPIC) of stakeholders regarding project activities. FPIC is an emerging international human rights norm, and private governance standards have arisen to verify and accredit FPIC (Forest Stewardship Council 2012: 6). There has been an acknowledgement of the need for a complaints mechanism to address concerns about FPIC (UN-REDD 2013: 33). The problem confronting REDD+ is that implementation of parts of the programme are largely voluntary, following the UN tradition of subordinating global agreements to national sovereignty.

QUALITY OF GOVERNANCE

CDM

Table 1.1   CDM – quality of governance by region (February 2015)

Principle	1. Meaningful participation Maximum score: 25 Minimum: 5							
Criterion	1. Interest representation Maximum score: 15 Minimum: 3				2. Organisational responsibility Maximum score: 10 Minimum: 2			Principle score
Indicator	Inclusiveness	Equality	Resources	Criterion Score	Accountability	Transparency	Criterion Score	
North (38)	3.0	2.7	**1.6**	7.3	2.7	2.7	5.3	12.6
South (52)	2.7	2.7	**2.4**	7.8	3.2	3.1	6.3	14.1
Principle	2. Productive deliberation Maximum score: 30 Minimum: 6							
Criterion	3. Decision-making Maximum score: 15 Minimum: 3				4. Implementation Maximum score: 15 Minimum: 3			Principle score
Indicator	Democracy	Agreement	Dispute settlement	Criterion Score	Behavioural change	Problem-solving	Durability	Criterion Score
North	**2.4**	2.8	**2.3**	7.4	2.7	**2.4**	2.6	7.8	15.2
South	2.9	3.0	3.0	8.9	2.8	2.9	2.9	8.6	17.4
Total (out of 55)								
North				27.8				
South				31.5				

Note: Light grey represents the highest scoring indicator by region; dark grey the lowest; numbers in **bold** are below the threshold value of 50 per cent.

Table 1.2   CDM – quality of governance by sector (February 2015)

Principle	1. Meaningful participation Maximum score: 25 Minimum: 5							
Criterion	1. Interest representation Maximum score: 15 Minimum: 3				2. Organisational responsibility Maximum score: 10 Minimum: 2			Principle score
Indicator	Inclusiveness	Equality	Resources	Criterion Score	Accountability	Transparency	Criterion Score	
Environment	3.2	2.7	2.3	8.2	3.0	3.0	6.0	14.2
Social	2.6	2.0	1.4	6.0	1.8	2.0	3.8	9.8
Economic	4.7	2.0	1.0	7.7	3.7	3.7	7.4	15.1
Government	3.3	3.0	2.1	8.4	3.5	3.3	6.8	15.2
Academic	2.9	2.8	1.9	7.6	2.9	2.9	5.8	13.4
Other	1.8	2.7	2.2	6.7	2.7	2.0	4.7	11.4
Principle	2. Productive deliberation Maximum score: 30 Minimum: 6							
Criterion	3. Decision-making Maximum score: 15 Minimum: 3				4. Implementation Maximum score: 15 Minimum: 3			Principle score
Indicator	Democracy	Agreement	Dispute settlement	Criterion Score	Behavioural change	Problem-solving	Durability	Criterion Score
Environment	2.5	2.9	2.7	8.1	2.8	2.6	2.7	8.1	16.2
Social	1.8	1.4	1.8	5.0	2.0	2.0	2.4	6.4	11.4
Economic	2.0	3.3	3.0	8.3	3.3	3.3	2.7	9.3	17.6
Government	3.2	3.3	3.2	9.7	3.2	3.1	2.8	9.1	18.8
Academic	3.0	3.0	2.8	8.8	2.8	2.7	3.0	8.5	17.3
Other	2.0	2.5	2.2	6.7	1.8	2.0	2.2	6.0	12.7
Total (out of 55)								
Environment				30.4				
Social				21.2				
Economic				32.7				
Government				34.0				
Academic				30.7				
Other				24.1				

Note: Light grey represents the highest scoring indicator by sector; dark grey the lowest; numbers in **bold** are below the threshold value of 50 per cent.

Commentary on the Results

Ninety respondents answered the survey, with a clear majority from the South. Respondents did not appear to be especially impressed with the CDM, which received a low 'pass' only. Southern respondents rated the mechanism more favourably – a result that was repeated across both principles. Northern respondents identified interest representation and decision-making as the weakest criteria. At the indicator level, both South and North gave resources a low score, and for Northern respondents, this was the lowest scoring indicator. Democracy and dispute settlement also received a low rating from the North. The highest performing indicators were inclusiveness (North) and agreement and dispute settlement (South).

Government provided the highest score, followed by the economic, academic and environmental sectors. The results from 'other' respondents as well as the social sector (which gave it the lowest score of all) constituted a 'fail'. This was repeated at the criterion level. Environment, government, academic, social and economic all identified resources as the weakest indicator, and it is interesting to note that economic respondents provided the lowest score of all. 'Other' identified inclusiveness as the lowest indicator, while conversely, the economic and environmental sectors both identified inclusiveness as the highest scoring indicator; for government it was accountability. Academics rated democracy, agreement and durability as equally high.

Commentary from Survey Respondents

Respondents provided a few CDM-specific comments. One Northern academic was concerned about the lack of inclusiveness in the CDM's policy agenda. Its 'focus on incentives' had diminished the extent to which those responsible for emissions had any 'accountability to the impacts'. 'Carbon linkages' were 'so many and interactive' that they were 'beyond the capability of bureaucratic decision-making' that only focused on incentives. Another Northern academic felt that small island states received unequal treatment even though they were most heavily affected by climate change. The emphasis on large-scale projects in the CDM meant that such countries, with their low populations, would only ever develop small-scale projects, which stood 'no chance' of being approved. Another environmental respondent from the South commented that the application of the CDM on the ground was 'too cumbersome and very expensive for developing countries to manage', and that it was 'mainly geared towards benefiting developed countries'. One Northern economic respondent, commenting on resources noted that for businesses it was 'rather the opposite' – they funded the CDM, not the other way round. Two respondents commented on implementation aspects of the CDM. A Northern academic noted that it was only market mechanisms with payments for 'practical projects' such as CDM that had any 'real effects'. Another Northern environmental respondent, speaking from the 'frustrated point of view of a CDM project developer' questioned the CDM's effectiveness, however. Since it had 'failed to provide a price on carbon, sustainable initiatives are no longer possible'.

REDD+

Table 1.3   REDD+ – quality of governance by region (February 2015)

Principle	1. Meaningful participation Maximum score: 25; Minimum: 5							
Criterion	1. Interest representation Maximum score: 15 Minimum: 3				2. Organisational responsibility Maximum score: 10 Minimum: 2			Principle Score
Indicator	**Inclusiveness**	**Equality**	**Resources**	Criterion Score	**Accountability**	**Transparency**	Criterion Score	
North (41)	3.7	2.9	**1.6**	8.1	2.8	2.7	5.6	13.7
South (49)	3.1	3.1	**2.8**	9.0	3.4	3.2	6.6	15.6
Principle	2. Productive deliberation Maximum score: 30 Minimum: 6							
Criterion	3. Decision-making Maximum score: 15 Minimum: 3				4. Implementation Maximum score: 15 Minimum: 3			Principle Score
Indicator	**Democracy**	**Agreement**	**Dispute settlement**	Criterion Score	**Behavioural change**	**Problem solving**	**Durability**	Criterion Score	
North	2.5	2.8	2.5	7.7	3.1	2.9	3.1	9.1	16.9
South	3.1	3.2	3.0	9.3	3.1	3.2	3.2	9.5	18.8
Total (out of 55)								
North				30.5				
South				34.4				

Note: Light grey represents the highest scoring indicator by region; dark grey the lowest; numbers in **bold** are below the threshold value of 50 per cent.

Table 1.4   REDD+ – quality of governance by sector (February 2015)

Principle	1. Meaningful participation Maximum score: 25 Minimum: 5							
Criterion	1. Interest representation Maximum score: 15 Minimum: 3				2. Organisational responsibility Maximum score: 10 Minimum: 2			Principle Score
Indicator	Inclusiveness	Equality	Resources	Criterion Score	Accountability	Transparency	Criterion Score	
Environment	3.6	3.0	2.3	8.9	2.9	2.8	5.7	14.6
Social	.0	2.0	1.8	6.8	2.0	1.3	3.3	10.1
Economic	4.3	2.7	1.0	8.0	3.3	3.7	7.0	15.0
Government	4.1	3.4	2.8	10.3	3.8	3.4	7.2	17.5
Academic	3.7	2.9	2.1	8.7	3.3	3.0	6.3	15.0
Other	3.2	3.3	2.3	8.8	3.0	3.2	6.2	15.0

Principle	2. Productive deliberation Maximum score: 30 Minimum: 6							
Criterion	3. Decision-making Maximum score: 15 Minimum: 3				4. Implementation Maximum score: 15 Minimum: 3			Principle Score
Indicator	Democracy	Agreement	Dispute settlement	Criterion Score	Behavioural change	Problem-solving	Durability	Criterion Score	
Environment	2.7	3.0	2.8	8.5	3.2	3.2	3.1	9.5	18.0
Social	1.5	1.8	2.0	5.3	2.5	2.5	2.8	7.8	13.1
Economic	2.3	3.7	3.0	9.0	3.3	3.7	4.0	11.0	20.0
Government	3.3	3.5	3.2	10.0	3.5	3.4	3.6	10.5	20.5
Academic	3.0	3.0	2.8	8.8	3.2	2.9	3.2	9.3	18.1
Other	2.8	2.7	2.5	8.0	2.0	2.5	2.5	7.0	15.0

Total (out of 55)	
Environment	32.6
Social	23.2
Economic	35.0
Government	38.0
Academic	33.1
Other	30.0

Note: Light grey represents the highest scoring indicator by sector; dark grey the lowest; numbers in **bold** are below the threshold value of 50 per cent.

Commentary on the Results

Ninety respondents participated in the survey, with a few more respondents from the South. REDD+ received a relatively high 'pass', but not a 'credit'. The mechanism did pass all principles and criteria across North and Southern respondents however, with Southern respondents providing consistently higher ratings. Resources was again the weakest indicator, with Northern respondents providing a much lower rating than their Southern counterparts (1.6 cf. 2.8). Interestingly, the indicator ratings provided by Northern respondents were more dynamic than those from the South, and included the highest rated indicator (inclusiveness). With the exception of resources, Southern participants rated REDD+ governance indicators within the 'high' band, with little differentiation. For the South, accountability was the highest performing indicator.

Government provided the highest total score, followed by economic, academic and environmental (following the CDM). The mechanism received a low 'pass' from the 'other' sector, but was again awarded a 'fail' from the social sector. These results were replicated at the criterion level. The lowest rated indicator was again resources, provided by the economic sector. Resources also received a 'fail' from the academic and the environmental sectors, and although the lowest indicator for government, it received a better rating (2.8). 'Other' identified behaviour change as the lowest indicator, while social respondents identified transparency. Inclusiveness was the highest performer across sectors, with the exception of 'other', which selected equality.

Commentary from Survey Respondents

Respondents provided a number of detailed observations regarding REDD+ governance. One Northern academic, also critical of CDM, was of the view that REDD+ 'ignored carbon linkages' as well, especially regarding biodiversity, but acknowledged that it was 'harder to measure than even carbon'. Another academic from the South similarly believed that REDD+ had 'little or no potential' to address carbon issues. They went further to assert that it was 'increasingly seen as a magic bullet promising much and delivering little anywhere'. One Southern government respondent was more positive, observing that the 'root cause of deforestation and forest degradation is weak forest governance' and was of the view that the initiative would 'support the improvement of governance'.

In terms of its inclusiveness, one Southern environmental respondent thought that 'REDD+ inclusiveness varies country to country'. However, when it was 'initiated by the collaboration of civil society and NGOs' at the 'local level' it could be more inclusive. But despite this, it was still not 'fully aligned to social and environmental safeguards'. A Southern academic was of the view that REDD+ 'does not meet needs of communities and rural people and in fact may make them worse off'. In commenting on equality, this respondent also questioned its capacity to 'assist the rural poor', a view that was shared by one 'other' Southern respondent. For them, the 'real ground level people' were 'less partici-pants', due to the prevalence of 'elite tapping and government control'. One Southern academic discussed the mechanism's methods for reaching agreement. They thought that it 'may not lead to as many emission reductions as initially were sought, but again, decisions influence policies and behaviour. Even the prospect of decisions affects policies and behaviour'. The main drawback with this approach was that it took 'too much time to come to agreement'. Basing their experience on REDD+, a Northern government respondent simply commented: 'current climate change agreements are not working'. Regarding dispute settlement, the Southern academic (quoted immediately above) thought that it needed to be recognised that 'dispute settlement should be at different scales. Internationally, disputes are managed but not settled (at least, not yet)', but they did think that at the 'project level some advancement has been achieved' by REDD+.

Finally, one environmental respondent from the South was unsure whether REDD+ would solve the problem of deforestation. As a mech-anism, it had the capability, but 'real payment is not practiced'. As it was a new initiative, local communities also had 'high expectations'. If REDD+ could not gain 'market access' it would encounter the same problems face by other initiatives. It needed to be designed in alignment with the 'local context' and have 'flexible standards' for monitoring, reporting and verification.

ANALYSIS AND CONCLUSIONS

The present scope of CDM projects has been challenged with respect to consistency and governance in developing countries. The fundamental issue among many regulatory aspects is instrumental to achieving pro-poor growth. A genuine but unresolved question of transparency in regulatory instruments has been challenging the developing world. Extreme corruption in these countries is one of the major elements that are preventing good governance. Legal uniformity of regulatory instru-ments is another issue to be addressed as this has created many loopholes in the economic use of resources, and increases corruption. The decentralisation of power to the local community is another urgent step that needs to be put in place in developing countries. Most of the decisions in CDM projects in developing communities are top down, leaving less chance for local strategy formulation, and local experience and capacity development.

A set of globally accepted CDM guidelines with identified processing and implementation times for both international and local approvals are urgently required, as challenges experienced by private investors are diluting interest. This then could also offer opportunities for private companies to move towards using better technology and achieve better operational performance and GHG reduction. A smooth inflow of investment and technology is possible if CDM projects can link their objectives with rural poverty alleviation. Such a 'win–win' strategy should be aimed at rural communities, and could be designed to accelerate agricultural growth in the rain-fed regions of developing countries. It would represent a genuine effort in improving farming technology that could also improve the availability of energy and other infrastructural facilities, as well as generate new non-farm employment that supplements the agricultural income.

In sum, there is an urgent need for an efficient CDM mechanism that would improve incentives for SD and OP. To achieve consistency in policy development, two-track CDM approaches as referred to in Torvanger et al. (2013: 473) could break the political logjam and facilitate the inclusion of SD benefits and OP benefits. Likewise, in developed countries, this mechanism could reduce the uncertainty of whether real emissions reductions have actually been achieved. The role of financial institutions could also be promoted with this approach. Reducing institutional and administrative constraints may lower the transaction costs that are currently resulting in slow and constrained market innovation. Institutional regulatory mechanisms could be developed on the basis of social experience and local knowledge, not merely economic rationalism. In this way, the overall goals of CDM can be achieved by using the carbon market as a catalyst for change and addressing market failures. Efficient mechanism for delivering finance through CDM projects can then be obtained in order to reduce the persisting poverty in developing countries.

The major scope of global REDD – preparing local communities to actively participate in national REDD+ – has been challenged by non-uniform sets of social actors and weak governance in developing countries. This raises the question of how efficiently the delivery of benefits has been achieved with systematic regulation. The fundamental issue among many regulatory aspects is the instrumental efficiency to deliver the benefits to achieve pro-poor growth. Therefore, a lack of legal uniformity has created many gaps in the economic use of resources, and has increased corruption. The situation is being worsened by the political instability in developing countries. To overcome this problem, power decentralisation to the local community is another urgent step that needs to be put in place.

BIBLIOGRAPHY

Abreu Mejía, D. 2010, 'The evolution of the climate change regime: Beyond a north-south divide?' *International Catalan Institute for Peace, Working Paper*, (2010/6).

Angelsen, A., Brockhaus, M., Kanninen, M., Sills, E., Sunderlin, W. D. and Wertz-Kanounnikoff, S. 2009, *Realising REDD+: National strategy and policy options*, Bogor Barat 16115, Indonesia: Center for International Forestry Research (CIFOR).

Angelsen, A., Brockhaus, M., Sunderlin, W. D. and Verchot, L. V. 2012, *Analysing REDD+: Challenges and choices*, Bogor, Indonesia: CIFOR.

Ares, E. 2014, 'Carbon Price Floor', *Science and Environment Section*, London: HM Treasury. Viewed 22 April 2015, http://researchbriefings.files.parliament. uk/documents/SN05927/SN05927.pdf.

Bäckstrand, K. 2008, 'Accountability of networked climate governance: The rise of transnational climate partnerships', *Global Environmental Politics*, **8** (3) 74–102.

Bäckstrand, K. and Lövbrand, E. 2006, 'Planting trees to mitigate climate change: Contested discourses of ecological modernization, green governmentality and civic environmentalism', *Global Environmental Politics*, **6** (1) 51–75.

Bäckstrand, K. and Lövbrand, E. (eds) 2007, *Climate governance beyond 2012: Competing discourses of green governmentality, ecological modernization and civic environmentalism*, Aldershot and Burlington: Ashgate.

Bernard, F., McFatridge, S. and Minang, P. A. 2012, 'The Private Sector in the REDD+ Supply Chain: Trends, challenges and opportunities', Manitoba, Canada: The International Institute for Sustainable Development (IISD).

Bumpus, A. G. and Cole, J. C. 2010, 'How can the current CDM deliver sustainable development?', *Wiley Interdisciplinary Reviews: Climate Change*, **1** (4) 541–7.

Cadman, T. 2000, 'The Clearcut Case: How the Kyoto Protocol could become a driver for deforestation', Amsterdam: Greenpeace International. Viewed 20 April 2015, http://www.greenpeace.org/norway/Global/norway/p2/other/report/ 2000/the-clearcut-case-how-the-kyo.pdf.

Cadman, T. 2013a, *Climate change and global policy regimes: towards institutional legitimacy*, Basingstoke, London: Palgrave Macmillan.

Cadman, T. (ed.) 2013b, *Introduction: Global governance and climate change*, Basingstoke, London: Palgrave Macmillan.

Cadman, T. 2014, 'Climate finance in an age of uncertainty', *Journal of Sustainable Finance and Investment*, **4** (4) 351–6.

Cadman, T. and Maraseni, T. N. 2012, 'The governance of REDD+: an institutional analysis in the Asia Pacific region and beyond', *Journal of Environmental Planning and Management*, **18** (1) 145–70.

Carbon Market Watch 2013, *Local realities of CDM projects: A compilation of case studies.* Viewed 20 April 2015, http://carbonmarketwatch.org/wp-content/uploads/2015/02/CDM-Cases-Studies.pdf.

Carbon Market Watch n.d., *Plantar – Pig iron project, Brazil.* Viewed 20 April 2015, http://carbonmarketwatch.org/campaigns-issues/plantar-pig-iron-project-brazil.

Carbonweb 2001, *Lobbyists harvest the fruits of their labour at COP-6bis.* Viewed 20 April 2015, http://www.carbonweb.org/documents/corporate europe.pdf.

CBD 2000, *Progress Report on the Implementation of the Programme of Work on the Biological Diversity of Inland Water Ecosystems (Implementation of Decision IV/4).* Viewed 14 May 2015, https://www.cbd.int/kb/record/decision/7144.

CBD 2003, 'Interlinkages between biological diversity and climate change. In Advice on the integration of biodiversity considerations into the implementation of the United Nations Framework Convention on Climate Change and its Kyoto Protocol', *CBD Technical Series (No. 10).* Viewed 14 May 2015, https://www.cbd.int/doc/publications/cbd-ts-10.pdf.

CBD 2004, *Decision adopted by the Conference of the Parties to the Convention on Biological Diversity at its seventh meeting.* Viewed 14 May 2015, https://www.cbd.int/doc/decisions/cop-07/cop-07-dec-04-en.pdf.

CDM 2014, 'CDM Board agrees improvements to stakeholder consultation', *Highlights – 80th meeting of the CDM Executive Board.* Viewed 20 April 2015, http://cdm.unfccc.int/press/newsroom/latestnews/releases/2014/0718_index.html.

CDM 2015a, 'Aviation emissions projects soon clear for take-off under the Kyoto Protocol's Clean Development Mechanism', *Press highlights – 82nd meeting of the CDM Executive Board.* Viewed 22 April 2015, http://cdm.unfccc.int/press/newsroom/latestnews/releases/2014/0213_index.html.

CDM 2015b, *CDM Statistics.* Viewed 8 May 2015, http://cdm.unfccc.int/Statistics/index.html.

CDM 2015c, 'Stakeholder communication form'. Viewed 3 July 2015, http://cdm.unfccc.int/sunsetcms/storage/contents/stored-file-20150302153926492/EB_Form05.doc.

CDM EB 2008, *Guidelines for Completing the Project Design Document (CDM-PDD) and the Proposed New Baseline and Monitoring Methodologies (CDM-NM).* Viewed 14 May 2015, http://cdm.unfccc.int/Reference/Guidclarif/pdd/PDD_guid04.pdf.

CDM Executive Board (CDM EB) 2009, *Approved consolidated baseline and monitoring methodology ACM0002. Consolidated baseline methodology for grid-connected electricity generation from renewable sources.* Viewed 14 May 2015, http://cdm.unfccc.int/EB/045/eb45_repan10.pdf.

CDM Policy Dialogue 2012, *Climate change, carbon markets and the CDM: A call to action.* Luxembourg: CDM Policy Dialogue, viewed 22 April 2015, http://www.cdmpolicydialogue.org/report/rpt110912.pdf.

CDMWatch 2002, *Action Alert.* Viewed 20 April 2015, https://web.archive.org/web/20020921054723/http://www.cdmwatch.org/alert_list.php.

Chiroleu-Assouline, M., Poudou, J.-C. and Roussel, S. 2012, 'North/South Contractual Design through the REDD+ Scheme'. Viewed 20 April 2015, http://www.feem.it/userfiles/attach/20121251614254NDL2012-089.pdf.

Corbera, E. and Schroeder, H. 2011, 'Governing and implementing REDD', *Environmental Science and Policy*, **14** (2) 89–99.

Crowe, T. L. 2013, 'The potential of the CDM to deliver pro-poor benefits', *Climate Policy*, **13** (1) 58–79.

Curtin, T. 2012, 'Ringbarking third world forestry', *Quadrant Online.* Viewed 3 July 2015, https://quadrant.org.au/opinion/doomed-planet/2012/09/ringbarking-third-world-forestry/.

Darragh, C., Streck, C. and Unger, M. v. 2014, 'REDD+ Finance in the European Union: Options for scaling-up near term support'. Viewed 3 July 2015, http://www.climatefocus.com/sites/default/files/redd_finance_in_the_european_union.pdf.

Davis, C., Daviet, F., Nakhooda, S. and Thuault, A. 2009, 'A Review of 25 readiness plan idea notes from the World Bank Forest Carbon Partnership facility'. Viewed 27 March 2013, http://www.wri.org/publication/world-bank-forest-carbon-partnership-facility-idea-note-review.

de Leaniz, C. G. 2008, 'Weir removal in salmonid streams: implications, challenges and practicalities', *Hydrobiologia*, **609** (1) 83–96.

de Oliveira, J. P., Cadman, T., Ma, H. O., Maraseni, T., Koli, A., Jadhav, Y. D. and Prabowo, D. 2013, *Governing the forests: An institutional analysis of REDD+ and community forest management in Asia*, Yokohama: International Tropical Timber Organization (ITTO) and the United Nations University Institute of Advanced Studies (UNU-IAS).

Depledge, J. 2006, 'The opposite of learning: Ossification in the climate change regime', *Global Environmental Politics*, **6** (1) 1–22.

Dooley, K., Griffiths, T., Martone, F. and Ozinga, S. 2011, 'Smoke and mirrors: A critical assessment of the forest carbon partnership facility'. Viewed 3 July 2015, http://www.forestpeoples.org/sites/fpp/files/publication/2011/03/smokeandmirrorsinternet.pdf.

Doyle, T. and Chaturvedi, S. 2010, 'Climate territories: A global soul for the global south?', *Geopolitics*, **15** (3) 516–35.

Eastwood, L. E. (ed.) 2013, *Gender and climate change: Stakeholder participation and conceptual currency in the climate negotiations regime*, Basingstoke, London: Palgrave Macmillan.

European Union 2008, *Guidelines on a Common Understanding of Article 11b (6) of Directive 2003/87/EC as Amended by Directive 2004/101/EC (non-paper).* Viewed 14 May 2015, http://ec.europa.eu/clima/policies/ets/linking/docs/art11b6_guide_en.pdf.

Food and Agriculture Organization, United Nations Development Programme and United Nations Environment Programme 2008, 'UN collaborative programme on reducing emissions from deforestation and forest degradation in developing countries', *FAO, UNDP, UNEP Framework Document.* Viewed 20 February 2013, http://mptf.undp.org/document/download/1740.

Forest Carbon Partnership Facility 2010, *Demonstrating activities that reduce emissions from deforestation and forest degradation.* Viewed 18 February 2013, http://www.forestcarbonpartnership.org/sites/forestcarbonpartnership. org/files/Documents/PDF/Sep2010/New%20FCPF%20brochure%20–%20low %20resolution%20051809_0.pdf.

Forest Carbon Partnership Facility 2012a, *2012 Annual Report.* Viewed 27 March 2013, http://www.forestcarbonpartnership.org/sites/fcp/files/2013/FCPF%20F Y12%20Anual%20Report%20FINAL%20Oct8.pdf.

Forest Carbon Partnership Facility 2012b, *Common approach to environmental and social safeguards for multiple delivery partners.* Viewed 30 March 2013, https://www.forestcarbonpartnership.org/sites/forestcarbonpartnership.org/files/ Documents/PDF/Aug2012/FCPF%20Readiness%20Fund%20Common%20 Approach%208-9-12.pdf.

Forest Carbon Partnership Facility 2012c, *Contributions to the FCPF Carbon Fund as of December 31, 2012 (US$m).* Viewed 20 April 2015, http:// www.forestcarbonpartnership.org/sites/fcp/files/2013/FCPF Readiness Fund Contributions as of Dec 31_2012.pdf.

Forest Carbon Partnership Facility 2012d, *The FCPF carbon fund: Pioneering performance based payments for REDD+.* Viewed 26 April 2013, http://www. forestcarbonpartnership.org/sites/forestcarbonpartnership.org/files/Documents/ PDF/June2012/FCPF%20Brouchure_June%2013_2012.pdf.

Forest Carbon Partnership Facility 2013a, 'Delivery partners'. Viewed 20 April 2013, http://www.forestcarbonpartnership.org/delivery-partners.

Forest Carbon Partnership Facility 2013b, *Readiness Fund.* Viewed 3 April 2013, http://www.forestcarbonpartnership.org/readiness-fund.

Forest Stewardship Council 2012, *FSC guidelines for the implementation of the right to Free, Prior and Informed Consent (FPIC).* Viewed 18 March 2013, http://www.unredd.net/index.php?option=com_docman&task=doc_download& gid=8973&Itemid=53.

Global Witness 2009, *Understanding REDD+: The role of governance, enforcement and safeguards in reducing emissions from deforestation and forest degradation.* Viewed 15 March 2015, http://www.forestcarbonpartnership.org/ sites/forestcarbonpartnership.org/files/Documents/PDF/Apr2011/Understanding %20REDD+.pdf.

Greenpeace Australia Pacific 2010, *Papua New Guinea: Not ready for REDD.* Viewed 21 April 2013, http://www.greenpeace.org/australia/en/what-we-do/ forests/resources/reports/papua-new-guinea-not-ready-fo/.

Griffiths, T. 2008, 'Seeing "REDD"? Forests, climate change mitigation and the rights of indigenous peoples and local communities'. Viewed 3 July 2015, http://www.forestpeoples.org/sites/fpp/files/publication/2010/08/seeingreddup datedraft3dec08eng.pdf.

Haites, E. 2011, 'Climate change finance', *Climate Policy*, **11** (3) 963–9.

Haya, B. 2007, 'How the CDM is subsidizing hydro developers and harming the Kyoto Protocol'. Viewed 14 May 2015, https://ideas.repec.org/p/ess/wpaper/id4822.html.

IGES 2014, *Snapshots of selected REDD+ project designs*. Kanagawa, Japan: Institute for Global Environmental Strategies.

International Rivers n.d., 'Spreadsheet of Hydro Projects in the CDM Project Pipeline'. Viewed 3 July 2015, http://www.internationalrivers.org/resources/spreadsheet-of-hydro-projects-in-the-cdm-project-pipeline-4039.

Kanowski, P. J., McDermott, C. L. and Cashore, B. W. 2011, 'Implementing REDD+: lessons from analysis of forest governance', *Environmental Science and Policy*, **14** (2) 111–17.

Karani, P. and Gantsho, M. 2007, 'The role of Development Finance Institutions (DFIs) in promoting the Clean Development Mechanism (CDM) in Africa', *Environment, Development and Sustainability*, **9** (3) 203–28.

La Vina, A. G. M., Labre, L., Ang, L. and de Leon, A. 2014, 'The Road to Doha: The future of REDD-Plus, agriculture, and land-use change in the UNFCCC', Philippines: Foundation for International Environmental Law and Development.

Lang, C. 2010, 'World Bank's FCPF in Indonesia fails to address civil society concern'. Viewed 21 April 2013, http://www.redd-monitor.org/2010/05/25/world-banks-fcpf-in-indonesia-fails-to-address-civil-society-concerns/.

Lang, C. 2013, 'COONAPIP, Panama's Indigenous Peoples Coordinating Body, withdraws from UN-REDD'. Viewed 18 March 2013, http://www.redd-monitor.org/2013/03/06/coonapip-panamas-indigenous-peoples-coordinating-body-withdraws-from-un-redd/.

Lecocq, F. and Ambrosi, P. 2007, 'The clean development mechanism: History, status, and prospects', *Review of Environmental Economics and Policy*, **1** (1) 134–51.

Lovell, H. C. 2010, 'Governing the carbon offset market', *Wiley Interdisciplinary Reviews: Climate Change*, **1** (3) 353–62.

Mann, M. L., Kaufmann, R. K., Bauer, D. M., Gopal, S., Baldwin, J. G. and Del Carmen Vera-Diaz, M. 2012, 'Ecosystem service value and agricultural conversion in the Amazon: implications for policy intervention', *Environmental and Resource Economics*, **53** (2) 279–95.

Maraseni, T. (ed.) 2013, *Evaluating the clean development mechanism*, Basingstoke, London: Palgrave Macmillan.

Martin, C. 2013, 'Protecting climate finance: An anti-corruption assessment of the UN-REDD programme'. Berlin: Transparency International, viewed 10 April 2015, http://files.transparency.org/content/download/723/3100/file/2013_ProtectingClimateFinance_UNREDD_EN.pdf.

Martin, C. and Elges, E. 2013, 'Protecting climate finance: an anti-corruption assessment of the Forest Carbon Partnership Facility'. Berlin: Transparency International, viewed 10 April 2015, http://files.transparency.org/content/download/1442/10766/file/2013_ProtectingClimateFinance_FCPF_EN.pdf.

Mohammadi, A., Abbaspour, M., Soltanieh, M., Atabi, F. and Rahmatian, M. 2013, 'Post-2012 CDM multi-criteria analysis of industries in six Asian countries: Iranian case study', *Climate Policy*, **13** (2) 210–39.

Multipartner Trust Fund Office (MTFO) 2013b, 'UN-REDD Programme Fund', *Trust Fund Factsheet.* Viewed 20 February 2013, http://mptf.undp.org/factsheet/fund/CCF00.

Newell, P. 2009, 'Varieties of CDM governance: some reflections', *The Journal of Environment and Development*, **18** (4) 425–35.

Nilsson, C., Reidy, C. A., Dynesius, M. and Revenga, C. 2005, 'Fragmentation and flow regulation of the world's large river systems', *Science*, **308** (5720) 405–8.

Office of the Secretary 2014, *U.S.– China joint announcement on climate change*, Washington DC: Whitehouse. Viewed 16 May 2015, https://www.white house.gov/the-press-office/2014/11/11/us-china-joint-announcement-climate-change.

Okereke, C. 2010, 'Climate justice and the international regime', *Wiley Inter-disciplinary Reviews: Climate Change*, **1** (3) 462–74.

Orr, C. 2001, 'Dams and development: A new framework for decision-making', *The report of the World Commission on Dams 2000.* London: Earthscan.

Pachauri, R. 2014, 'Chairperson of the intergovernmental panel on climate change, presentation to the sixth international forum for sustainable Asia and the Pacific (ISAP)', Yokohama: ISAP, 23 July.

Parks, B. C. and Roberts, J. T. 2008, 'Inequality and the global climate regime: breaking the north-south impasse', *Cambridge Review of International Affairs*, **21** (4) 621–48.

Paterson, M. and Stripple, J. (eds) 2007, *Singing climate change into existence: On the territorialization of climate policymaking*, Aldershot and Burlington: Ashgate.

Person, B. 2002, 'The Plantar CDM project: Why it must be rejected by the CDM Board and PCF investors'. Viewed 20 April 2015, https://web.archive.org/web/20030128020205/http://www.cdmwatch.org/plantar.html.

Pittock, J. 2010, 'A pale reflection of political reality: Integration of global climate, wetland, and biodiversity agreements', *Climate Law*, **1** (3) 343–73.

Pittock, J. 2011, 'National climate change policies and sustainable water man-agement: conflicts and synergies', *Ecology and Society*, **13** (2) 25.

Pottinger, L. 2008, 'Bad deal for the planet: Why carbon offsets aren't working. And how to create a fair global climate accord'. Viewed 14 May 2015, http://www.internationalrivers.org/resources/bad-deal-for-the-planet-why-carbon-offsets-aren-t-working-and-how-to-create-a-fair-global.

REDD Monitor 2008, *The World Bank forest carbon partnership facility: REDDy or not, here it comes!* Viewed 23 March 2013, http://www.redd-monitor.org/2008/11/10/the-world-bank-forest-carbon-partnership-facility-reddy-or-not-here-it-comes/.

Resanond, A., Jittsanguan, T. and Sriphraram, D. 2011, 'Company's Competi-tiveness Enhancement for Thai Agribusiness through the Clean Development Mechanism (CDM) under the Kyoto Protocol', *Journal of Sustainable Devel-opment*, **4** (2) 80.

Rey, D. and Swan, S. 2014, *A Country-Led Safeguards Approach: Guidelines for National REDD+ Programmes.* Ho Chi Minh City, Vietnam: The Netherlands Development Organisation, REDD+ Programme.

Richards, M. and Swan, S. 2014, *Participatory Subnational Planning for REDD+ and other Land Use Programmes: Methodology and Step-by-Step Guidance*, Ho Chi Minh City, Vietnam: SNV Netherlands Development Organisation, REDD+ Programme.

Shrestha, R. M. and Timilsina, G. R. 2002, 'The additionality criterion for identifying clean development mechanism projects under the Kyoto Protocol', *Energy Policy*, **30** (1) 73–9.

SinksWatch 2003, *Background information: Plantar project*. Viewed 15 May 2015, http://www.sinkswatch.org/node/4554.

Sirohi, S. 2007, 'CDM: Is it a "win–win" strategy for rural poverty alleviation in India?' *Climatic Change*, **84** (1) 91–110.

Somorin, O. A., Smit, B., Brown, H. C. P., Sonwa, D. J. and Nkem, J. 2011, 'Institutional perceptions of opportunities and challenges of REDD+ in the Congo Basin', *The Journal of Environment and Development*, **20** (4) 381–404.

Tanwar, N. 2007, 'Clean development mechanism and off-grid small-scale hydropower projects: Evaluation of additionality', *Energy Policy*, **35** (1) 714–21.

The Forest Peoples Programme (FPP) 2008, *The Forest Carbon Partnership Facility: Facilitating the weakening of indigenous peoples' rights to lands and resources*. Viewed 1 April 2013, http://www.forestpeoples.org/sites/fpp/files/publication/2010/08/fcpffppbriefingfeb08eng.pdf.

Thompson, M. C., Baruah, M. and Carr, E. R. 2011, 'Seeing REDD+ as a project of environmental governance', *Environmental Science and Policy*, **14** (2) 100–10.

Torvanger, A., Shrivastava, M. K., Pandey, N. and Tornblad, S. H. 2013, 'A two-track CDM: improved incentives for sustainable development and offset production', *Climate Policy*, **13** (4) 471–89.

UN 1993, *Agenda 21: Programme of action for sustainable development, Rio declaration on environment and development, statement of forest principles*, New York: United Nations Publications Department of Public Information.

UN 2015, *Delivering as one*. Viewed 4 March 2015, https://undg.org/home/guidance-policies/delivering-as-one/.

UNEP 2014, *Forests in a Changing Climate: A Sourcebook for Integrating REDD+ into Academic Programmes*. Nairobi, Kenya: UNEP.

UNFCCC 1992, *United Nations framework on climate change*. Viewed 25 January 2015, https://unfccc.int/files/essential_background/background_publications_htmlpdf/application/pdf/conveng.pdf.

UNFCCC 2011, *Report of the conference of the parties on its sixteenth session, held in Cancun from 29 November to 10 December 2010. Addendum part two: Action taken by the conference of the parties at its sixteenth session*. Viewed 18 February 2013, http://unfccc.int/resource/docs/2010/cop16/eng/07a01.pdf.

UNFCCC 2012a, *News release: Kyoto protocol's clean development mechanism reaches milestone*. Viewed 9 April 2015, http://unfccc.int/files/press/press_releases_advisories/application/pdf/pr20121304_cdm_4000.pdf.

UNFCCC 2012b, *Report of the Conference of the Parties on its Seventeenth Session, held in Durban from 28 November to 11 December 2011. Addendum. Part two: Action taken by the Conference of the Parties at its Seventeenth*

Session. Viewed 23 January 2015, http://unfccc.int/resource/docs/2011/cop17/eng/09a01.pdf#page=2.

UNFCCC 2014a, *New market-based mechanism.* Viewed 28 December 2014, http://unfccc.int/cooperation_support/market_and_non-market_mechanisms/items/7710.php.

UNFCCC 2014b, *Status of the Doha amendment.* Viewed 15 May 2015, http://unfccc.int/kyoto_protocol/doha_amendment/items/7362.php.

United Nations Development Group Viet Nam, n.d., *Joint programmes.* Viewed 3 July 2015, http://www.un.org.vn/en/what-we-do-mainmenu-203/joint-programmes-a-teams-mainmenu-208.html.

UN-REDD 2009, *Report of the Third Policy Board Meeting Washington D.C., U.S.* Viewed 18 February 2013, http://www.unredd.net/index.php?option=com_docman&task=doc_details&gid=1234&Itemid=53.

UN-REDD 2011a, 'REDD+ participatory governance assessments piloted in Indonesia and Nigeria', *UN-REDD Newsletter.* Viewed 28 April 2015, http://www.un-redd.org/Newsletter20/ParticipatoryGovernanceAssessments/tabid/54365/Default.aspx.

UN-REDD 2011b, *The UN-REDD programme strategy 2011–2015.* Viewed 20 February 2013, http://mptf.undp.org/document/download/5623.

UN-REDD 2012, *Programme handbook for national programmes and other national-level activities.* Viewed 4 March 2013, http://www.unredd.net/index.php?option=com_docman&task=doc_download&gid=8148&Itemid=53.

UN-REDD 2013, *Guidelines on free, prior and informed consent.* Viewed 18 March 2013, http://www.unredd.net/index.php?option=com_docman&task=doc_download&gid=8717&Itemid=53.

UN-REDD n.d., 'Putting REDD+ safeguards and safeguard information systems into practice', *Policy Brief #3.* Viewed 20 March 2013, http://www.unredd.net/index.php?option=com_docman&task=doc_download&gid=9167&Itemid=53.

USAID 2013, *Emerging compliance markets for REDD+: An assessment of supply and demand*, San Francisco, CA: USAID.

Voldovici, V. and Lauder, D. 2014, 'Republicans vow EPA fight as Obama touts China climate deal'. Viewed 16 May 2015, http://www.reuters.com/article/2014/11/12/us-china-usa-climatechange-mcconnell-idUSKCN0IW1TZ20141112.

World Bank 2015, *Prototype carbon fund.* Viewed 20 April 2015, http://wbcarbonfinance.org/PCF.

World Commission on Dams 2002, *The report of the World Commission on Dams (WCD) and its relevance to the Ramsar Convention.* WCD, viewed 14 May 2015, http://archive.ramsar.org/pdf/res/key_res_viii_02_e.pdf.

World Rainforest Movement (WRM) 2010, *Brazil: Once again opposing Plantar's CDM project'.* Viewed 20 April 2015, http://www.wrm.org.uy/oldsite/bulletin/151/Brazil.html.

Young, O. R. 2010, *Institutional dynamics: Emergent patterns in international environmental governance*, Cambridge, MA: MIT Press.

Zarin, D., Angelsen, A., Brown, S., Loisel, C., Peskett, L. and Streck, C. 2009, 'Reducing Emissions from Deforestation and Forest Degradation (REDD): An options assessment report'. Meridian Institute, viewed 20 April 2015, http://redd-oar.org/links/REDD-OAR_en.pdf.

2. Combatting deforestation I – FSC and PEFC

HISTORY AND DESCRIPTIVE BACKGROUND OF THE RISE OF FOREST CERTIFICATION

A rising awareness of tropical deforestation in the 1980s led to increased action by environmental NGOs to protect forests globally (Pattberg 2005: 358–61). The success of their efforts was largely a result of growing alliances between groups in developed and developing countries, disillusioned by the failure of intergovernmental processes to effectively tackle the problem of unsustainable logging (Humphreys 1996: 18–19, Keck and Sikkink 1998: 150–2, Elliott 2000: 43–9, Ozinga 2001: 13). Initially, the primary target was the tropical timber trade, but this was subsequently expanded in the 1990s to include forests in the industrialised nations as well, notably in the temperate and boreal forest regions. A number of strategies were developed, such as targeting timber retail outlets and international timber companies through boycotts, and pressurising local and national governments (as well as regional bodies such as the EU) to ban imports. This led to bans from the European Parliament, Austria and Switzerland between 1988–93, all of which were reversed as a consequence of counter-measures developed by Malaysia. Under pressure from NGOs, the Dutch government and importers agreed to an alternative approach to end imports from sources identified as not being sustainable (Keck and Sikkink 1998: 154–6).

Other NGOs also sought to achieve similar objectives by working through existing intergovernmental agencies, demanding that producer and consumer country members sourced and supplied tropical timber from sustainable sources (Gale 1998: 159–61, Elliott 2000: 45–6, Humphreys 1996: 155–6). Their primary target was the International Tropical Timber Organisation (ITTO), founded in 1983. There was some reaction to increasing NGO concerns regarding tropical deforestation within ITTO. In the same year, the ITTO commissioned the International Institute for Environment and Development (IIED) to prepare a report, which found less than 1 per cent of the global timber trade to be from sustainable sources. The result of this report was to encourage both NGOs and the ITTO membership to look more closely at promoting sustainable forest management (Humphreys 1996: 74). In 1985, an International Tropical Forest Timber Agreement (ITTA) was ratified, and a Tropical Forest Action Plan (TFAP) developed in 1986.

These were not the only state-based processes to attempt to tackle the problem of illegal and unsustainable logging. Nine separate proposals for a global forest initiative were developed between January and December of 1990, all of which failed to gain traction (Humphreys 1996: 83–8). Swedish Prime Minister Ola Ulstein has been attributed as first putting forward the proposal 'in response to the failure of existing international forest protection programmes' (Boyer 2005: 304). But despite the belief at the time that Rio would be able to produce a global-level solution, none eventuated, as was mentioned earlier (Keck and Sikkink 1998: 160). Although there were agreements that would ultimately lead to conventions on biological diversity, climate change and desertification, there were no legally binding outcomes for forests, only the 'Non-Legally Binding Authoritative Statement of Principles for a Global Consensus on the Management, Conservation and Sustainable Development of All Types of Forests', known as the *Statement of Forest Principles* (Department of Economic and Social Affairs/Secretariat of the United Nations Forum on Forests and Department of Economic and Social Affairs/UNFF Secretariat 2004).

The approach to environmental management that emerged in the wake of Rio reflects the high level of influence exercised by business interests and their preference for self-regulation. It ultimately marks the end of an unsuccessful campaign by NGOs to use UN processes to control corporate behaviour (Clapp 2005: 25). The International Chamber of Commerce, the Business Council for Sustainable Development (BCSD, now World Business Council for Sustainable Development – WBCSD) and the Rio organisers approached the International Organization for Standardization (ISO) to develop an environmental management system (EMS) (Parto 1999: 182, Clapp 1999: 201). Voluntary standards were essentially legitimated at UNCED, which was reflected in the contents of *Agenda 21*. Private industry and business associations were exhorted to increase clean technologies and decrease pollution (Clapp 1999: 199 and 208). This had the effect of encouraging voluntary programmes, which certified compliance against standards (Hortensius 1999: 14).

The desire to pursue a voluntary approach before and after Rio has been explained as a means of avoiding national environmental laws, which, some representatives of industry argued, might be challenged as a technical barrier to trade, and potentially in violation of WTO rules

(Raines 2006: 50). ISO established a technical committee, TC 207 to develop the new '14000' series of standards, and published an explicit statement on the committee's website that it would not 'set limit levels or performance criteria for operations or products' (ISO TC 207 1998).

But the failure of Rio to deliver a forest convention did not mean that forest policy at the intergovernmental level ground to a halt. Forests were still contained in the Rio document, *Agenda 21* (Chapter 11, Combatting deforestation). Governments also agreed to establish a body to continue work on resolving the forest issue, and in 1995 the Intergovernmental Panel on Forests (IPF) was established as a policy forum for forest-related decisions (Department of Economic and Social Affairs/Secretariat of the United Nations Forum on Forests and Department of Economic and Social Affairs/UNFF Secretariat 2004). The IPF lasted until 1997 when it was replaced by the Intergovernmental Forum on Forests, which itself continued until 2000 when it, in turn, was superseded by the United Nations Forum on Forests (UNFF) (ECOSOC 2000).

UNFF and its predecessors adopted a different route, focusing instead on national forest policies and developing a series of regional governmental processes to create criteria and indicators (C&I) to assess the sustainability of forest management (Ozinga 2001: 23). The largest regional efforts were the Montreal Process for Temperate and Boreal Forests (initiated by Canada in 1994) and the Helsinki (later pan European) Process (established prior to Rio in 1990). Other regional processes were also developed: Tarapoto for the Amazon, in 1995; the Dry Zone Africa Initiative (Kenya 1995), North Africa and Near East Initiative (1996) and the Central American Initiative of Leparterique (1997) (Hortensius 1999: 13).

Criteria were defined as conditions or elements within forest management that needed to be consistent with principles of sustainable forest management. *Indicators* represented measurable aspects that were to be assessed against each criterion, and which were used together to determine the quality of forest management (Lammerts van Beuren and Blom 1997: 34). *SFM* was defined as constituting forest management practices that ensured ongoing wood production, but also (reflecting the discourse of Rio) ensured environmental and social productivity. *Standards* were ideally meant to consist of a set of principles, criteria and indictors that served as a tool to promote SFM, to act as a basis for monitoring and reporting, and to provide a reference for assessment of actual forest management (Lammerts van Beuren and Blom 1997: 34). *Certification* was defined as 'a process, which results in a written quality statement (a certificate) attesting to the origin of raw wood material and its status

and/or qualifications following validation by an independent third party'
(Baharuddin and Simula cited in Lammerts van Beuren and Blom 1997:
35)

But the *principles* (that is, the rules or values informing C&I)
underlying SFM at the national level remained somewhat nebulous.
Instead the focus was placed on using C&I as a voluntary approach to
putting international agreements into practice and defining how SFM
could be put into operation. Governments' closeness to business interests,
in these C&I processes, it has been argued, ultimately resulted in weak
measures (Gale and Burda 1999: 280). They were to be seen rather as
'guidelines' for the development of voluntary standards, indicative of
SFM and negotiated largely in consultation with the forest industry
(MCPFE 1998: 258–9). Under the Montreal process for example, which
covered 60 per cent of the world's forests, SFM and the measures
required to achieve it, were left undefined. Instead, C&I became a
'common understanding' for achieving 'progress towards' SFM (Commonwealth of Australia 1997: v).

In 1995 the ISO national standards bodies of Canada and Australia
proposed the development of a guide for the forest industry with the clear
intention of creating a link between SFM and certification under the
14001 standard (ISO TC 207 1995b: 3). One impetus for the proposal
appears to have been the Canadian forest industries' wish to gain
international recognition for the Canadian Standard Association (CSA)
standard for SFM, which was being developed at that time (Elliott 2000:
16). The development of the Canadian CSA standard had occurred in a
highly charged political context. Environmental NGOs, already wary of
the C&I approach, were heavily critical of the CSA. They objected to
clear-cut forest management permitted under the standard, and the use of
chlorine bleaching in pulp production. A successful international campaign had secured the cancellation of pulp orders and NGOs were
concerned that the guide could be misused. Canadian environment
groups, including Greenpeace, refused to participate in the Canadian
technical committee on the grounds that the CSA standard lacked
performance requirements without which, they argued, an EMS was not
an adequate measure of sustainability (Elliott 2000: 147–56).

Despite this background, TC 207 resolved to develop a technical
reference document, ISO TR 14061, and CSA was made the secretariat
(Elliott 2000: 16). Once again, the responsible working group was
instructed not to specify performance levels for forestry (ISO TC 207
1995a: 13). This led one commentator to observe that the potential now
existed for companies to use the EMS framework and link it to the
Helsinki and Montreal C&I processes (Hauselmann 1997: 13). Indeed,

ISO's own literature claimed that there was 'a link between the management system approach of ISO 14001 and the range of forest policy and
forest management performance objectives, including principles, criteria
and indicators of SFM' (Hortensius 1999: 17). At the same time ISO
avoided having to take responsibility for any linkage made by asserting
that it was 'up to the forestry organisations to decide whether they want
to meet externally developed performance objectives such as the sets of
SFM' (Hortensius 1999: 20). Supporters of 14061 argued that ISO was
compatible with all of the various non-governmental and intergovernmental initiatives that have been established in the wake of
Agenda 21 and the *Statement of Forest Principles* (Hortensius 1999: 13).

In addition, ISO 14020, the standard covering the general principles
for environmental labels and declarations, was also designed to be
broadly compatible with the materials being developed by the IPF (Elliott
2000: 14). Canada's CSA standard also used criteria similar to those of
the IPF (Elliott 2000: 156). NGO efforts to change the content and
direction of ISO 14020 were consistently overruled within TC 207
(Hauselmann 1997: 8). All of these activities succeeded in creating the
impression that C&I driven industry forest management standards had a
performance basis, where none such existed. All of these developments
provided the backdrop to the 'certification wars' between industry and
environmental NGOs that ensued (Humphreys 2005).

The intergovernmental approach has been criticised for delivering
reductionist outcomes and typifying the ongoing inability of the intergovernmental community to end unsustainable and illegal logging (Humphreys 2006: 215, Bernstein and Cashore 2004: 39, Cashore et al. 2004:
11–12, Gulbrandsen 2004: 76, Pattberg 2005: 361, Tollefson et al. 2008:
25). Despite the failure of UNCED to deliver a forest convention,
intergovernmental forest-related initiatives continued to develop a life of
their own, notably at the national and regional level, and UNFF continues
to this day. Negotiations for the ITTA also continued, and the Agreement
entered into legal force in 1994. But it was not particularly strong in its
language, referring only to 'undocumented trade'. Subsequent negotiations for a new, more comprehensive agreement, were resisted by a
number of countries including Brazil, India and China, part of the
so-called Amazonian Pact countries, who objected to the comprehensive
language relating to illegal logging in the document (Humphreys 1996:
33–57). This new agreement was finally negotiated in 2006 and entered
into force in 2011. But it was without a number of important countries,
including Canada, which ratified the agreement in 2006, but subsequently
withdrew (effective as of 2013) (ITTO n.d.).

One interesting development to emerge in recent times has been the shift in the forest management discourse away from SFM to 'sustainable management of forests' (FAO 2012). This term first appeared in text associated with the Bali climate change talks of 2007 relating to forest activities proposed under REDD. It appears to have gone relatively unchallenged until the climate talks Bonn June 2009, when efforts to introduce SFM back into the text negotiations were met with some resistance from ENGOs. By the next round of discussions in Bangkok in October of the same year, SMF was back in contention. This shift runs contrary to other intergovernmental initiatives, notably UNFF, a major advocate of SFM (UN 2007: 2). This conflict between conservation and (by implication) production-orientated language has even made it to the popular media:

> SFM is the villain – a meaningless greenwash phrase adopted widely by the global logging industry to allow it to carry on business as usual. SMF, however, emphasises conservation and protection and is backed by the likes of Greenpeace and Global Witness, as well as many countries. (*The Guardian*, n.d.).

These developments have created some discomfort in the pro-SFM camp, notably in FAO, which commented that the move to SMF was the result of activities by 'stakeholder groups advocating a restricted, conservation oriented REDD instrument' (FAO 2012: 1).

The extent to which global forest protection policies are working has come under further scrutiny in more recent times, and the focus on tropical deforestation has been questioned. Russia is now the country with the greatest rate of deforestation, with over 37 million hectares of tree cover lost between 2001 and 2013, followed by Brazil with nearly 36 million, Canada with just over 28, and the US with over 27. At 7 million hectares, forest losses in 2013 in boreal forests are rapidly catching up with deforestation in the tropical zones (8 million hectares in the same year) (Global Forest Watch 2015). If the figures are extrapolated to 2011–2013, Russia had by far the greatest rate (over 43 million ha), followed by Canada (24.5 million ha) with Brazil third (21 million ha) and followed by the US (17 million ha). These statistics led one commentator to speculate whether 'there was sufficient evidence now to pass the villain baton on to other national actors' (Freemen 2015).

FOREST STEWARDSHIP COUNCIL

NGOs had begun looking at systems for labelling 'good wood' as a means of protecting tropical rainforests as early as 1985 (Cadman 2011: 31). By 1988, those still seeking to engage with such bodies as the ITTO finally lost patience with the intergovernmental approach and determined to look at certification more seriously as an alternative option (Humphreys 2005: 4). These measures resulted in NGO-driven market-based systems of forest certification, designed specifically to challenge industry-driven standards (Humphreys 1996: 66–74). NGOs rejected the development of domestically generated C&I and related certification standards (particularly in Europe), and began a new series of consumer campaigns targeting major paper purchasers (Elliott 2000: 22–3, Mantyranta 2002: 93–103). They tapped into the consuming public's scepticism over the validity of claims made by 'self-certifying' individual companies, and emphasised the need for arm's length approaches, which led to the development of their own certification schemes and the ensuing market competition between industry certification programmes (based on C&I), and their own (Gale and Burda 1999: 280).

Serious discussions around the creation of an international certification programme began in 1991, and by 1992 an interim board had been elected. In an attempt to differentiate from the C&I approach and to avoid the use of the term 'sustainable', a decision was made to create principles and criteria (P&C) for 'well-managed' forests. Initially it was decided that the P&C should only cover native forests. But after some internal debate, pressure from forest industry members, and their inclusion in industry schemes, plantations were also included in a tenth principle. In 1996 the Forest Stewardship Council A.C. was incorporated in Oaxaca, Mexico, partly due to the support offered by the host state, but also in recognition of the importance of including developing countries. The decision-making body was based around a general assembly of members, divided into economic, social and environmental chambers, with each chamber being further divided into North and South (Cadman 2011).

In the same year, sales of wood products with the FSC logo began in the UK, and in Sweden in 1997 the first national standard was endorsed, making a non-tropical country the first to gain FSC accreditation. In the same year, an Indonesian programme, LEI (Lembaga Ekolabel Indonesia) entered into a cooperative agreement with the scheme (Cadman 2011: 45–8). The scheme commenced a process of institutional consolidation from 1998, commencing with a project to include small forest owners in

the programme, and continuing in 1999 with a series of policy clarifi-
cations around high conservation value (HCV) forests, pesticide use and
labour issues. Despite pressure from the forest science community, FSC
maintained its opposition to the use of genetically modified organisms in
its certification programme (Strauss et al. 2001: 7). These policy positions were followed in 2002 by an initiative to increase social stakeholder
participation in the programme, the creation of a more decentralised
organisational structure in 2003 and the release of a range of new
standards in 2004. In 2005 a review to investigate plantation certification
was commenced, and by 2008, given the review's recommendations to
return to a single set of P&C, the issue was rolled over into an ongoing
review of the P&C. A governance review was commenced in 2007 and
was adopted in 2008 (Cadman 2011: 48–52).

More recently, a further revision of the P&C was initiated in January
2009. The review lasted nearly three years; in February 2012, 75 per cent
of FSC members accepted the revisions, and a fifth version was created
(Forest Stewardship Council 2014b). A significant development was a set
of International Generic Indicators (IGIs) with the intent of providing
global consistency. This was in response to the absence of national
standards in some countries and the need for certification bodies to
properly evaluate and confirm compliance with the P&Cs (Forest
Stewardship Council 2014b). A Modular Approach Programme (MAP)
was approved in 2005 to prioritise support for community and smallholders to achieve FSC full certification. In 2011 a draft standard went into
the development stages, with pilot projects in 2013. Related standards
started to be released in 2014. The stepwise approach (long under
discussion in FSC) was designed to include legality verification, in
response to market demand (Forest Stewardship Council 2014a, FSC
International 2015b). The development of indicators to expand on HCV
definitions to protect intact forest landscape (IFLs) is scheduled for
release in 2016 by a HCV Technical Working Committee (Greenpeace
2014a).

FSC has played an increasing role in the climate negotiations, as a
consequence of the increasing interest in reducing emissions from
forest-based activities. FSC representatives attended UNFCCC COP-15
in 2009 and held a 'side event' to discuss the role of the FSC in the
context of REDD+. It has had a continuous presence since, and also
increased its relations with voluntary carbon standards organisations,
including The Gold Standard. At the 2011 General Assembly a motion
was adopted recognising forest carbon as an environmental value. In
November of the same year at COP 17 in Durban it released its climate
change strategy, and at COP 19 in Warsaw it presented its own,

newly-developed 'due diligence' system for carbon schemes (FSC International 2015b). These are also connected to increased efforts to develop effective methods for assessing the FPIC of Indigenous people and other rights holders in forest certification. Although FSC had requirements for granting or withholding consent in place as early as 1994, there were 'not many documented examples of good practices', and in 2012 the process of incorporating FPIC more formally into the P&C commenced (FSC Canada 2012). In 2014, a series of field trials were implemented in developing and developed countries, including Chile, Nepal, Spain and Russia (FSC International 2014). As of the beginning of 2015, over 180 million ha of native forests and plantations were certified under the FSC brand (FSC International 2015a).

Much of the FSC's controversies mirror the development of its policies and programmes, and the reaction to them from supporters and opponents. Initial debate as to whether economic interests could become voting members was also intense. Thirteen social and environmental groups, including Greenpeace, Friends of the Earth and Indigenous groups then withdrew their support, arguing that economic interests had been given too much power (Mantyranta 2002: 21).

Discussions regarding plantation certification also proved a subject of intense debate (Mantyranta 2002: 20). The initial P&C only referred to plantations in so far as their establishment was expressly forbidden on sites of primary and well-established secondary forests, or of environmental, cultural or social significance (Humphreys 1996: 150). The FSC issued a revised set of P&C, further amended in 2000, permitting the certification of plantations with certain provisos (Humphreys 1996: 150). This confirmed the fears of some of those NGOs that had withdrawn from the founding assembly in 1993 (Humphreys 2005: 6).

Serious concerns regarding FSC accredited certifiers also began to emerge from the mid 1990s. The most controversial case was the certification by the Rainforest Alliance's SmartWood Program of teakwood plantations in Costa Rica. While the plantation was 'decertified' in 1998, false and misleading claims had been issued regarding its investment potential and certification status, seriously undermining the reputation of FSC and NGOs involved in the scheme (Romeijn and Wageningen 1999). Heavy criticism of the FSC's P&C and the role of certifiers ensued, and concerns about a wide range of matters including transparency, accountability and equity were raised (Elliott 2000: 22). In 1999 NGO frustration over the failings within the FSC system culminated in the production of a highly critical report published by the Rainforest Foundation. It challenged the effectiveness of the FSC secretariat, the commitment of certifiers to stringent – and consultative –

certification assessments, and the true extent of democracy, representation, transparency and 'multistakeholderism' across the system (Counsell 1999).

The FSC's percentage-based claims policy also proved controversial. This was a process whereby certified and uncertified sources could be mixed. One leading figure within the FSC, Julio César Centeno, already angered by the Costa Rica issue, resigned over the policy (Mantyranta 2002: 25, Counsell and Terje Loraas 2002: 21). A decision was adopted to allow sawmills dealing with only small quantities of non-certified wood to participate in FSC system, but an effort by NGOs to set the minimum volume of certified timber in solid wood products at 70 per cent was defeated (Forest Stewardship Council n.d.: 5).

Dissatisfaction with the FSC led to increasing levels of scrutiny by NGOs. In May 2001, European environmental and social NGO Forests and the European Union Resource Network (FERN) published its report *Behind the Logo*, a comprehensive analysis of FSC and its competitor schemes, and although more favourable to the FSC than other schemes, the report identified problems with FSC consultation, communication and dispute resolution (Ozinga 2001: 47). A number of NGO complaints were also raised both formally and informally with FSC during this period. These included an ongoing dispute around the unpopular practice of undertaking evaluations using 'interim' standards in the absence of national standards (Royal Forest and Bird Protection Society (RFBPS) et al. 2001). It was agreed that the use of interim certification using the certifiers' own generic standards would also be phased out over time. National standards under development by a national initiative, even if they were in draft form, were to be incorporated in assessments undertaken by certification bodies (Forest Stewardship Council n.d.: 10). An external team of consultants was also brought in to develop a guidance document on the interpretation of Principles Two and Three for certifiers using generic standards (Forest Stewardship Council 2004: 2–7). This was in response to concerns about certification assessments in Indonesia (Forest Stewardship Council 2004: 6).

In November 2001 the Rainforest Foundation published the report, *Trading in Credibility*, which systematically outlined a number of structural and procedural weaknesses in the FSC system, as well as some of the shortcomings of its certification and standard-setting activities in a number of countries (Counsell and Terje Loraas 2002: 12). Alarm was also engendered in some NGOs (and ironically, FSC competitors) due to the decision under the FSC Swedish national standard to allow 'mutual accreditation' with the rival industry scheme, PEFC, under the 'Stock Dove' arrangement (Mantyranta 2002: 245–9).

Fears about percentage-based claims, or 'mixed' sources, also fed into scepticism among some NGOs regarding the handling and accreditation of non-FSC 'controlled wood' from uncertified forests (Forest Steward-ship Council 2004: 3). The FSC created a new standard, the intention of which was to eliminate 'controversial' sources of timber from supply chains, particularly illegally harvested wood (Forest Stewardship Council 2004: 11). The new standard was defended by the FSC as addressing the G8's action plan to combat illegal logging and assist national procure-ment policies favouring legally harvested timber (Forest Stewardship Council 2004: 3).

In 2004, a follow-up report to *Behind the Logo* published by FERN, *Footprints in the Forest*, compared FSC to an increasing number of competitor schemes (Ozinga 2004). Although kinder to FSC than most of the other schemes investigated, the report was nevertheless critical of FSC on matters relating to both policy and performance (Ozinga 2004: 38). In particular it needed to 'seriously address' the problems that were associated with plantation certification (Ozinga 2004: 21). The continu-ous opposition to plantation certification was substantively addressed by FSC in its plantation review, and a final report was issued in 2006 (Forest Stewardship Council 2007). The report recommended one common set of integrated P&C, arguing the higher the impacts of management, 'the greater the emphasis needed for prevention, mitigation and compensation measures' (Forest Stewardship Council 2006a: 1). Certifiers were also targeted, and it was recommended that their role should be one of auditing the extent to which the forest management genuinely involved stakeholders in discussions and resolved conflicts (Forest Stewardship Council 2006b: 7–11). Much of this work was lost, however, when the review entered its technical phase in 2007 and was merged with the P&C review in 2008, which ultimately reversed the decision of the review committee, perhaps reflecting, once again, the controversial and unresolved role of plantations in FSC certification.

Opposition to FSC certification from within its own ranks continued through 2008. In October a group of environmental NGOs and forestry companies including FERN, Greenpeace, Inter-African Forest Industry Association, Precious Woods, Swedish Society for Nature Conservation and Tropical Forest Trust produced a joint statement voicing concerns about controlled wood, the role of certification bodies and the (revised) complaints mechanism (FERN et al. 2008). Attention was also drawn to the lack of 'sufficiently stringent procedures within FSC Accreditation Services International (ASI)' (FERN et al. 2008: 1). The statement also called for a phasing out of controlled wood certificates by 2018.

The P&C review of 2009 went some way to acknowledging these issues. One was the announcement of the development of a set of IGIs aimed at strengthening the credibility of the FSC system. Certification bodies previously had to develop and implement generic standards on a country-by-country basis, resulting in inconsistency across countries and standards. IGIs were developed as the 'starting point' leading to 'adapted standards' (Forest Stewardship Council 2014c). This had been one of the major grievances of NGOs earlier in the decade around the use of 'interim' standards, and inconsistency at the national level between countries.

Shortly after the review began, Greenpeace published a non-flattering report, *Under the cover of forest certification*, claiming that the FSC failed to prevent the destruction of HCV forests in Sweden. Greenpeace claimed that inadequate standards were used in Sweden and companies knowingly destroyed old growth forests (Tas and Rodrigues 2009). Other environmental NGOs went further, claiming that 60 per cent of FSC-certified products come from primary forests, arguing that the FSC had not released any data to prove otherwise (Goetzman 2010). Partially in response, FSC formed an expert group to develop guidance documents for the identification and maintenance of HVCs. A draft was released in late 2012 (Forest Stewardship Council 2014a).

But the criticisms continued. In March 2013 Greenpeace released another report, entitled *FSC at Risk,* summarising shortcomings within the FSC system including the failure to maintain HCV forests, logging IFLs overlooking social conflicts and human rights violations, and claiming that controlled wood was 'uncontrolled'. Much of this was blamed on weak interpretation and application of standards by certifi-cation bodies (Greenpeace 2013). This too seemed to generate some action, and IFLs were included in the FSC's definition of HCV forests, which were subsequently included in the P&Cs and adopted in 2014 (Forest Stewardship Council 2014a).

Greenpeace issued a progress report in December 2014, noting that the development and implementation of indicators to achieve IFL protection were scheduled for release in 2016. But it also indicated that as of 2014 there were no policies in place for addressing human rights violations in high-risk regions. It concluded that FSC needed to develop measures around stakeholder participation in land-use planning around HCV issues, and address lack of transparency, corruption issues and poor governance. Certification bodies were singled out for an inherent conflict of interest in auditing companies who paid them to do so (Greenpeace 2014a).

Sources and Means of Delivery of Finance

The success of FSC as a market mechanism to deliver sustainable forest management is unclear. A study compared the FSC systems of Argentina and Brazil and found that 'the main cross-national difference in this regard is that Brazil has a much larger extractive industry selling products from native forests. There is not enough difference, however, in market demand in these industries to explain the dramatic variation in the effectiveness of the FSC' (Espach 2006: 81). It also found that government agencies in Argentina and Brazil have little or no direct influence over firms' decisions on whether to participate. Government policies and incentives in this regard are widely held to lack credibility.

A comparative study of FSC in USA by Rickenbach and Overdevest (2006) found differences in satisfaction across enterprise type. They found that small private enterprises reported lower satisfaction than public and large private enterprises. The research also found no relationship between overall satisfaction and recertification intention. Certification for those already certified may be the exception in the future (Rickenbach and Overdevest 2006: 147). Sample et al. (2003: 25) analysed agencies' views to certification in the USA. They found that few agencies cited economic incentives, such as the potential for increased income from the sale of certified wood, as important to their decision to seek independent certification. Therefore, certification is becoming increasingly important as a voluntary mechanism for improving forest management practices on both public and private lands, and for recognising the achievements of resource managers whose efforts can serve as tangible, observable models for improving the conservation and sustainable management of America's forests (Sample et al. 2003: 25).

However, a similar study in Latin America and Mexico found that neither the fair trade coffee nor FSC initiatives were likely to be adopted by local people themselves to transform their markets into institutions that place people and the environment at the centre of production, trade and consumption. It also found that 'FSC's efforts to make certification more accessible to small, low-intensity and community-based forest operators could be weakened without an appreciation of how mainstream market logics and practices systematically encourage a privileged attention to Northern forests and actors' (Taylor 2005: 144). Here the study found that in both cases, tensions between conventional and alternative market logics and practices are inevitable as products while being in the market were not quite of it.

The FSC's merits as a market mechanism for contributing to effective forest management at the national level have been challenged. Hain and

Ahas (2007) reviewed an Estonian case and questioned whether FSC really improved forest management. They found that sceptical forest officials and entrepreneurs do not like very strict environmental measures as it limits their ability to make free decisions during forest management. They also reported that certification of private forest (less than 10 ha) organisation and cooperation among private forest owners are minimal, making it difficult to exchange information, promote certification and communicate effectively. Therefore, certification has not solved the problem of unsustainable over-logging and illegal forestry in Estonian private forest (Hain and Ahas 2007).

PROGRAMME FOR THE ENDORSEMENT OF FOREST CERTIFICATION

In 1993 North American forestry interests responded to the creation of FSC commencing the development of their own competitor certification schemes: the CSA and the US Sustainable Forestry Initiative (SFI). European forest industries determined to pursue their own market scheme distinct from FSC by the late 1990s (Finnish Forest Industries Federation 1998a). European forestry interests felt that FSC was not supportive of small-scale private forest owners, by far the largest source of wood products for industry, and determined to pursue a 'pan-European' approach, comprised of national certification schemes that could provide an alternative international scheme (Cashore et al. 2007: 6).

Following their experiences in Sweden and Finland, Scandinavian associations of forest owners felt that the FSC was excluding them from participating in the scheme, which they considered costly and intrusive. The inability for small forest owners to group together essentially also forced small-scale family holdings to seek alternative options. NGOs were seen to have overstepped themselves in matters where they had no right to regulate. The FSC was seen as overly stringent and lacking interpretive flexibility in its rules, as well as favouring larger companies with greater economies of scale. Overall, the system was seen as being far too environmentally and socially stringent, and landowners and forest industries wanted a scheme that paid greater attention to economic criteria. There was also a perception that environmental and social interests dominated the decision-making processes, and since the FSC lacked the legitimacy of a state institution it was interpreted as suffering from an accountability deficit (Gulbrandsen 2004: 92).

The idea of recruiting the EU to the cause was first floated by the Finnish Forest Industries Federation in 1998, based upon the idea of developing a scheme that promoted European forest products as coming from sustainably managed forests (Mantyranta 2002: 128). The European Commission was lobbied to create a certification framework EU-wide, and there were discussions with directorates general as well as parliament members, but no directives or regulations were issued on the subject (Humphreys 2005: 15–19, Mantyranta 2002: 132). The lack of action by the EU may have been another spur to the creation of the PEFC (Humphreys 2006: 127). Industry representatives from Finland and Germany met to discuss the way forward, having determined that the FSC was not suitable, and set about recruiting other European countries to the cause (Mantyranta 2002: 132–5).

Several technical working group meetings throughout 1998–9 were held to oversee and develop the content of the proposed scheme (Mantyranta 2002: 6–7). The time was right, it was observed, 'to construct a European alternative to the FSC' (Mantyranta 2002: 146). After initial meetings, a draft certification framework was developed and it was determined to invite 'market partners' and an enlarged number of participant countries to subsequent events (Mantyranta 2002: 153). Membership would be based around country representation, with votes being allocated according to the scale of cutting in a given country. Other organisations could attend, but they could not vote (Mantyranta 2002: 184–5). The scheme was launched in Paris under the name Pan European Forest Certification (PEFC) in June 1999 (Mantyranta 2002: 214). Eleven country representatives participated (PEFC 2007b). The PEFC's interim board was established at the same meeting, consisting of five forest owner associations and one seat each for industry, processors and NGOs (Mantyranta 2002: 214). The first PEFC schemes from Finland, Norway, Sweden, Germany and Austria were endorsed in 2000, and in May 2001 the CSA joined the PEFC Council (PEFC 2007b: 1).

PEFC passed the FSC's area of certified forest for the first time in July 2001 (36.42 million ha to 22.38 million ha) (PEFCC Newsletter 2001). PEFC's attitude towards FSC can be interpreted as one of competitive rivalry, based on a strategy of building support in the state, community and private forest sectors, and the FSC supply chain (Cashore et al. 2004: 180). In Germany the competition reached the point where an initial commitment to FSC certification from state forest ministry was extended to include PEFC certification (Teegelbekkers 2001a: 5). This has been explained as a method of protecting market share (Humphreys 2005: 22). Considerable effort was also put into keeping forest owners in the scheme. Revisiting the tactics of the early 1990s, forest owners were encouraged to organise protests outside timber retailers stocking FSC-only products, necessitating some retailers to negotiate with forest owners to de-escalate the confrontation (Teegelbekkers 2001a: 5). This had the effect of alienating some FSC supporters, but it also led to the removal of the FSC logo from their products and encouraged others to adopt both brands (Cashore et al. 2004: 181–2).

In 2002 in a push to further internationalise itself, PEFC permitted four more national schemes into the General Assembly (Gunnerberg 2002a: 1). This stimulated discussions about redesigning the system to be more global. PEFC was also approached by Gabon about developing a pan-African forest certification system (PEFCC News Special 2002: 2, PEFCC Newsletter 2002: 3). A Globalisation Working Group was established to work out the details for brand development and expansion, and a new scheme retaining the original initials but now named the 'Programme for the Endorsement of Forest Certification schemes' was approved by the General Assembly in October 2003 (PEFCC Newsletter 2003: 1, PEFC News 2003: 4). In an interesting show of the degree of closeness between the intergovernmental policy world and industry-driven certification, Pekka Patosaari, UNFF Coordinator and Head of Secretariat, was invited to speak at the meeting. He noted that the PEFC's 'lack of support from some NGOs seems to determine the public perception and this can also have some relevance from a marketing point of view'. He was also quoted as saying that 'PEFC was already strong enough to stand alone, and deliver' (PEFC 2003: 9). The scheme's global expansion continued in 2004 and the Australian, Italian, Chilean and Portuguese national programmes were endorsed as member schemes. In 2005, the certification schemes of Canada, Brazil, Luxembourg and the Slovak Republic were also formally endorsed, as well as the US-based SFI (PEFC 2007a).

With this growth in international membership there also came a shift in governmental attitudes towards PEFC. European markets and government procurement policies began a process of mutual recognition of both FSC and PEFC – a consequence of mobilisation around procurement issues (PEFC News 2005). In Germany, PEFC had mounted a counter-attack to the Federal Government's pro-FSC policy, arguing that it would violate legislation (Teegelbekkers 2003a: 6). PEFC claimed that demand for its products was so high that 'even the chairman of the German FSC working group has recently certified his own forests to PEFC' (Teegel-bekkers 2003b: 5). In Denmark the environment minister moved to have state forests certified to both certification systems (Olsen 2004: 5). In 2005, a Belgian government procurement policy review criticised a number of PEFC affiliates on account of the low recognition of Indig-enous peoples' rights. PEFC dismissed this as 'opinion rather than fact' (PEFC News 2006a: 2).

PEFC expansion continued into 2006 with more companies handling its timber in Asia and Africa, and multiple country schemes were under assessment to join the programme (PEFC News 2007b: 3, PEFC News 2007a: 3). By the end of the year, thanks to its endorsement of a number of previously discrete schemes such as the SFI, PEFC controlled 69 per cent of the world's certified timber, in comparison to FSC's 24 per cent (PEFC News 2006c: 1).

If FSC's developments in policy and the problems it engendered were largely fought inside the organisation, PEFC's problems are better characterised as conflicts with external opponents, most notably environmental NGOs, but also with Indigenous people. Environmental NGOs were initially included in discussions in Finland around forest certification, although Greenpeace Finland did not and was actively critical. However, the draft that was negotiated between June 1996 and March 1997 was short-lived, and consensus between the parties collapsed. This has been attributed to the desire among NGOs to have the standard FSC certified, a rush to beat Sweden to publication of its (FSC) standard, and pressure from non-participating (pro-FSC) domestic and international NGOs, who also objected to a lack of proper consultation (Mantyranta 2002: 67–85). Another perspective argues that outcome was predictable due to control of the forest policy agenda by state-centric, neo-corporatist interests (Howlett and Rayner 2006: 261). A decision was made in 1998 to restart the negotiating process for a Finnish Forest Certification System (FFCS) but environmental groups did not attend (Mantyranta 2002: 188). The standard was finalised in their absence under the argument that NGOs were not needed since their dissatisfaction had been addressed in the new criteria (Finnish Forest Industries Federation 1998b). A similar pattern of initial cooption of some NGOs followed by rejection of others was pursued in Germany. There, only environmental NGOs willing to cooperate were included, which excluded Greenpeace and World Wildlife Fund (WWF) (Mantyranta 2002: 146–7). This was justified on the grounds that NGO non-participation was due to ideological motives (Teegelbekkers 2003a). Indigenous people, notably the Sámi of northern Scandinavia also experienced problems around participation and inclusion in national PEFC schemes. They came into conflict with the FFCS over not being properly included in the standard-setting process. This came to the attention of World Bank, which refused to extend capacity-building grants for forest certification initiatives to PEFC on account of the fact that Indigenous rights were not being adequately recognised. PEFC Council responded by producing a policy paper in late 2005. This effectively repeated the status quo position that PEFC schemes followed intergovernmental arrangements and national requirements (Cadman 2011: 126–7).

During the period 2009–2015, the focus of PEFC activities was on revising and updating standards, improving stakeholder participation and generally increasing the amount of global forest certified. While representation was still dominated by Northern hemisphere nations and organisations, a number of PEFC systems were approved in Asia, Africa and South America.

In July 2010 Greenpeace published a report titled *How Sinar Mas is Pulping the Planet*, concerning illegal harvesting of rainforest timber in peatland and the destruction of critical tiger and orang-utan habitat by Asia Pulp and Paper (APP), part of the Sinar Mas group and PEFC certificate holder (Greenpeace 2010). PEFC lodged a formal complaint with the certifying body *Société Générale de Surveillance* (SGS) South Africa (Gunnerberg 2010a). An investigation by SGS reported that the timber used was legal and permitted due to certain technicalities (Marais 2011). However, Greenpeace dismissed SGS's findings, arguing that the certifier was effectively being asked to police its own work (Tait 2010).

A debate involving the United States Green Building Council (USGBC) that had been initiated two years previously resurfaced in 2010, continuing through to 2012. The two points of contention were the limited scope of USGBC's Leadership in Energy and Environmental Design (LEED) tool, and the stringency of its requirements. In 2010, the tool only recognised FSC-certified materials (PEFC News 2010b). PEFC was one of many accusing USGBC of raising the sustainability benchmarks for wood products too high, making certification unattainable for the majority of forest managers (Gunnerberg 2010b). USGBC still did not recognise PEFC-certified materials in 2012 (PEFC News 2012).

Finally, the ongoing rivalry between PEFC and the FSC resurfaced, with FSC publishing a report summarising and comparing the sustainability requirements of the two certification systems (PEFC News 2009). In his response, PEFC Secretary General Ben Gunneberg stated:

> It's a nonsensical exercise comparing apples to oranges. The perceived differences in FSC's analysis are based on differences in interpretation of specific criteria, and the mistakes in the report highlight the difficulty of comparing alternative certification systems. (PEFC News 2009)

Despite ongoing differences, the two certification bodies came together in 2013 to oppose the proposal to create an ISO standard for forest certification. The joint statement read:

> PEFC and FSC strongly believe that an ISO chain of custody standard would not add value to global efforts to promote sustainable forest management through forest certification ... A separated chain of custody delivered by another institution such as ISO cannot deliver similar synergies [to FSC and PEFC certification] and will lead to uncertainty due to its dislocated nature with respect to forest management certification. (PEFC and FSC 2010)

Notable changes to PEFC leadership during 2009–2015 included the appointment of Indigenous and developing country representatives to the Board of Directors. Indigenous representatives were appointed in November 2010 (Minnie Degawan) (PEFC News 2010a) and March 2013 (Juan Carlos Jintiach) (PEFC News 2013). A developing country representative, Sheam Satkuru-Granzella, was elected Vice Chair to the Board of Directors in November 2011 (PEFC News 2011). Other positions within the Board of Directors also changed hands during this time.

Workshops to revise PEFC's Chain of Custody Standards began in 2009. Revisions are still ongoing. In 2010 the General Assembly decided to incorporate social requirements into the PEFC Chain of Custody Standard (PEFC Council 2015, 5). These revisions included ensuring freedom of association, prohibition of forced labour and underage workers, equal opportunity and working conditions that did not endanger safety or health (PEFC Council 2015, 12–15).

The major focus of revisions during 2011–2013 was 'the further development of PEFC's risk assessment procedures in the due diligence system [DDS] part of the standard' (PEFC Council 2014: 9). The DDS was applied to all certificate holders and supplies with PEFC claim, while self-declaration was cancelled, and a new risk assessment and mitigation system was put in place. Importantly, provisions were put in place to ensure that complaints were investigated and substantiated (PEFC Council 2014).

Sources and Means of Delivery of Finance

Many studies clearly show that adoption choices are influenced by the character of the forest operation, market and product characteristics, trade dependence, associational structures in the forestry sector, NGO pressure and government support (Auld et al. 2008: 205). Governments of Latin America (and elsewhere) have used certification schemes as a means of meeting sustainability requirements. Being able to use major forest certification schemes greatly increases the prospect of obtaining competitive bids for legal and sustainable timber (Anonymous 2005a). Government buyers have also been able to accept PEFC certificates as an assurance that they are purchasing timber from sustainable sources. PEFC certification has been claimed to address problems of sustainability for importers of Brazilian timber in particular (Anonymous 2005b). In Norway and Sweden non-industrial forest owners showed a preference for PEFC, based on the belief that environmental, social and forest company interests dominate the FSC decision-making process (Gulbrandsen 2005a). An important issue in this scenario is that although the governments in both countries facilitated and legitimised certification processes (like PEFC), environmental group activism and supply chain pressure were more important for certification initiatives. Therefore, a group of large Swedish forest companies responded to market and advocacy group pressures by choosing the widely recognised FSC scheme instead. Further studies of Norway and Sweden cases found that certification processes in both countries have resulted in high participation in certification schemes, high market penetration by certified forest organisations and reduced conflict prevalence over forestry practices (Gulbrandsen 2005b). One of the interesting findings here is that although forest certification seems to have modified on-the-ground practices in ways that lead to less environmental deterioration of forests, people still know too little about forest certification's environmental impact and efficacy as a problem-solving instrument.

There is also some evidence that existing forest laws influence market preferences when considering which global commodity chain to adopt. In the case of Malaysia and Australia for example, government-initiated (and PEFC-affiliated) forest certification and ensuring standards were an attempt to create a new basis for market access (Stringer 2006: 701). The introduction of certification standards was seen as a means of reorganising production and overcoming particular trade barriers created by competitors. This resulted in a consolidation of economically dominated forestry management models (and companies). Instead of facilitating the opening up of international markets to tropical wood per se, certification has resulted in companies choosing specific certification schemes to gain a competitive edge internationally for their particular supply chain (Stringer 2006: 718)

NORTH/SOUTH RELATIONS AND STATE AND NON-STATE ACTORS

At the 1993 FSC founding assembly, Northern NGOs were accused of wanting certification to relate solely to the tropics, and some social

interests were unhappy about the consultation and discriminatory treatment of tropical countries (Mantyranta 2002: 21–4). At the beginning of
1996 its membership was drawn from only 25 countries, and Asia and
Africa were not well represented. This increased to 37 by 1997, but
numbers in the economic chamber were still criticised as being too low
to ensure proper interest representation. Under-representation of social
interests, particularly from Africa and Asia, was also identified as being a
problem during this period, perhaps even more severe than economic
participation. On a separate but related issue, small forest owners
continued to accuse FSC of being discriminatory, in view of the fact that
large-scale tropical forestry certification was both easier to achieve and
more cost-effective than small-scale operations. By 1997 only 4 per cent
of FSC's area under certification was from small-scale or community
operations (Elliott 2000: 21).

Concerns about plantation certification were consistently expressed by
Southern environmental and social NGOs in the 1990s, which argued that
industrial-scale monoculture plantations were having a disproportionate
impact in developing countries. The World Rainforest Movement released
a number of reports criticising the impact of tree plantations on the
struggles of local people in the global South to protect their rights
(Lohmann 2003: 3–4). This unhappiness with plantation certification
continued to remain unresolved to the satisfaction of Southern NGOs,
and WRM published further hostile reports, cataloguing ongoing problems in Thailand and Brazil, in 2003 (ibid.). The plantations policy
review also failed to appease Southern interests who wanted to retain a
separate Principle Ten, and one social and one environmental representative from the South out of the twelve participants objected to the review's
recommendation (Forest Stewardship Council 2006b: 16).

The impacts of controlled wood certification have also fallen heavily
on developing countries, largely on account of greater levels of social
conflict and human rights abuses – two of the 'controversial' issues
related standards were meant to address. Greenpeace issued two critical
reports in 2013 and 2014, arguing for the development of framework
policies for FSC-certified logging operations in high-risk regions (Greenpeace 2014a). These are to be addressed by 2016 (Greenpeace 2014a).

Nevertheless, FSC's three-chamber General Assembly and the North/
South balance required within each chamber has been identified as being
an innovative institutional model (Pattberg 2005: 365). However, in 1999
interim board member Julio César Centeno accused FSC of lacking
balanced participation from developing countries and of being dominated
by Northern NGOs and their Northern industry allies. FSC also cared
mostly about certifying large-scale producers at the expense of small

forest owners, for whom certification was unachievable unless they were in Europe and had access to other certification programmes (Mantyranta 2002: 24–5). The North/South imbalance in economic representation has been attributed to the increased compliance costs associated with ecologically complex tropical forest certification and the prevalence of better regulatory standards in the North, which makes compliance comparatively easier and certification more attractive (Pattberg 2005: 366–70).

Although PEFC has stressed that NGOs can participate in national PEFC institutions and vote in them, several NGOs have challenged the validity of that participation. In Austria, WWF's challenge was simply dismissed as 'attempts to shame the successful PEFC Initiative' (Herzog 2001: 5). In Germany, when an attempt at negotiating an agreement between NGOs, trade unions and the timber industry failed, NGOs were accused of not signing for tactical reasons and launching 'groundless attacks' (Teegelbekkers 2001b: 5). In Norway, WWF launched further attacks on the system's credibility during this period (Gill 2001). In Finland, PEFC's revised standards were published in 2002 and encountered NGO objections, as did those of Norway, published in 2003.

PEFC commissioned a report to review the criticisms and arguments of its opponents. The analysis in the PEFC leadership was that it was 'unwarranted, and unfounded', but part of a learning process to accept positive criticisms and to ignore 'the destructive, misleading and untrue' (Gunnerberg 2002b: 1). It succeeded in recruiting some NGOs into its scheme, and one French NGO, France Nature Environnement (FNE), chose to do so, but it should be noted that a French PEFC Council Board member also sat on the FNE Board (Ozinga 2004: 51). Over the following years the organisation increased its efforts at NGO recruitment and was successful in Luxembourg, gaining an environmental NGO member, NATURA (Thinnes 2006: 4).

In 2006 Peter Seligmann, co-founder, chair and CEO of Conservation International (CI) presented the keynote speech at the General Assembly (PEFC News 2006b: 2). He concurred with PEFC's model of strategic engagement, observing that 'cooperation not confrontation' was the same method CI used (PEFC News 2006b: 2). In 2004 CI had established a forum in collaboration with pulp company Aracruz Celulose (previously an FSC-certified entity) and the Partnership Fund for Critical Ecosystems to facilitate dialogue between environmental NGOs and forest plantation pulp companies in Brazil. This process led to the development of 'forestry partner programs' in 2007 with farmers. The history of Aracruz and certification in Brazil is worth a short examination. The company had come under criticism during the assessment of its plantations for PEFC certification for sitting in on stakeholder consultations, making it difficult for people to present their concerns, and for not undertaking consultations in a timely and sufficiently widespread manner (Ozinga 2004: 62–4).

In April 2007 PEFC issued a brochure, which claimed it was supported by environmental NGOs. The intention of the brochure was to provide the facts 'behind a number of incorrect assertions', concerning Indigenous peoples' participation, environmental NGO support of PEFC and its social dialogue (PEFC News 2007c: 2). The programme also continued to engage unsuccessfully with international environmental NGOs. In 2009 WWF was invited to attend the PEFC 'Stakeholder Forum', an initiative designed to demonstrate its commitment to non-voting interests. It declined to participate, claiming that the programme remained dominated by industry. PEFC challenged the decision not to attend and questioned the organisation's objectivity (Cadman 2011: 116–17).

Indigenous people have also had a problematic relationship with PEFC. In Finland, the Indigenous Sámi reindeer herders were particularly dependent on state forestlands managed by Metsähallitus. They needed grazing access to the arboreal and ground lichens in the unprotected old growth forest areas, and had been arguing for logging moratoria in late winter grazing areas since the 1990s. Sámi representatives had been forced to institute lawsuits and file appeals to the UN's Human Rights Committee. The Committee found the logging a violation of the Sámi Indigenous rights, but forestry activities continued to expand, and the Sámi were again required to take Metsähallitus to court. The Sámi Parliament had earlier demanded that forest management be conducted in Sámi areas under the P&C of the FSC. Herders claimed that the criterion relating to the Sámi's traditional means of livelihood was not being met under the Finnish PEFC standard, nor had they been involved in developing the criterion relating to cooperation regarding husbandry and forestry (Liimatainen and Harkki 2001: 26–7). An executive committee was established between the Reindeer Herders' Association, the Sámi Parliament, Metsähallitus and the Forest Owners Union (MTK) to address unresolved 'special issues' (Kaivola 2002: 7). Discussions between the reindeer herding cooperatives, the Sámi Parliament, Greenpeace and Metsähallitus resulted in the cessation of logging affected by the conflict, but conflict reignited as game hunters and fishers objected to the proposed area set aside for grazing, which would have reduced logging by 50 per cent (Kaivola 2005: 8). FFCS had the option to use its dispute settlement process, but it was not activated (Yrjo-Koskinen et al.

2004: 9). On account of the 'Stock Dove' arrangement with FSC, the PEFC Swedish standard was obliged to make a number of key amendments, including setting aside areas from logging and banning logging in certain biotopes in accordance with FSC provisions, but this was not the case for privately owned forests (Mantyranta 2002: 245–9, Ozinga 2004: 24–7).

QUALITY OF GOVERNANCE: FSC

Table 2.1   FSC – quality of governance by region (February 2015)

Principle	1. Meaningful participation — Maximum score: 25, Minimum: 5							
Criterion	1. Interest representation — Maximum score: 15, Minimum: 3				2. Organisational responsibility — Maximum score: 10, Minimum: 2			Principle Score
Indicator	**Inclusiveness**	**Equality**	**Resources**	Criterion Score	**Accountability**	**Transparency**	Criterion Score	
North (45)	3.4	2.8	**1.6**	7.9	2.8	2.7	5.5	13.4
South (48)	3.0	3.0	2.5	8.5	3.2	3.1	6.3	14.8

Principle	2. Productive deliberation — Maximum score: 30, Minimum: 6							
Criterion	3. Decision-making — Maximum score: 15, Minimum: 3				4. Implementation — Maximum score: 15, Minimum: 3			Principle Score
Indicator	**Democracy**	**Agreement**	**Dispute settlement**	Criterion Score	**Behavioural change**	**Problem-solving**	**Durability**	Criterion Score	
North	2.7	2.9	2.5	8.1	2.9	2.9	3.0	8.8	16.8
South	3.0	3.1	3.0	9.1	3.2	3.2	3.3	9.6	18.7

Total (out of 55)	
North	30.2
South	33.4

Note: Light grey represents the highest scoring indicator by region; dark grey the lowest; numbers in **bold** are below the threshold value of 50 per cent.

Table 2.2   FSC – quality of governance by sector (February 2015)

Principle	1. Meaningful participation Maximum score: 25 Minimum: 5							
Criterion	1. Interest representation Maximum score: 15 Minimum: 3				2. Organisational responsibility Maximum score: 10 Minimum: 2			Principle Score
Indicator	Inclusiveness	Equality	Resources	Criterion Score	Accountability	Transparency	Criterion Score	
Environment	2.9	2.9	2.2	8.0	2.9	3.0	5.9	13.9
Social	2.3	2.3	1.3	5.9	1.5	1.5	3.0	8.9
Economic	4.3	3.7	1.0	9.0	4.0	4.3	8.3	17.3
Government	3.7	3.1	2.2	9.0	3.2	3.1	6.3	15.3
Academic	3.5	2.8	2.2	8.5	3.1	2.8	5.9	14.4
Other	3.2	3.0	2.0	8.2	3.3	2.8	6.1	14.3

Principle	2. Productive deliberation Maximum score: 30 Minimum: 6							
Criterion	3. Decision-making Maximum score: 15 Minimum: 3				4. Implementation Maximum score: 15 Minimum: 3			Principle Score
Indicator	Democracy	Agreement	Dispute settlement	Criterion Score	Behavioural change	Problem-solving	Durability	Criterion Score	
Environment	2.9	2.9	2.9	8.7	3.1	3.1	3.2	9.4	18.1
Social	1.5	1.5	1.5	4.5	2.3	2.3	2.3	6.9	11.4
Economic	2.7	4.3	3.0	10.0	3.7	3.7	4.3	11.7	21.7
Government	2.9	3.5	3.0	9.4	3.4	3.3	3.1	9.8	19.2
Academic	3.0	2.8	2.9	8.7	2.9	2.9	3.2	9.0	17.7
Other	2.6	3.3	2.2	8.1	2.8	2.6	3.0	8.4	16.5

Total (out of 55)	
Environment	32.0
Social	20.3
Economic	39.0
Government	34.5
Academic	32.1
Other	30.8

Note: Light grey represents the highest scoring indicator by sector; dark grey the lowest; numbers in **bold** are below the threshold value of 50 per cent.

Commentary on the Results

There were 93 respondents to the survey, spread almost evenly across regions. FSC received a 'pass' but not a 'credit' from both North and South, at the principle and criterion levels. Southern respondents provided the highest scores, with no 'fails' at the indicator level. The weakest indicator was resources, which received a 'fail' rating from Northern respondents and a low 'pass' from the South. The North rated inclusiveness as the highest indicator; durability was the highest indicator for the South.

The economic sector gave FSC the highest score by far, followed by government, academic, environmental and 'other'. Only the social sector gave a 'fail' score, a result that was replicated at the principle and criterion levels. Significantly, all sectors gave resources a 'fail' at the indicator level. Despite its high overall score, the economic sector rated this indicator the lowest of all (1.0). The highest indicator ratings were provided by the economic sector for inclusiveness, transparency, agreement and durability. Government and academic provided the next highest ratings for inclusiveness; 'other' selected agreement. Environment rated 'durability' the highest, but it should be noted that the environmental sector results are not impressive. Conversely, the fact that the economic sector rated FSC so highly is also of interest. So too is the government rating for inclusiveness, as government membership of FSC is restricted under the Statutes (Forest Stewardship Council).

Commentary from Survey Respondents

Respondents provided a large number of comments. One Northern academic challenged the inclusiveness of FSC, asserting that it was 'just an advocacy-biased perspective of what constitutes good management'. One environmental respondent from the North provided comments for all indicators relating to interest representation, as well as organisational responsibility, and it is worth looking at these two criteria as a whole. As an NGO, they were of the view that their interests were 'rather well taken into account if not always acted upon'. Their concern about inclusiveness related to the fact that their specific FSC project was not well integrated into the broader 'FSC network' including 'national offices and others who are part of the FSC system'. They were of the view that their project treated all participants equally 'even to the point of it hindering the project goals'. In a revealing comment about resources they observed that:

> More resources should have been budgeted to capacity building and technical
> assistance in the FSC project where I work. This does not reflect that the
> project was not concerned about those aspects of the project but rather the
> amount of capacity building and technical assistance needed was significantly
> higher than estimated.

They thought the FSC was both accountable and transparent, but that in
both regards the demonstration of responsibility to stakeholders 'could be
improved'.

Looking at the issues of both inclusiveness and accountability, a
Northern academic was extremely critical of FSC. They felt it was
'strongly dominated by environmental groups, and forest managers have
low influence'. They thought it was 'more focused on its own political
power than on the interests of sustainable forestry'. This was exemplified
by the fact that 'rules in Europe' were 'much more strict than in
elsewhere' – so much so that 'human rights sometimes are not considered
in developing countries'. Another Southern academic was critical of what
they saw as a conflict of interest between FSC and Accreditation Services
International (ASI), the FSC's accreditation body. They argued that there
was 'no independent control' because FSC had 'suspended independent
certification'. According to this respondent, this was 'not compatible with
ISO 17011'. As an editorial observation, it should be noted that ASI is
certified under the ISO standard (ASI 2014). This same academic also
commented on FSC's decision-making, which they thought 'takes time,
is not always implemented, and is not always coherent'. Its dispute
settlement mechanisms were 'fairly transparent' but they did 'not always
convince all stakeholders'.

Environmental sector respondents were unsure of FSC's ability to
combat deforestation. One Southern environmental respondent noted that
local communities had a 'negative impression because of lack of market
access of certified products'. Another environmental respondent from the
North thought that the 'requirements associated with FSC certification
may slow or deter certification uptake'. Also, there was 'as yet little
evidence that the initiative works'. They thought that the new 'evaluation
requirements' under development were an 'improvement'; the downside
was that 'they add complexity and hence may decrease the appeal of FSC
certification'. A second environmental respondent from the North reiterated FSC's ongoing 'problems to address small owners of forests and
small companies as well'. This perspective was echoed by one Southern
academic who thought that 'in community forestry contexts FSC is
potentially very relevant', but it was 'expensive and not really practical at
small scales'.

QUALITY OF GOVERNANCE: PEFC

Commentary on the Results

Table 2.3   PEFC – quality of governance region (February 2015)

Principle	1. Meaningful participation Maximum score: 25 Minimum: 5							
Criterion	1. Interest representation Maximum score: 15 Minimum: 3				2. Organisational responsibility Maximum score: 10 Minimum: 2			Principle Score
Indicator	Inclusiveness	Equality	Resources	Criterion Score	Accountability	Transparency	Criterion Score	
North (43)	3.5	3.1	**1.5**	8.1	2.8	2.8	5.6	13.7
South (46)	2.7	2.7	**2.4**	7.8	2.9	2.9	5.8	13.7
Principle	2. Productive deliberation Maximum score: 30 Minimum: 6							
Criterion	3. Decision-making Maximum score: 15 Minimum: 3				4. Implementation Maximum score: 15 Minimum: 3			Principle Score
Indicator	Democracy	Agreement	Dispute settlement	Criterion Score	Behavioural change	Problem-solving	Durability	Criterion Score	
North	2.7	2.8	2.6	8.0	3.0	2.8	2.9	8.7	16.8
South	2.8	2.7	2.7	8.2	2.9	3.0	2.9	8.9	17.1
Total (out of 55)								
North				30.4				
South				30.7				

Note: Light grey represents the highest scoring indicator by region; dark grey the lowest; numbers in **bold** are below the threshold value of 50 per cent.

Table 2.4 PEFC – quality of governance by sector (February 2015)

Principle	1. Meaningful participation Maximum score: 25 Minimum: 5							
Criterion	1. Interest representation Maximum score: 15 Minimum: 3				2. Organisational responsibility Maximum score: 10 Minimum: 2			Principle Score
Indicator	Inclusiveness	Equality	Resources	Criterion Score	Accountability	Transparency	Criterion Score	
Environment	2.7	2.7	2.0	7.4	2.7	2.9	5.6	13.0
Social	2.5	1.5	1.5	5.5	1.5	1.5	3.0	8.5
Economic	4.3	3.7	1.0	9.0	3.7	4.0	7.7	16.7
Government	3.2	3.2	2.1	8.5	3.1	2.9	6.0	14.5
Academic	3.5	3.1	2.0	8.6	3.1	3.0	6.1	14.7
Other	3.0	3.0	2.0	8.0	2.4	2.2	4.6	12.6

Principle	2. Productive deliberation Maximum score: 30 Minimum: 6								
Criterion	3. Decision-making Maximum score: 15 Minimum: 3				4. Implementation Maximum score: 15 Minimum: 3				Principle Score
Indicator	Democracy	Agreement	Dispute settlement	Criterion Score	Behavioural change	Problem-solving	Durability	Criterion Score	
Environment	2.6	2.6	2.8	8.0	3.1	3.0	2.9	9.0	17.0
Social	1.7	1.5	1.5	4.7	1.8	2.0	2.0	5.8	10.5
Economic	2.3	3.3	2.7	8.3	2.7	3.0	3.0	8.7	17.0
Government	3.0	3.2	2.8	9.0	3.4	3.3	3.2	9.9	18.9
Academic	2.9	2.8	2.8	8.5	2.9	2.9	3.0	8.8	17.3
Other	2.4	3.0	2.0	7.4	2.6	2.4	2.6	7.6	15.0

Total (out of 55)	
Environment	30.0
Social	19.0
Economic	33.7
Government	33.4
Academic	32.0
Other	27.6

Note: Light grey represents the highest scoring indicator by sector; dark grey the lowest; numbers in **bold** are below the threshold value of 50 per cent.

Eighty-nine respondents, almost evenly divided between North and South, answered the survey. Both regions produced remarkably similar results, with little difference between the two overall scores – a modest 'pass' from both. This was repeated at the principle level: for participation, the scores were identical, and for deliberation they were very close. There was also little variation at the criterion level. This was not the case for the indicators, which were more variable for Northern respondents. Resources was the lowest scoring indicator for both North and the South, and a 'fail' for both, but with different margins (North 1.5 *cf.* South 2.4). Northern indicator ratings were more dynamic than the South. Inclusiveness was the highest indicator for the North, and overall; for the South it was problem-solving, but with less divergence from the other indicators.

The economic sector provided PEFC with the highest score, marginally more than government, followed by academic and environment. 'Other' was next, with social a very distant last (33.7 highest score, *cf.* 19.0). These results were replicated at the principle and criterion levels, with clear 'fails' from social sector respondents. Resources was the lowest rated 'fail' indicator for all sectors, with the lowest rating from the economic sector. Social respondents 'failed' PEFC on four other indicators (equality, accountability, transparency, agreement and dispute settlement); 'other' also rated dispute settlement as a 'fail', as well as dispute settlement. Economic provided the highest rating overall, followed by academic, for inclusiveness. Government was next, for behaviour change. 'Other' provided equally high scores for inclusiveness and agreement.

No respondents provided PEFC-specific comments. Those views that were expressed were in comparison to FSC or other sustainable development initiatives. These are contained in the comparative analysis chapter.

ANALYSIS AND CONCLUSIONS

Can forest certification improve forest management? It certainly plays an important role in securing long-term financial stability for forest enterprise, particularly when there is a possibility for moving from an independent non-profit agent to a business of its own (Pattberg 2005: 371). To function as an effective mechanism of governance towards sustainable development, market-based systems have to overcome problems regarding the demand (high) and supply (low) of certified products. In addition, economic management of forest-based market mechanisms appears to require governmental rules and regulation, as well as certification, to make efficient delivery of finance.

Nevertheless, the power of the certification concept is driving the development of a huge global range of certification and labelling schemes. For example, EU national official 4 referred to the following:

> The Green Development Initiative is focusing on certifying land management and therefore delivering certificates, if you will, that can be bought by the private sector. So if it's all meant to facilitate the private sector to provide 'transparency' on what's happening with their euro or dollar or whatever they put into biodiversity or into land management … [a]nd of course, where you already have certification schemes in place, we don't need to duplicate that and we can simply say, well, if you have this forest, then a part of it is already under FSC, well, that's fine.

This interviewee further elaborated:

> Now, there is a reluctance to put money into biodiversity or in land – in sustainable land management I should say – simply because we don't know what the results are. We have no assurance that an invested euro will actually deliver *not only* biodiversity but also development, and that situations where you have a biodiversity outcome but where you discard the rights of Indigenous people – those sort of situations are avoided.

A key question with certification is the relationship to regulatory schemes. This interviewee said the following:

> I would hope that in the long run [voluntarily certification] would be a basis for a compulsory action, but that's not tomorrow, it's not next year. It will take a lot of time. Actually, we started this project in 2008. And our first question was: 'How can we force a global market in financing biodiversity and exploring the possibilities for carbon trade?' Well, that's a very nice exercise, but it doesn't take you anywhere useful. But it *did* trigger the whole debate on how can we then attract new and additional resources for biodiversity.

Forest certification has become a significant factor in achieving good governance in environmental management, particularly in extending decision-making to local communities – even if the extent to which this occurs in both systems investigated is limited. It is also important to understand why producers certify, and which scheme they select, before knowing to what extent certification is actually having a positive effect on behavioural change. Governments in different countries have major roles in forest certification. In some cases, pressure from private sector initiatives such as certification have encouraged governments to provide more checks and balances, as exemplified in the US, where the government developed an initiative to ascertain if timber imports met legality criteria (Stirling 2005: 13). This is explored in more detail in the following chapter. However, the problem of competing schemes in different jurisdictions creates a problem of overlapping responsibilities, practices and outcomes. While 'forest certification' as a whole can generate sources of income, it is important to look beyond the specific scheme itself (Auld et al. 2008: 205) to understand positive and negative unattended consequences, spill-over effects, and longer term impacts that flow from the emergence of certification.

Data on the instruments show that certified lands are skewed in favour of temperate and boreal forests (Auld et al. 2008: 205). This continues to raise questions about the effectiveness of forest certification. The evidence from the case studies and empirical studies in this section indicate that the said instruments can impact positively on livelihoods if the projects are carefully designed and implemented. Forest management and regulation have a significant economic impact on the livelihoods of poor people in developing communities. Through the absence of active participation of these people, inequality between rich and poor increases and leads to a huge gap in the efficiency of the outcome of the projects. Another issue that needs urgent consideration is the certification of private forest. As organisation and cooperation among private forest owners is minimal, it is difficult to exchange information, promote certification and communicate effectively. Therefore, it is imperative to form a comprehensive framework for forest certification that would avoid underestimating the costs of projects, and minimising the costs that exist.

BIBLIOGRAPHY

Anonymous 2005a, 'Sustainable timber grows in popularity', *Contract Journal*, **428** (6523) 21.

Anonymous 2005b, 'Two new forestry schemes gain government approval (brief article)', *Contract Journal*, **429** (6538) 13.

ASI 2014, *ASI presents findings from the ISEAL peer review*. Viewed 2 May 2015, http://www.accreditation-services.com/archives/asi-presents-findings-from-the-iseal-peer-review.

Auld, G., Gulbrandsen, L. H. and McDermott, C. L. 2008, 'Certification schemes and the impacts on forests and forestry', *Annual Review of Environment and Resources*, **33** (1) 187–211.

Bernstein, S. and Cashore, B. 2004, 'Non-state global governance: Is forest certification a legitimate alternative to a global forest convention', *Hard choices, soft law: Voluntary standards in global trade, environment and social governance*, 33–63.

Boyer, B. 2005, 'Multilateral negotiation simulation exercise: The sustainable management and conservation of forests', in Berglund, M. (ed.) *International*

Environmental Lawmaking and Diplomacy Review 2005, Joensuu: University of Joensuu Press.

Cadman, T. 2011, *Quality and legitimacy of global governance: case lessons from forestry*, Basingstoke, London: Palgrave Macmillan.

Cashore, B., Auld, G. and Newsom, D. 2004, *Governing through markets: Forest certification and the emergence of non-state authority*, New Haven, London: Yale University Press.

Cashore, B., Egan, E., Auld, G. and Newsom, D. 2007, 'Revising theories of nonstate market-driven (nsmd) governance: Lessons from the Finnish Forest Certification Experience', *Global Environmental Politics*, **7** (1) 1–44.

Clapp, J. 1999, 'Standard inequities', in Gibson, R. B. (ed.) *Voluntary initiatives: The new politics of corporate greening*, Peterborough: Broadview Press.

Clapp, J. 2005, 'Global environmental governance for corporate responsibility and accountability', *Global Environmental Politics*, **5** (3) 23–34.

Commonwealth of Australia 1997, *Australia's first approximation report for the Montreal Process*, Canberra: Montreal Implementation Group.

Counsell, S. 1999, *Trickery or truth? An examination of the effectiveness of the Forest Stewardship Council*, London: The Rainforest Foundation.

Counsell, S. and Terje Loraas, K. 2002, *Trading in credibility: The myth and reality of the Forest Stewardship Council*, London, Oslo: Rainforest Foundation.

Department of Economic and Social Affairs/Secretariat of the United Nations Forum on Forests and Department of Economic and Social Affairs/UNFF Secretariat 2004, 'United Nation forum on forests. Global partnership: For forests for people', *Fact Sheet 1*.

ECOSOC 2000, *Report of the fourth session of the intergovernmental forum on forests*.

Elliott, C. 2000, *Forest certification: A policy perspective*, Bogor: Center for International Forestry Research.

Espach, R. 2006, 'When is sustainable forestry sustainable? The Forest Stewardship Council in Argentina and Brazil', *Global Environmental Politics*, **6** (2) 55–84.

FAO, 2012, *Sustainable management of forests and REDD+: Negotiations need clear terminology*. Viewed 3 July 2015, http://www.unredd.net/index.php?option=com_docman&task=doc_download&gid=1148%Itemid=53.

FERN, Greenpeace, Inter-African Forest Industry Association, Precious Woods, Swedish Society for Nature Conservation and Tropical Forest Trust 2008, *Regaining credibility and rebuilding support: Changes the FSC needs to make*. Viewed 16 November 2014, http://www.fern.org/sites/fern.org/files/changes%20the%20FSC%20needs%20to%20make.pdf.

Finnish Forest Industries Federation 1998a, 'Increased credibility for Finnish forest certification approach through European co-operation', *Media release.*

Finnish Forest Industries Federation 1998b, 'Industry fully supports the Finnish Forest Certification System (FFCS): FSC-labelling of products becomes available, too?', *Media release.*

Forest Stewardship Council, *Statutes (Version 1.3, Revised August 2000, November 2002 and June 2005)*. Viewed 1 July 2015, http://au.fsc.org/download.fsc-ac-statutes.389.pdf.

Forest Stewardship Council 2004, 'Annual review 2003', *FSC News and Notes*, **3** (1).

Forest Stewardship Council 2006a, 'FSC plantations review policy working group completes its task', *FSC News and Notes*, **4** (9) 1.

Forest Stewardship Council 2006b, *FSC plantations review policy working group final report*. Viewed 1 July 2015, http://plantations.fsc.org/.

Forest Stewardship Council 2007, *Plantations review*. Viewed 1 July 2015, http://plantations.fsc.org.

Forest Stewardship Council 2014a, *FSC general assembly 2014 motion outcomes*. Viewed 16 November 2014, http://ga2014.fsc.org/motion-updates.

Forest Stewardship Council 2014b, *FSC principles and criteria international guidelines to forest management*. Viewed 8 December 2014, https://ic.fsc.org/principles-and-criteria.34.htm.

Forest Stewardship Council 2014c, *IGI International Generic Indicators background information*. Viewed 8 December 2014, http://igi.fsc.org/background.5.htm.

Forest Stewardship Council n.d., 'Final motions and results from FSC general assembly 2002'.

Freemen, A. 2015, *Canada and Russia beat tropical countries to top global deforestation list*. Viewed 16 April 2015, http://mashable.com/2015/04/09/canada-russia-top-deforestation-list/.

FSC Canada 2012, *FSC Guidelines for the implementation of the right to Free, Prior and Informed Consent released*. Viewed 10 April 2015, https://ca.fsc.org/newsroom.239.116.htm.

FSC International 2014, *Putting free, prior and informed consent into practice: FSC and indigenous peoples*. Viewed 10 April 2014, https://ic.fsc.org/newsroom.9.791.htm.

FSC International 2015a, *Facts and figures*. Viewed 7 April 2015, https://ic.fsc.org/facts-figures.839.htm.

FSC International 2015b, *FSC Modular Approach Program (MAP)*. Viewed 7 April 2015, https://ic.fsc.org/map.656.htm.

Gale, F. 1998, *The tropical timber trade regime*, Basingstoke, London: Macmillan Press.

Gale, F. and Burda, C. (eds) 1999, *The pitfalls and potential of eco-certification as a market incentive for sustainable forest management*, Vancouver: UBC Press.

Gill, E. 2001, 'Unfounded criticism of Norway's forest owners federation by WWF', *PEFCC Newsletter*, **8** 3–4.

Global Forest Watch 2015, *Countries with greatest tree cover loss (2001–2013)*. Viewed 16 April 2015, http://www.globalforestwatch.org/countries/overview.

Goetzman, K. 2010, 'Ecological internet: Radical, green, and wired', *UTNE Wild Green*, Kansas, MI: Ogden Publications, Inc.

Greenpeace 2010, *How Sinar Mas is pulping the planet*, Greenpeace International. Viewed 7 May 2015, http://www.greenpeace.org/international/en/publications/reports/SinarMas-APP/.

Greenpeace 2013, *FSC at risk. A join 4-step action plan to strengthen and restore credibility*. Viewed 15 November 2014, http://www.greenpeace.org/international/Global/international/briefings/forests/2013/FSC-at-risk.pdf.

Greenpeace 2014a, *FSC progress report on Greenpeace's key issues of concern, and progress on its recommendations*. Viewed 15 November 2014, http://www.greenpeace.org/international/Global/international/briefings/forests/2014/FSC-Progress-Report-2014-Q3.pdf.

The Guardian n.d., 'Bangkok diary: acronyms, ambition and underwater meetings'. Viewed 19 August 2015, http://www.theguardian.com/environment/blog/2009/oct/08/bangkok-climate-change-talks.

Gulbrandsen, L. H. 2004, 'Overlapping public and private governance: Can forest certification fill the gaps in the global forest regime?', *Global Environmental Politics*, **4** (2) 75–99.

Gulbrandsen, L. H. 2005a, 'Explaining different approaches to voluntary standards: A study of forest certification choices in Norway and Sweden', *Journal of Environmental Policy and Planning*, **7** (1) 43–59.

Gulbrandsen, L. H. 2005b, 'Sustainable forestry in Sweden: The effect of competition among private certification schemes', *Journal of Environment and Development*, **14** (3) 338–55.

Gunnerberg, B. 2002a, 'General assembly synopsis', *PEFCC News Special*, **1**.

Gunnerberg, B. 2002b, 'PEFC forging ahead', *PEFCC Newsletter*, **11** 1.

Gunnerberg, B. 2010a, 'Letter to Andy Tait regarding Greenpeace report and letter'. Viewed 20 April 2015, http://www.pefc.org/news-a-media/general-sfm-news/534-statement-regarding-greenpeace-report-and-letter-to-pefc-and-pefc-stakeholders-7th-july-2010.

Gunnerberg, B. 2010b, 'Letter to Steve Baer, Chair of USGBC's Materials & Resources Technical Advisory Group'. Viewed 7 May 2015, http://www.pefc.org/news-a-media/general-sfm-news/302-usgbc-urged-to-support-forest-certification.

Hain, H. and Ahas, R. 2007, 'Can forest certification improve forest management? Case study of the FSC certified Estonian State Forest Management Centre', *International Forestry Review*, **9** (3) 759–70.

Hauselmann, P. 1997, *ISO inside out: ISO and environmental management*, Godalming: WWF International.

Herzog, G. 2001, 'PEFC Austria – Totally compliant with Austrian law – Issues first logo licenses', *PEFCC Newsletter*, **8** 5.

Hortensius, D. 1999, 'ISO 14000 and forestry management: ISO develops "bridging" document'. Viewed 1 July 2015, http://infohouse.p2ric.org/ref/39/38678.pdf.

Howlett, M. and Rayner, J. 2006, 'Globalization and governance capacity: Explaining divergence in national forest programs as instances of "next generation" regulation in Canada and Europe', *Governance: An International Journal of Policy, Administration and Institutions*, **19** (2) 251–75.

Humphreys, D. 1996, *Forest politics: The evolution of international cooperation*, London: Earthscan.

Humphreys, D. 2005, 'The certification wars: Forest certification schemes as sites for trade-environment conflicts', *The privatizing environmental governance panel at the 46th annual convention of the International Studies Association*. Honolulu, Hawaii.

Humphreys, D. 2006, *Logjam: Deforestation and the crisis of global governance*, London: Earthscan.

ISO Technical Committee 207 1995a, 'Environment', *Articles and News*, 3.

ISO Technical Committee 207 1995b, 'Environment – ISO/TC 207 considers industry's needs', *Articles and News*, 3.

ISO Technical Committee 207 1998, *About ISO/TC 207*. Viewed 13 April 2015, https://web.archive.org/web/20000229103912/http://www.tc207.org/aboutTC2 07/index.html.

ITTO. No date, 'Grouping definitions'. Viewed 19 August 2015, http://www. itto.int/group_definitions/.

Kaivola, A. 2002, 'Revision of forest certification requirements under way in Finland', *PEFCC Newsletter*, 11. Viewed 1 July 2015, http://pefc.org/index. php?option=com_sumointeractivecontent&view=itemdetail&id=577.

Kaivola, A. 2005, 'Ongoing debate about forestry and reindeer husbandry in Upper Lapland in Finland', *PEFC Newsletter*, 25. Viewed 1 July 2015, http://pefc.org/index.php?option=com_sumointeractivecontent&view=itemdetail &id=563.

Keck, M. E. and Sikkink, K. 1998, *Activists beyond borders: Advocacy networks in international politics*, New York: Cornell University Press.

Lammerts van Beuren, E. M. and Blom, E. M. 1997, *Hierarchical framework for the formulation of sustainable forest management standards*, Leiden: The Tropenbos Foundation.

Liimatainen, M. and Harkki, S. 2001, *Anything goes? Report on PEFC certified forestry*, Helsinki: Greenpeace Nordic and the Finnish Nature League.

Lohmann, L. (ed.) 2003, *Certifying the uncertifiable: FSC certification of tree plantations in Thailand and Brazil*, Montevideo and Moreton-in-Marsh: World Rainforest Movement.

Mantyranta, H. 2002, *Forest certification – an ideal that became an absolute, translation by Heli Mantyranta*, Helsinki: Metsalehti Kustannus.

Marais, G. 2011, 'Letter from SGS to PEFC International regarding results of investigation into APP'. Viewed 30 April 2015, www.pefc.org/news-a-media/ general-sfm-news/1166.

MCPFE 1998, 'Sustainable forest management in Europe, special report on the follow-up on the implementation of resolutions H1 and H2 of the Helsinki ministerial conference', in Liaison Unit in Lisbon (ed.) *Follow-up Reports on the Ministerial Conferences on the Protection of Forests in Europe*, Lisbon: Ministry of Agriculture, Rural Development and Fisheries of Portugal.

Olsen, T. 2004, 'PEFC certification Denmark', *PEFC News*, **23** 5.

Ozinga, S. 2001, 'Behind the logo: An environmental and social assessment of forest certification schemes'. Moreton-in-Marsh: FERN.

Ozinga, S. 2004, *Footprints in the forest: Current practice and future challenges in forest certification*, Moreton-in-Marsh: FERN.

Parto, S. 1999, *Aiming low*, Peterborough: Broadview Press.

Pattberg, P. H. 2005, 'The Forest Stewardship Council: Risk and potential of private forest governance', *Journal of Environment and Development*, **14** (3) 356–74.

PEFC 2003, 'Summary of presentation by Mr Pekka Patosaari, UNFF coordinator and head of secretariat', *PEFC News*, 17.

PEFC 2007a, *About PEFC*. Viewed 14 June 2007, https://web.archive.org/web/ 20090707224018/http://www.pefc.org/internet/html/about_pefc.htm.

PEFC 2007b, *A short history*. Viewed 14 June 2007, https://web.archive.org/web/20090707234547/http://www.pefc.org/internet/html/about_pefc/4_1137_498.htm.

PEFC and FSC 2010, *Joint statement by the Forest Stewardship Council (FSC) and the Programme for the Endorsement of Forest Certification (PEFC) recommending ISO members to vote against the new work item proposal chain of custody of forest based products – requirements.* Viewed 08 May 2015, http://www.pefc.org/images/documents/external/Joint_Statement_FSC_PEFC_July_8_2013.pdf.

PEFC Council 2014, *Chain of custody of forest-based products – Guidance for use*, Geneva, Switzerland: PEFC Council. Viewed 28 April 2015, http://pefc.org/images/documents/guides/PEFC_GD_2001-2014_Guidance_for_use_of_Chain_of_Custody_2014-06-23.pdf.

PEFC Council 2015, 'Chain of custody of forest-based products – Social requirements: Guidance for use (Enquiry draft)', *PEFC Guides*, Geneva: PEFC. Viewed 8 May 2015, http://www.pefc.org/news-a-media/general-sfm-news/1832-public-consultation-on-guidance-on-social-requirements-in-chain-of-custody-certification.

PEFC News 2003, 'Alteration to the PEFC name', **17** 4.

PEFC News 2005, 'EU parliament regards PEFC and FSC as equally suitable', **30** 1.

PEFC News 2006a, 'Belgian public procurement policy includes PEFC', **31** 2.

PEFC News 2006b, 'Key note speech by Peter Seligmann from Conservation International', **34** 2.

PEFC News 2006c, 'PEFC – World's largest resource of certified wood', *PEFC Newsletter* 29. Viewed 1 July 2015, http://pefc.org/index.php?option=com_sumointeractivecontent&view=itemdetail&id=559.

PEFC News 2007a, 'Assessment of forest certification systems', *PEFC Newsletter* 37. Viewed 1 July 2015, http://pefc.org/index.php?option=com_sumo interactivecontent&view=itemdetail&id=551.

PEFC News 2007b, 'PEFC Council global statistics', **37** 3.

PEFC News 2007c, 'PEFC: Only European? Based on merely a handful of criteria? Not for indigenous people? No social dialogue ...?' **37** 2.

PEFC News 2009, *Who gains from FSC's latest effort to undermine other forest certification systems?* Viewed 17 April 2015, http://www.pefc.org/news-a-media/general-sfm-news/617-who-gains-from-fsc.

PEFC News 2010a, *Indigenous peoples representative joins PEFC board of directors.* Viewed 21 April 2015, http://www.pefc.org/news-a-media/general-sfm-news/659-pefc-adds-three-new-board-members.

PEFC News 2010b, *Pressure mounts for USGBC to accept multiple forest certification programmes.* Viewed 20 April 2015, http://www.pefc.org/news-a-media/general-sfm-news/589-pressure-mounts-for-usgbc-to-accept-multiple-forest-certification-programmes.

PEFC News 2011, *Developing country representative elected as vice chair to PEFC board of directors.* Viewed 27 April 2015, http://www.pefc.org/news-a-media/general-sfm-news/662-developing-country-representative-elected-as-vice-chair-to-pefc-board-of-directors.

PEFC News 2012, *USGBC LEED: A never-ending story?* Viewed 27 April 2015, http://www.pefc.org/news-a-media/general-sfm-news/1085-usgbc-leed-a-never-ending-story.

PEFC News 2013, 'Indigenous Leader Joins PEFC Board of Directors'. Viewed 27 April 2015, http://www.pefc.org/news-a-media/general-sfm-news/1165-indigenous-leader-joins-pefc-board-of-directors.

PEFCC News Special 2002, 'Continuing globalisation of the PEFC council', 2.

PEFCC Newsletter 2001, 'Statistics on main forest certification schemes', *PEFCC Newsletter*, **7** 1.

PEFCC Newsletter 2002, 'PEFC chairman to visit Gabon to discuss feasibility of pan African forest certification system', December, 3.

PEFCC Newsletter 2003, 'Globalisation', *PEFCC Newsletter*, **14** 1.

Raines, S. S. 2006, 'Judicious incentives: International public policy responses to the globalization of environmental management', *Review of Policy Research*, **23** (2) 473–90.

Rickenbach, M. and Overdevest, C. 2006, 'More than markets: Assessing Forest Stewardship Council (FSC) Certification as a policy tool', *Journal of Forestry*, **104** (3) 143.

Romeijn, P. and Wageningen, L. 1999, *Green gold: on variations of truth in plantation forestry*, Hedsum, Netherlands: Treemail Publishers.

Royal Forest and Bird Protection Society (RFBPS), Greenpeace NZ, World Wide Fund For Nature NZ, Environment and Conservation Organisations of NZ, Native Forest Action, F. o. t. E. N., Native Forest Network – Southern Hemisphere & Federated Mountain Clubs of NZ 2001, 'Letter to FSC accredited forest management certifiers'.

Sample, V. A., Price, W. and Mater, C. M. 2003, 'Certification on public and university lands: Evaluations of FSC and SFI by the forest managers', *Journal of Forestry*, **101** (8) 21.

Stirling, R. 2005, 'Rival groups slam PEFC endorsement (Programme for the Endorsement of Forest Certification Schemes)', *Contract Journal*, **429** (6530) 13.

Strauss, S. H., Campbell, M. M., Pryor, S. N., Coventry, P. and Burley, J. 2001, 'Plantation certification and genetic engineering: FSC's ban on research is counterproductive', *Journal of Forestry*, **99** (12) 4.

Stringer, C. 2006, 'Forest certification and changing global commodity chains', *Journal of Economic Geography*, **6** (5) 701–22.

Tait, A. 2010, 'Letter from Greenpeace to PEFC International regarding APP controversy'. Viewed 30 April 2015, http://www.pefc.org/news-a-media/general-sfm-news/672.

Tas, A. and Rodrigues, J. 2009, *Under the cover of forest certification*, Sweden: Greenpeace Nordic.

Taylor, P. L. 2005, 'In the market but not of it: fair trade coffee and Forest Stewardship Council certification as market-based social change', *World Development*, **33** (1) 129–47.

Teegelbekkers, D. 2001a, 'ENGOs invited to witness the auditing process in Germany', *PEFCC Newsletter*, **7** 5–6.

Teegelbekkers, D. 2001b, 'Germany – Over 5 million hectares already certified', *PEFCC Newsletter*, **9** 5.

Teegelbekkers, D. 2003a, 'Chain-of-Custody certificates increasing in Germany', *PEFCC Newsletter*, **14** 6.
Teegelbekkers, D. 2003b, 'Germany: Chain-of-Custody', *PEFC News*, **16** 5.
Thinnes, M. 2006, 'ENGOs join PEFC', *PEFC News*, **33** 4.
Tollefson, C., Gale, F. and Haley, D. 2008, *Setting the standard: Certification, governance and the forest stewardship council*, Vancouver: UBC Press.
UN 2007, *UN Resolution 62/98, establishing the Non-Legally binding instrument on all types of forests*. Viewed 19 August 2015, http://www.un.org/ga/search/view_doc.asp?symbol=A/RES/62/98.
Yrjo-Koskinen, E., Liimatainen, M. and Ruokanen, L. 2004, *Certifying extinction? An assessment of the revised standards of the Finnish forest certification system,* Helsinki: Greenpeace Finland, Finnish Association for Nature Conservation, Finnish Nature League.

3. Combatting deforestation II – FLEGT

HISTORY AND DESCRIPTIVE BACKGROUND OF EFFORTS TO COMBAT ILLEGAL LOGGING

The intergovernmental initiatives discussed in Chapter 2 were not greatly supported by environmental NGOs or Indigenous peoples' organisations, who dismissed them as exercises in 'window dressing' (Cadman 2011: 145). They were especially critical of the initiatives' abilities to combat deforestation and tackle illegal logging. Illegal logging has been attributed to a wide range of causes including population growth, poverty, drug cultivation, wars and the military, as well as land tenure inequities (Humphreys 1996: 2–15).

Processes to address forest law enforcement and governance, distinct from UNFF, got underway in 2001. They have been characterised as originating both from industry, which was concerned that the illegal timber trade was depressing prices, and NGO concerns that demand for legal timber was being undermined. A series of bilateral trade agreements and regional processes were developed to address these problems: in the supply regions of Asia (2001), Africa (2003) and Europe and North Asia (2005), with the assistance of the World Bank; and in the consumer countries, the EU's FLEGT Action Plan of 2003, which, in contrast to UNFF, was made legally binding on its 25 member states (Humphreys 2006: 149–67). These were connected to a series of voluntary partnership agreements (VPA) with timber-producing countries and a licensing scheme for imports of timber into the European Community (2005) (Lawson and MacFaul 2010). These were identified as having made efforts to include a broader range of actors and issues (Capistrano et al. 2007: 9).

Illegal logging is a significant transnational crime with impacts on the environment, on notions of good governance, economies of timber-producing countries, and serious impacts on human rights and the ability to carry out traditional ways of life (Australian Government 2012: 2, Interpol 2013a: 1). It shares many factors in common with other transnational crimes and their dependence on corruption. Globalisation has facilitated product flows with transit through third countries, enabling the hiding of illegal origins of timber. Imports into developed countries are considerable, with the US, EU and Australia bringing in legislation to counter the illegal imports. Issues around enforcement, definition of illegal logging, tracking chain of custody, and involvement of banking systems in laundering money from illegal logging mean that it is still a complex task to ensure that imports of timber are from legal sources.

Definitions of illegal logging vary. While not consistent, an illegal wood product is understood as having at least one link in the supply chain affected by at least one illegality. Illegality pertains to the legislation in the country or countries of production, in the country from which the product in its current form has been exported, and international legislation to which any of the countries are committed. It can refer to timber harvesting, transportation, processing and export/import, and has been linked to negative environmental, social and economic outcomes (WWF 2015a, FAO 2004: 53–6). Complying with laws in the country in which timber is harvested is, however, central. But this can be quite complex, as much timber is imported through third countries, and information about source country may be hidden or simply not provided. According to Bricknell (2010: 95), in reality illegal logging encompasses all steps in the chain of custody. Ozinga and Gerard note the difficulty of using in-country legislation as a guide, as laws can be ambiguous and unclear, citing an overview of Indonesian logging where up to 90 per cent of state forest lands had not been legally transferred from traditional landholders (Ozinga and Gerard 2005: 439). Papua New Guinea Forest Industry Association (PNGFIA) expressed concern that definitions of illegal logging stay in tandem with their preferred ITTO definition of 'harvesting, transporting, processing and trading of forest products in violation of national laws', and not broaden 'in ways desired by environmental campaigners' (PNGFIA 2011: 10).

Data collection about the scope of the problem is difficult to collect at all stages of the process, with Bricknell noting an inability for analysts to accurately describe trends (Bricknell 2010: xii). A relatively recent change to a more sophisticated laundering approach by criminals adds to the difficulty in collecting data, with illegally logged timber being described as 'plantation' to cover its true origins (Nellemann and Interpol Environmental Crime Programme 2012: 7). Cindy Squires, executive director of International Wood Products Association, noted that to ensure that trade with Peru was legal, 'You need to get out there and see' (Neuman and Zarate 2013).

Figures describing illegal logging are estimates, usually drawn together from a number of sources and often containing risk indicators (for instance, Gupta et al. 2012). UNODC puts the annual market loss worldwide at greater than USD10 billion, with additional losses to governments at USD 5 billion (UNODC 2010: 167–8). They use an estimate of 20–40 per cent of global timber production as being illegal, with 20 per cent of this imported into the EU. While there can be variability in estimates, there is agreement that the problem is large, and damaging. Russia is now the country with the greatest deforestation rate with over 43 million ha logged between 2011 and 2013, so even at a conservative estimate of 10 per cent being illegal, the problem is huge (Global Forest Watch 2015).

China's imports of timber have been increasing rapidly, so fast that estimates swiftly become outdated (UNODC 2010: 167–8). In 2006 it was estimated that between 30 and 45 per cent of Chinese timber imports were illegal, with another assessment giving 50 per cent in 2007, mostly from the Russian Federation. One reason given for these high amounts between Russia and China is the 'porous' nature of the border (Schloenhardt 2008: 103). It is also estimated that in the three years to 2004, 98 per cent of the timber which China imported from Myanmar was illegal (UNODC 2010: 167). China is now dominating imports into Australia and growing in quantity and variety of lines, including furniture and paper (Gupta et al. 2012: 26–7). Illegal logging is contributing to an environmental problem of enormous costs with effects on biodiversity and global warming, causing environmental change in a large dimension (Goncalves et al. 2012: 2, Setiono 2007: 27). Risks also include loss of species and habitat, soil erosion and flooding (UNODC 2010: 161), yet these environmental harms do not tend to be reflected in legislation. While global impacts on forest degradation, climate change and habitat loss are mentioned in recent anti-illegal logging legislation, this does not take into account the harms caused by legal logging, or the impact on future generations. The emerging field of green criminology adds issues of 'harm' to those of legal 'injury' and takes into account factors affecting ecological and sociological implications (Ruggiero and South 2013: 360). Theories of white-collar crime suggest that environmental harm can fall outside what is illegal, and in fact be part of 'business as usual' (Halsey and White 2006: 196). While, for instance, in some developed countries there may be no evidence of systematic illegal logging (Schloenhardt 2008: 79), practices of the timber industry can be both destructive and lawful: 'what counts as "crime" depends upon the standpoint that criminologists choose to adopt' (Green et al. 2007: 8).

Illegal logging shares many aspects with other transnational crimes. Corruption is 'front and centre' (Bricknell 2010: 95) and has now overtaken growth in rural population as the most prominent determinant of deforestation (Koyuncu and Yilmaz 2009: 220). This corruption includes bribery and intimidation to gain logging leases, the ignoring of illegal activities, and the facilitation of the movement of illegal logs (Bricknell 2010: 95). Involvement of corrupt officials is essential in a crime that is so visible, with logs needing to pass through checkpoints and across borders (Setiono 2007: 28). In Russia, corruption is seen as 'endemic', with bribes being used to buy services such as permits from government officials or to release seized timber. There are reports of salvage permits being given to log 'fire-damaged forests', with logging done first and fires lit afterwards either by government officials or the loggers themselves (Schloenhardt 2008: 67).

There is a great profitability in illegal logging, making it attractive to transnational organised crime and leading to vulnerability at all levels to corruption, fraud and lack of payment of tax (McElwee 2004: 123). It has been linked to organised crime in the Russian Far East with connections to both the Chinese and Russian mafia (Schloenhardt 2008: 65). In South East Asia, traffickers are often based in Singapore, Taiwan or Hong Kong, with Chinese ex-patriots being key players. Illegal logging in the source countries is carried out by gangs, with assistance from corrupt officials (UNODC 2010: 166–7). Profits are large, with traffickers able to double their money exporting from Papua New Guinea (PNG) to China, and gangs organising the logging in Indonesia also make a good profit (UNODC 2010: 167). Interpol and the World Bank have found that because of the profitability, illegal logging concerns have become more 'organised, sophisticated and transnational', including using computer hacking to obtain fraudulent permits (Interpol and World Bank 2009: 2), and the use of advanced telecommunications to enable high volumes of money laundering, tax evasion and the creation of false trails (Interpol and World Bank 2009: 20).

Like other transnational organised crime, globalisation has facilitated the flow of illicit goods through third countries. This is an important factor, as it is a method of disguising illegal origins. Illegally harvested logs from PNG can become integrated with 'legal' logs from an intermediary country (Setiono 2007: 28), and Indonesian timber labelled as coming from Malaysia can be transhipped through China. China imports Indonesian timber through the port of Zhangjiagang, close to factories making flooring and decking (UNODC 2010: 163–5). A 2006 brief published by Greenpeace described the laundering of illegal timber from Russia through Finland to the European and other markets (Green-peace 2006). This was echoed by an Australian report noting the preponderance of paper imported to the country from Finland, with source timber from Russia being of suspect origin (Schloenhardt 2008:

121). Knowing country of origin is crucial to assessing risk as part of the due diligence process required by the new Australian regulations for example. Gupta et al. noted that finding the first port of lading is not easy information to gather, nor is record-keeping of chain of custody (Gupta et al. 2012: 35). Schloenhardt (2008: 120–1) noted a deficiency in certification and documentation of product pathways.

Like other organised crime, illegal logging syndicates use quasi-legitimate businesses, money laundering and seemingly legitimate corporate structure to hide their crime (Interpol and World Bank 2009; 2). Banks are key players when it comes to the operation of these corporations, as large amounts of money are needed for mills, machinery, trucks and the paying of bribes (Setiono 2007: 27), as well as establishing plantations to launder illegal timber (Nellemann and Interpol Environmental Crime Programme 2012: 7). The returns are high, with revenues up to ten times higher than legal alternatives, and it is often funding from investors in the US, Asia and the EU that make the laundering of illegal timber possible (ibid.: 7). Setiono and Husein describe the operations of Indonesian financiers called 'cukongs', who are criminal masterminds and make arrangements for spending such as bribes, fees and laundering (Setiono and Husein 2005: 9). Most of the large timber conglomerates in Indonesia own their own banks but despite this fail to pay debts, regulatory reforestation funds or taxes (ibid.: 6).

It is not necessarily a simple process to divest from dubious companies. In 2010 the Norwegian Sovereign Wealth Fund excluded Samling Global from its portfolio due to its 'suspected involvement in illegal logging in Sarawak' and other areas (Nellemann and Interpol Environmental Crime Programme 2012: 57–8). Despite this, money could reach the company through stakes in other entities that were still investing in Samling Global, including Goldman Sachs, Charles Schwab and BlackRock.

Developed countries play a role in money laundering from PNG's illegal logging. A representative of PNG's anti-corruption Task Force Sweep described Australia as the 'Cayman Islands' of the Pacific for money laundering (Mason 2012), noting that the billion dollars which PNG invests in Australia could not possibly be legitimate. Australian Federal Police estimate that AUD170 million a year is laundered in Australian banks and property from the proceeds of crime perpetrated in PNG.

EU states have legislation covering money laundering, but as of 2005 no EU country had used the legislation to fight illegal logging (Ozinga and Gerard 2005: 445). A key strategy is to follow customer due diligence to ensure that account holders and the source of their money are legitimate (Setiono 2007: 31). Goncalves et al. note that due diligence should always be carried out by banks for customers in the timber or furniture trades (Goncalves et al. 2012: 21). This could be applied, for instance, where customers involved in forestry have a high level of timber transactions in countries such as Kalimantan and PNG (Setiono 2007: 32–5). The use of due diligence has the advantage of targeting the industrial level of activity, rather than poor forest dwellers.

Despite its ability to assist in preventing corruption and human rights abuses, due diligence is not necessarily used by banks in developed countries. A report by Oxfam notes that none of Australia's 'big four' banks are committed to a due diligence approach that would prevent involvement in 'land grabs' (where there has been no FPIC of communities), that leave vulnerable communities exposed to 'hunger, violence, homelessness and the threat of a lifetime of inescapable poverty' (Narayanasamy 2014: 5). In 2006 community groups from PNG and Australia filed a complaint against ANZ Bank for its support of Malaysian logging company Rimbunan Hijau, citing its 'serious human rights abuses, environmentally devastating logging practices and repeated, serious illegal conduct' (ACF 2006). In addition, OXFAM noted Westpac's involvement with logging company WTK Group in PNG, a company known for violence and sexual misconduct towards local women (Narayanasamy 2014: 3). Westpac signed the Equator Principles in 2003, a voluntary agreement working with the World Bank to ensure that projects they fund are socially responsible and environmentally sound (Equator Principles 2003).

Clearly defined land ownership is a key issue in timber harvesting. Ozinga and Gerard (2005:439) note the complexities of the legal situation in Canada, with, for instance, in British Columbia, Indigenous people holding the rights to the land but the government maintaining jurisdiction over forest concessions and resource management. Ambiguous and unclear land tenure creates opportunities for fraudulent claims, and the use of bribery and corruption of government officials (Interpol 2013a: 11). Bouriaud (2005: 285) in a study on Central and Eastern European countries found that in Lithuania, the larger the amount of land with unclear ownership, the greater the incidence of illegal logging.

Audits show that most logging operations in PNG have not gained appropriate informed consent of the local resource owners, with some agreements being signed under gunpoint. Women are especially susceptible to human rights abuses, with those working in isolated camps claiming that they are 'forced to have sex with company officials and the police who work with them', again at gunpoint (Greenpeace 2004: 7–8). Inter Press Service reports the case of Pomio District in PNG, where illegal logging destroyed soil and forests relied on by communities for water, natural medicine and resources to build homes (Wilson 2014), and police riot squads work with the logging companies to intimidate communities. Companies gaining Special Agricultural Business Leases were found by the National Court not to have garnered proper consent, but by the time the developer ceased operations, over AUD50 million worth of timber had been exported and 7000 ha of forest cleared.

Like profits from other transnational crime, money made through illegal logging has been used to fund conflict in countries like Democratic Republic of Congo, Cambodia and Liberia (Ozinga and Gerard 2005: 438). A report from Al Jazeera notes that in Pakistan the timber mafia worked with the Taliban in illegal logging, resulting in large sums to fund terrorist activities between 2007 and 2009 (Khan 2010). The subsequent deforestation resulted in an inability for water to be slowed, thus exacerbating flood damage. Stored illegal timber was dislodged, destroying bridges and cutting off villages from access to supplies and medication. According to the Environmental Protection Agency, the deforestation also contributed to an increase in severe weather patterns.

Conflict is associated with illegal logging in other ways. In South East Asia the dropping of Agent Orange and associated bombing during the Vietnam War resulted in the loss of 1.7 million ha of forest cover. While timber was needed for the war effort, the huge demand for reconstruction and the decreased forest cover were factors encouraging illegal logging (McElwee 2004: 101–7). A discussion paper from the New Zealand Ministry of Agriculture and Forestry notes that illegal logging 'strikes at the heart of values it supports: "good governance, strong law enforcement and robust environmental management of ecosystems"' (Watson 2006: 5), and provides examples of strategies where countries are working together to combat illegal logging that operate on multilateral, regional and bilateral levels, as well as in public/private partnerships, such as NGOs working with industry (ibid.: 21).

While the US, EU and Australia have introduced legislation to prohibit illegal timber imports, corruption can still undermine the process. With up to 80 per cent of Peru's timber exports being identified as illegal, it still reaches the US market using doctored paperwork (Neuman and Zarate 2013), with for instance mahogany labelled as an alternative species, and illegally harvested Russian oak sold as flooring in the US. According to industry group the International Wood Products Association, it is possible to continue to trade with countries like Peru, but it needs to be done with great vigilance.

There have been claims that despite the epidemic nature of forestry crimes, 'forestry's criminal justice system is broken', with crimes going 'undetected, unreported or are ignored' and investigations 'amateurish and inconclusive' (Goncalves et al. 2012: 1). They argue that instead of directing attention at the well-resourced criminal organisations that are difficult to catch and may be protected by powerful friends, attention is focused on low-level criminals, whose activities are a response to extreme poverty. Crime at this level may best be addressed using preventive methods and dealing with the causes of poverty (Goncalves et al. 2012: 7). Ozinga and Gerard also noted that efforts to prevent illegal logging should not result in discrimination against women, poor people and ethnic minorities (Ozinga and Gerard 2005: 439).

There are a number of reasons for this lack of attention to enforcement, including illegal logging being seen as a 'victimless crime' partly due to its lack of visibility (Interpol and World Bank 2009: 20). There are perceptions that illegal logging is not a criminal activity. In developing countries, objectives can be set by industrial organisations and large forestry businesses rather than placing environmental objectives first, with the result of governments 'choosing' to under-resource monitoring and enforcement systems (Setiono 2007: 29). UNODC suggests that the importation of illegal timber is seen to damage the source country, not the importer, resulting in 'little moral stigma attached to looking the other way for fraudulent imports' (UNODC 2010: 162). While there is an increasing disquiet regarding the need to protect the environment and punish transgressors, environmental crimes are being dealt with un-systematically and leniently, usually only punished with fines at much less than the maximum prescribed (Bricknell 2010: iii- xii). This is due in part to the lack of training among members of the judiciary of the consequences of harm in environmental crime. The low rate of fines and the ability to attribute penalties as one of the costs of doing business means that recidivism is endemic. This inconsistent regulatory framework, the perception that illegal logging is not a crime and the lack of commitment to enforcing regulations all contribute to the causes of illegal logging (Tacconi 2007: 280). Interpol has expressed concerns regarding the FLEGT Action Plan, claiming that it falls short of being able to deal with illegal operations (Nellemann and Interpol Environmental Crime Programme 2012: 62).

According to Ozinga and Gerard (2005: 440) security and anti-terrorism measures are seen as more deserving of funding than measures to combat illegal logging in a post-9/11 world. Interpol is concerned that national police are not utilising proven methods to catch international forest criminals, and notes that in 2009 while 1885 Red Notices were published for terrorism-related activities, and 1600 Red Notices for drug trafficking, only 4 Red Notices were given out for illegal logging (Interpol and World Bank 2009: 25). Interpol has suggested the need for initiatives like FLEG to bring illegal logging into the international criminal justice regime, rather than operating at a national level (Interpol and World Bank 2009: 42). Changes in governance or regulatory measures provide opportunities for exploitation, and they note the growing criminal interest in processes such as carbon trading (ibid.: 24). They suggest new partners for FLEGT including customs officers, those researching tracking such as through DNA or satellite surveillance, and investigative NGOs. In 2014 a collaborative international enforcement operation conducted jointly by Peru Customs (SUNAT), Interpol and the World Customs Organisation (WCO) was successful in seizing USD 20 million of wood and wood products along with two vessels and logging equipment from criminal groups linked to the Peruvian illegal timber trade (Interpol 2014). This was the first collaboration between Interpol and WCO against forest crime. It had followed intelligence gathered by SUNAT that exposed organised crime involvement in illegal logging and fraud. Operation Amazones involved law enforcement and customs authorities from Brazil, China, Dominican Republic, Mexico and Peru, in addition to Interpol's National Central Bureaus in Brazil and Peru and regional bureaus in Argentina and El Salvador.

FLEGT

It should be noted that in the UN system, there is a preference for the term FLEG (notably in UNFF). This refers more broadly to efforts by the international community to address issues around forest law, enforcement and governance. But it is in the trade arena, and notably in Europe, that the most concrete action has been taken to address illegal logging. In October 2003, the EU adopted the FLEGT Action Plan to combat illegal logging and the resultant timber trade (European Commission 2003: 1–32). EU member states, some of them major global importers of timber and timber products, including the UK and the Netherlands, as well as the European Commission had become aware that there was no practical mechanism for identifying and excluding illegal timber from the EU market. Other major EU countries, including Germany, France, Italy and Spain were less relevant in driving the FLEGT process at an initial stage, but growing consensus among all EU member states has led to a fully fledged development of the FLEGT mechanism and the adoption of the EU Timber Regulation. However, some countries lag behind in the implementation of the regulation (European Commission 2015).

The principal instrument to implement the FLEGT Action Plan is the bilateral VPA between individual timber-producing countries in Africa,

Asia and Latin America, and the EU. The main objectives of the VPAs are to reinforce the ability of partner countries to control their forest sectors and to offer a mechanism to exclude illegal timber products from EU markets. Although the details of each partnership agreement will vary depending on the conditions of each prospective partner country and the nature of their timber trade with the EU, some elements will be common to all VPAs (European Forest Institute 2009).

All VPAs set out a range of measures to increase the capacity of producer countries to control illegal logging, while reducing the trade in illegal timber products between these countries and the EU. One major element is to provide support for improved governance and capacity-building in the forest sector of producer countries, and to develop legality standards through a participatory stakeholder process within individual producer countries. This includes improving transparency and information exchange between producer and consumer countries, including support for independent forest monitoring. A key instrument to improve governance, which the VPA relies on, is a timber legality assurance and licensing scheme that is developed and established in the producer country. This scheme provides both support for the development of community-based forest management empowering local communities to help prevent illegal logging, as well as for private sector initiatives aimed at combatting the trade in illegally harvested timber and timber products. The EU commits itself to curbing investments by EU institutions that may encourage illegal logging (European Commission 2007d: 2–3).

Following protracted preliminary discussions, negotiations for the first VPAs started at the end of 2006. Thus far, six countries (Cameroon, Central African Republic, Ghana, Indonesia, Liberia and the Republic of the Congo), known as 'VPA partner countries', have signed a VPA with the EU and are currently developing the systems needed to control, verify and license legal timber before actual implementation can commence. Nine additional countries are in formal negotiations with the EU, some of them for a considerable number of years: Côte d'Ivoire, Democratic Republic of the Congo, Gabon, Guyana, Honduras, Laos, Malaysia, Thailand and Vietnam. Eleven other countries have signalled their interest in considering VPAs, according to the EU FLEGT Facility (EU FLEGT Facility 2015b).

Under each VPA each partner country will implement a timber legality assurance scheme (TLAS) that contains a definition of legal timber and guarantees that timber exports to the EU have been legally produced by means of a licensing procedure (European Forest Institute 2009: 6). Under the licensing scheme, import into the EU of timber exported from a partner country will be prohibited (unless the timber is covered by a valid licence). The issuance of FLEGT licences requires credible evidence that the products in question have been produced in compliance with the specified laws of the partner country. In order to issue a licence, the licensing authority will require evidence to confirm that the timber was produced legally and that it can be traced through the supply chain back to its legal origin (European Commission 2007c: 2).

The TLAS include three basic elements that VPA partner countries need to develop. One is a national definition of legally produced timber that is developed in a multi-stakeholder process and sets out all the laws and regulations that must be complied with in the production process (European Commission 2007e: 1–2). The second key element is the establishment of a secure chain of custody that tracks timber from the forest where it was harvested through different owners and stages in processing to the point of export (European Commission 2007a: 2). The third component is a verification system developed to provide reasonable assurance to the licensing authority that the requirements of the definition have been met for each export consignment (European Commission 2007c: 2). Once these elements are set up, each VPA country will issue licences to validate the results of legality verification and chain of custody and to allow for customs clearance of the timber products in the EU. Lastly, independent monitoring of the whole timber legality assurance system will provide transparency and guarantee its credibility. The monitoring will be conducted by a 'third-party monitor', which needs to be a non-political body and possess the necessary skills and systems to ensure its independence and objectivity. It will include checking all aspects of the TLAS using best auditing practice, identifying non-compliances and system failures, and reporting its findings to a joint implementation committee with representation of the partner country, the European Commission and member states (European Commission 2007b: 3–5).

Once the timber licensing schemes are established, the EU member states' customs agencies will allow imports only of FLEGT-licensed timber products from FLEGT partner countries (Hudson and Paul 2011: 12).

If the ongoing VPA negotiations lead to the conclusion of a large number of VPAs, the FLEGT Action Plan is likely to become an increasingly comprehensive framework for the exclusion of illegal timber products from the EU, while at the same time improving forest management in producer countries. Development assistance will focus on establishing credible technical and administrative structures with adequate systems to verify that exported timber is legal, which could entail considerable institutional strengthening and capacity-building. The licensing system will reward the implementation of these systems through an improved position on the EU market.[1]

However, a particularly serious risk is 'circumvention' whereby unlicensed products originating from a producer country that has signed a VPA enters the EU through a non-signatory country. The scheme would benefit from all producer countries in a particular region that are major suppliers, directly or indirectly, to the EU-signing VPAs. A major concern in the Asia-Pacific region is the role of re-exporting countries – above all China and Vietnam – where large volumes of timber are imported to be processed and exported as finished products to Western markets and Japan. These intermediary countries in the trade chain would have to formally recognise the VPAs by only accepting licensed products from VPA producer countries for further processing and onward export to the EU. To this end, in November 2010 the EU initiated formal negotiations with Vietnam on a VPA (EU FLEGT Facility 2015a) and has also established a Bilateral Coordination Mechanism against illegal logging with China (EU FLEGT Facility 2015).

As with other demand-side measures against illegal logging in consumer countries, such as the amended US Lacey Act or the Australian Illegal Logging Prohibition Act, FLEGT VPAs require legality verification as one of the 'enforcement' mechanisms associated with their broader 'non-regulatory' mechanisms. Private sector companies with experience of certifying forest concessions against sustainability certification standards now offer a service to independently verify forest concessions against a narrower standard that focuses only on legality. Each company has developed its own generic standards, including country-specific standards (Lawson and MacFaul 2010: 77).

The largest providers of legality verification currently operating are the SGS, the Rainforest Alliance's Smartwood programme, and Bureau Veritas. All legality verification systems have adopted a two-step legality verification approach. The first step is usually called 'verification of legal origin' or VLO, or sometimes just 'verification of origin'. Its scope is generally limited to confirming that timber originated in a particular forest concession and that the company logging there has the necessary licences and permits to do so. The second step is typically referred to as 'verification of legal compliance' (VLC) and is more rigorous because it requires evidence of compliance with regulations governing harvesting. Compared to full certification of sustainability, legality verification standards are easier and faster for concessions to comply with (Lawson and MacFaul 2010: 77).

Regardless of the level or standard that the verification of legality is for, the assessment also involves chain-of-custody procedures. These aim to ensure that verified and unverified wood are kept separate. Most demand-side regulations (such as the FLEGT VPA licensing schemes) require at least the equivalent of a typical VLC standard to be achieved (Lawson and MacFaul 2010: 77).

In addition to these bilateral measures the European Commission has adopted a legislative measure against the trade in illegally harvested timber and timber products. The EU Timber Regulation (EUTR) is based on the due diligence principle and obliges European traders to provide reasonable assurance that the timber products traded are produced in accordance with the relevant legislation of the producing country (European Commission 2010). FLEGT licences are regarded as proof of legality and will thus exempt European traders or their suppliers in FLEGT partner countries from further administrative requirements. The combined implementation of the VPAs and the EUTR is expected to have three important effects. One is the creation of a level playing field in the European market for those companies that are trying to address illegality and those that are under-cutting the market by selling cheaper but illegally harvested timber products. Other expected synergies of implementing both the VPAs and the EUTR are to induce traders to buy and sell low-risk timber rather than high-risk timber, thereby reducing the use of illegally harvested timber by EU consumers. Third, both instruments would provide incentives for other producer countries to conclude VPAs and for exporters in non-VPA countries to establish timber tracking and legality verification schemes (Scheyvens and López-Casero 2010: 38–40).

However, the implementation of the EUTR still faces major challenges. According to the WWF, the EUTR is currently not yet able to tackle the trade in illegal timber effectively. This is partly because not all countries have implemented the regulation as mentioned above. While some member states are relatively advanced in the implementation process, others are still at the beginning (European Commission 2015: 1–3).

Another challenge to an effective contribution of the regulation to reducing illegal logging relates to the exclusion of a range of important wood products from the scope of the regulation. Initial trade flow analysis indicates that more than half of timber imports (by value) into the EU are left out, some deliberately, others by default (WWF 2015b: 1). The European Commission is expected to review the function-ing and effectiveness of the EUTR by 3 December 2015, following the submission of reports on the application of the regulation from EU member states by 30 April 2015 and a stakeholder consultation (WWF 2015b). The WWF argues that the EUTR should now cover all timber and timber products traded on the EU market in order to increase pressure to halt the illegal timber trade.

There are also issues with VPAs that the EU has signed with specific partner countries. Greenpeace called on the EU and Cameroon to integrate the question of timber from forest conversion (for agricultural, mining or infrastructure projects) into the VPA legality grid, including all ongoing implementation mechanisms and dialogue platforms. As part of the VPA implementation, the Cameroonian government has committed to enhancing transparency by publishing forest sector documents on its website, but according to Greenpeace the ownership structure of companies that benefit from logging permits was not included in that pledge. This information would be required for detecting any evidence of conflict of interest, corruption or other violations of international law, national law or laws of companies' country of origin (Greenpeace 2014b: 13). Similarly, based on an analysis of official Ghana logging permit lists, Global Witness found that three-quarters of Ghana's logging permits could break Europe's new timber law (Global Witness 2013: 1–2).

The connection between legality verification, sustainability certification and illegal logging is at times a problematic one, and symptomatic of a broader malaise within the certification system: the role of the certifier. This led one commentator to make the following observations:

> FSC and PEFC claim to account for some 98 per cent of the world's certified forests and chain of custody certificates. The FSC system provides a useful tool for Chinese factory managers to market their products. FSC accredited certification bodies (CBs) certify factories regardless of whether they process FSC wood or not, and it is claimed a process has emerged that has the potential to increase use of illegal wood despite FSC objectives. Small, medium sized enterprises in China processing wood buy their wood on the open market, often with problematic origins. Consulting companies advised SMEs [Small to Medium Enterprise] they could train them to implement a CoC [Chain of Custody] system and to introduce them to their CB partner, who could audit them and award a certificate. The number of FSC CoC certificates in China has exploded. These certified factories buy their wood from all over the world and few have any idea of its legal status. Factories often only run their CoC system for a few days a year when the CB visits, announced in advance, to check. The association of FSC's name becomes a stamp of environmental and social approval, demonstrating diligence under the EUTR and Lacey Act. This does not transform the industry, but provides a mechanism for many organizations to profit from business as usual. More needs to be done to ensure proper due diligence and traceability. Only those SMEs actually using FSC or PEFC wood should be allowed to hold and promote a COC certificate. (Poynton 2013)

This is a clear challenge to both certification and legality verification, and the CBs that support these schemes need to be far more rigorous in ensuring that their own supply chains are not contaminated with illegal timber.

Sources and Means of Delivery of Finance

Forest law enforcement and its governance is another part of measurement in efficient delivery of finance. There are different arguments on how to enforce forest laws, although there is consensus around efficient trading of forest products and equitable distribution of benefits – with implications for laws and regulations. However, some conflicts remain on whether to invest in enforcement via foreign aid or local resources. Some of the issues related to FLEGT are discussed below.

There are some case studies on FLEGT. Bollen and Ozinga (2013: 1) have compared VPAs in six countries, and suggest that Liberia is an exceptional case in that the VPA negotiating groups are not only from CSOs but also from local forest community groups. Involvement of forest community groups not only helps to manage the forest resources sustainably. This approach ensures an adequate supply of fuel wood to meet energy demands through the establishment of forest plantations, especially community-based plantations, which has been identified as the missing part in the case of Timor-Leste (Chiew et al. 2012: 18). Therefore, the objective of forest governance should focus on further increases in the contribution of the forestry sector towards the country's gross domestic product (GDP) through the development of downstream processing and a value-added industry, as well as through low impact use of forests like ecotourism and biotechnology industry (Chiew et al. 2012: 12).

An important issue of benefit distributions in the communities is the perceived benefits, which include the elimination of illegal players, a reduction in corruption and poverty, the promotion of business opportunities and the valorisation of investment (Carodenuto and Cerutti 2014: 55). The best example of not achieving these benefits is fragmentation of the forest in Cameroon. The success of VPA implementation in Cameroon depends on its ability to go beyond the timber legality verification for European markets, and uphold its stated socioeconomic development objectives (Carodenuto and Cerutti 2014: 55). In the Congo basin, a simultaneous marginalisation and fragmentation of smaller forestry enterprises is slowly growing due to a lack of congruence between the aims of Cameroon's VPA and private sector expectation.

However, a similar study in Cameroon by Eba'a Atyi et al. (2013) shows that those timber procurement policies such as FLEGT have the potential to contribute to the sustainable management of forest resources in central Africa. The report recommended to Cameroon's government that it should devote special attention to community forests. Furthermore, it stresses that local officials involved in granting community forest titles should provide more assistance to local communities in meeting VPA requirements. Therefore, within the informal sector, community forests would be the easiest segment to monitor since their resource allocation is already documented and forestry administration can go straight into monitoring the production process.

Institutionalising information-sharing and learning is another issue of interacting with local communities. In this regard, Ochieng et al. (2013: 39) recommend that the theoretical debate on regime interaction and interaction management, concepts applied at the international level, need to be further linked to the debate on Environmental Policy Integration (EPI), a concept mainly used to analyse the relationship between environmental and other policies at national and regional levels. For example, VPA and REDD+ in Ghana have a positive influence through the two regime interactions, although much depends on the future implementation of both regimes (Ochieng et al. 2013: 32).

Free trade agreements (FTAs) have positive as well as negative roles; they have more negative impacts on VPAs that demand more land for the production (Hoare 2014: 9). Contrary to this, according to Lesniewska and McDermott (2014: 4), the overemphasis on timber regulations fails to address the leading role of the agricultural sector in driving forest loss, constrains civil society participation and creates disproportionate market barriers for local producers. FTAs bring foreign direct investment which often requires the clearing of natural forest areas and has led to land disputes with local communities (Woods and Canby 2011: 5). In this broader challenge, Woods and Canby (2011: 6) say that 'VPAs are falling short across several widely accepted indicators of sustainability, including reversing forest loss, assuring long term civil society participation or supporting local benefit-sharing'.

NORTH/SOUTH RELATIONS AND STATE AND NON-STATE ACTORS

In Australia in 2010 there was bilateral support for legislation that would require verification that imports were not illegally harvested. Input from a subsequent Senate Committee resulted in the removal of industry codes of conduct and timber industry certifiers from the legislation, due to concerns regarding additional bureaucracy for industry (Milliken 2013: 17). However, in 2008 the Australian Timber Importers Federation adopted a code of ethics that included verification of chain of custody from importers, and some individual companies are using genetic profiling to confirm timber origins (Bricknell 2010: 99).

Legislation in the US and Australia has been subject to attack. In 2012 House Republicans flagged scaling back the requirements of the Lacey Act, describing enforcement of the bill as 'over-zealous' following the prosecution of Gibson Guitar under its aegis, with conservative groups seeing the corporation as being a 'victim of burdensome regulation' (Kesperowicz 2012). Before the Australian legislation was passed it was subject to a concerted campaign by former trade ambassador Alan Oxley (for example, Oxley 2013), who lobbied on behalf of logging and palm oil companies in South East Asia, and has been associated with Asia Pulp and Paper (McIntyre et al. 2011: 20, Milliken 2013), a problematic timber company that lost its FSC certificate (Hance 2012). Australia's conservative government is now reviewing the regulations to its Illegal Logging Prohibition Bill quoting from Alan Oxley as justification (Frydenberg 2014). The group Oxley chairs, World Growth International, had previously called on the US to roll back the Lacey Act, and provided information to a meeting of Asia Pacific Economic Cooperation (APEC) forestry ministers towards them isolating the US and Australia for their legislation stating that it acted as a non-tariff trade barrier (Lubis 2013). Curtin suggests that the prioritising of competitiveness over concerns of legality has meant that blanket approaches to assessing governance has, for instance, led to the UK government endorsing reports that include timber from established plantations being placed under the 'suspicious' label (Curtin 2007: 127–8).

Commentators have recommended building bridges between the world of law enforcement and that of environmentalists (ibid.: 43–4). NGOs are key to providing information in a field where data has been difficult to assemble, with law-makers, academics and researchers relying on the work carried out by NGOs in addition to Interpol (for example, Australian government in Gupta et al. 2012: 2, UNODC 2010: 294). In a 2015 collaboration between the non-profit organisation Digital Democracy and computer hackers, a new project 'Hack the Rainforest' is developing applications for Indigenous people and community-run monitoring programmes to document and share environmental and human rights violations in Peru (Digital Democracy 2010). The Carbon Disclosure Project (CDP), a business NGO, looks to convert commitments by business into action (CDP 2014). Among its members there is support for robust law enforcement, and transparent grievance mechanisms and clear standards regarding the rights of Indigenous people. They report an interest by business for consistency across jurisdictions, so that expectations regarding commodity use are standardised, and a desire for a 'level playing field', to ensure that legitimate businesses are not competing with illegal sources in the market. They note that legislations such as the EUTR and the US Lacey Act can help towards this, but not when large quantities are being sold into the Asian market.

QUALITY OF GOVERNANCE

Table 3.1   FLEGT – quality of governance by region (February 2015)

Principle	1. Meaningful participation Maximum score: 25 Minimum: 5							
Criterion	1. Interest representation Maximum score: 15 Minimum: 3				2. Organisational responsibility Maximum score: 10 Minimum: 2			Principle Score
Indicator	Inclusiveness	Equality	Resources	Criterion Score	Accountability	Transparency	Criterion Score	
North (37)	3.3	2.7	**1.5**	7.5	2.8	2.5	5.3	12.8
South (49)	3.0	3.0	2.6	8.7	3.1	3.2	6.3	14.9
Principle	2. Productive deliberation Maximum score: 30 Minimum: 6							
Criterion	3. Decision-making Maximum score: 15 Minimum: 3				4. Implementation Maximum score: 15 Minimum: 3			Principle Score
Indicator	Democracy	Agreement	Dispute settlement	Criterion Score	Behavioural change	Problem-solving	Durability	Criterion Score	
North	2.5	2.7	2.5	7.7	2.8	2.8	3.0	8.5	16.2
South	3.0	3.2	2.9	9.0	3.3	3.1	3.2	9.6	18.6
Total (out of 55)								
North				29.0				
South				33.6				

Note: Light grey represents the highest scoring indicator by region; dark grey the lowest; numbers in **bold** are below the threshold value of 50 per cent.

Table 3.2   FLEGT – quality of governance by sector (February 2015)

Principle	1. Meaningful participation Maximum score: 25 Minimum: 5							
Criterion	1. Interest representation Maximum score: 15 Minimum: 3				2. Organisational responsibility Maximum score: 10 Minimum: 2			Principle Score
Indicator	Inclusiveness	Equality	Resources	Criterion Score	Accountability	Transparency	Criterion Score	
Environment	3.4	2.9	2.2	8.5	2.7	2.9	5.6	14.1
Social	2.3	1.5	1.3	5.1	1.3	1.3	2.6	7.7
Economic	4.0	3.3	1.0	8.3	3.7	3.7	7.4	15.7
Government	3.0	3.1	2.3	8.4	3.3	3.0	6.3	14.7
Academic	3.4	2.9	2.1	8.4	3.3	3.0	6.3	14.7
Other	3.2	3.0	2.7	8.9	2.7	2.5	5.2	14.1

Principle	2. Productive deliberation Maximum score: 30 Minimum: 6							
Criterion	3. Decision-making Maximum score: 15 Minimum: 3				4. Implementation Maximum score: 15 Minimum: 3			Principle Score
Indicator	Democracy	Agreement	Dispute settlement	Criterion Score	Behavioural change	Problem-solving	Durability	Criterion Score
Environment	2.6	2.8	2.6	8.0	3.3	2.9	3.2	9.4	17.4
Social	1.5	1.5	1.5	4.5	2.3	1.8	1.8	5.9	10.4
Economic	2.7	4.0	2.7	9.4	3.3	3.7	3.3	10.3	19.7
Government	2.9	3.6	3.0	9.5	3.3	3.3	3.4	10.0	19.5
Academic	3.1	2.9	3.0	9.0	2.9	3.0	3.1	9.0	18.0
Other	2.3	3.0	2.0	7.3	2.5	2.5	2.3	7.3	14.6

Total (out of 55)	
Environment	31.5
Social	**18.1**
Economic	35.4
Government	34.2
Academic	32.7
Other	28.7

Note: Light grey represents the highest scoring indicator by sector; dark grey the lowest; numbers in **bold** are below the threshold value of 50 per cent.

Commentary on the Results

Eighty-six participants responded to this survey, with a majority from the South. There was some difference in the overall scores between regions, with the South awarding a moderately high 'pass', while the North provided only a low 'pass'. This distinction was repeated at the principle and criterion levels. In both cases resources was the lowest indicator, but with a 'fail' from the North and a low 'pass' from the South. Agreement and durability were the two highest indicators from Southern respondents, for the North, inclusiveness.

Economic respondents provided the highest score by sector, followed by government, academics, environment and 'other'. Only the social sector awarded a 'fail'. This was repeated at the principle and criterion levels, but it should be noted that 'other' 'failed' FLEGT at the principle and criterion level for deliberation (decision-making and implementation). Resources was the weakest indicator, and rated a 'fail' by all sectors, with the exception of 'other', which selected dispute settlement. The social sector gave an equally low rating for accountability and transparency. The lowest rating for resources overall was from the economic sector. Inclusiveness received the highest ratings from economic, environmental and academic respondents, and from the social sector (although at 2.3 this was still a 'fail'). Economic respondents awarded agreement a similarly 'high' rating to inclusiveness. Government respondents selected agreement as their highest indicator.

Commentary from Survey Respondents

Only one Northern academic commented specifically on FLEGT. They pointed to the inequalities in the scheme, as it 'did not consider poor people' who were 'illegally cutting timber to survive'. They also thought that the timber trade resulting from the mechanism helped 'developed countries benefit', and that this was 'against developing countries'. They were also of the view that 'typically, laws like FLEGT will force illegal activities if they do not open alternative chances for income'.

ANALYSIS AND CONCLUSIONS

Illegal logging is a significant global problem environmentally, socially and economically. While enacting anti-illegal logging legislation is a welcome initiative, there is more that can be done to combat it. It is important that countries continue to participate in international endeavours to combat corruption and money laundering, and work with developing and developed countries to ensure that their logging is legal. Data collection needs to build on detailed research conducted by NGOs. Processes such as certification, due diligence with regard to sources of timber, and funding and continual emphasis on processes of good governance can assist with this. Special attention needs to be given to products sourced from China, given the size of its role in our markets, the fact that it is increasing, and the role that China has in importing timber from illegal sources in our region.

When making laws, the needs and rights of traditional landholders need to be taken into account. Developed countries have a particular role in the funding of dubious landholder arrangements by its major banks, and it is important that those involved in banking are aware of the results of their investments. Resources and attention need to be allocated to enforcement and helping source countries police operations. The crime of illegal logging and the consequent environmental degradation, disruption to communities and damage to concepts of good governance and economies need to be taken seriously.

Since the VPAs and the EUTR still require full implementation, it is too early to draw strong conclusions on the impacts that the FLEGT and the Regulation will have on reducing illegal logging, and which possible shortcomings will need to be addressed in the future. However, some inferences can be made at this stage. In terms of governance there is considerable room for improvement. Local communities have not yet been appropriately involved in the negotiation process for the implementation of the VPAs as the European Forest Institute, which has hosted the EU FLEGT Facility since 2007, acknowledges (European Forest Institute 2015: 4). It is also safe to assume that a more comprehensive coverage of wood products under the EUTR would increase the positive impacts of the policy in terms of curbing the imports of illegal timber. The possible policy impact on trade flows also needs to be considered, as the EUTR may drive the demand for temperate hardwood products at the expense of tropical timber product imports despite the VPAs with selected tropical producer countries. Moreover, there is a need for research to assess the concrete contribution of FLEGT and the Regulation to curbing illegal logging, given the risk that producers in source countries redirect illegal timber products to domestic markets or other countries without comparable policy measures. The EU therefore needs to address these potential loopholes and advance in its negotiations with other major importer countries of wood products, such as China, the US and Japan.

Efforts to ensure that loggers and other entities in the forestry industry comply with forestry regulation must go well beyond the chain-of-custody system (checking documentation and provenance) and examine the overall legal environment (Dooley et al. 2011: 170). In this regard, it is important to look at the global picture of resource consumption and work towards a more equal distribution of resources, while strengthening civil society organisation in forest abundant countries to allow them to hold their government accountable for the development and implementation of national forest and land-use policies.

NOTE

1. Personal interviews with a European Commission expert, 5 August and 1 December.

BIBLIOGRAPHY

ACF 2006, *NGOs lodge complaint against ANZ Bank for PNG illegal logging ties*, Australian Conservation Foundation. Viewed 28 April 2015, http://www.acfonline.org.au/news-media/media-release/ngos-lodge-complaint-against-anz-bank-png-illegal-logging-ties.

Australian Government 2012, *Illegal logging prohibition act 2012: Explanatory memorandum*. Viewed 28 April 2015, http://www.austlii.edu.au/au/legis/cth/bill_em/ilpb2012270/memo_0.html.

Bollen, A. and Ozinga, S. 2013, *Improving Forest Governance: A Comparison of FLEGT VPAs and their Impact*, Brussels, Belgium: FERN.

Bouriaud, L. 2005, 'Causes of illegal logging in Central and Eastern Europe', *Small-scale Forests Economics, Management and Policy*, **4** (3) 269–92.

Bricknell, S. 2010, 'Environmental crime in Australia', Australian Institute of Criminology. Viewed 2 April 2015, http://www.aic.gov.au/media_library/publications/rpp/109/rpp109.pdf.

Cadman, T. 2011, *Quality and legitimacy of global governance: case lessons from forestry*, Basingstoke, London: Palgrave Macmillan.

Capistrano, D., Kanninen, M., Guariguata, M., Barr, C., Sunderland, T. and Raitzer, D., 2007, 'Revitalizing the UNFF: Critical Issues and Ways Forward, Country-led Initiative on Multi-year Programme of Work of the United Nations Forum on Forests: Charting the Way Forward to 2015', February, Bali, Indonesia, 13–16.

Carodenuto, S. and Cerutti, P. O. 2014, 'Forest Law Enforcement, Governance and Trade (FLEGT) in Cameroon: Perceived private sector benefits from VPA implementation', *Forest Policy and Economics*, **48** 55–62.

CDP 2014, 'Deforestation-free supply chains: From commitments to action', *Carbon Disclosure Project*. Viewed 10 May 2015, https://www.cdp.net/CDPResults/CDP-global-forests-report-2014.pdf.

Chiew, T. H., Hewitt, J. and Keong, C. H. 2012, *Timor Leste: Scoping Baseline Information for Forest Law Enforcement, Governance and Trade*. Kuala Lumpur: EU FLEGT Action Plan in Asia.

Curtin, T. 2007, 'What constitutes illegal logging?', *Pacific Economic Bulletin*, **22** (1) 125–34.

Digital Democracy 2010, *Technologists and indigenous activists convene in the Peruvian Amazon*. Viewed 10 May 2015, http://www.hacktherainforest.org/new-blog-1/.

Dooley, K., Griffiths, T., Martone, F. and Ozinga, S. 2011, *Smoke and mirrors: A critical assessment of the forest carbon partnership facility*, Moreton-in-Marsh: FERN. Viewed 20 April 2015, http://www.forestpeoples.org/sites/fpp/files/publication/2011/03/smokeandmirrorsinternet.pdf.

Eba'a Atyi, R., Assembe-Mvondo, S., Lescuyer, G. and Cerutti, P. 2013, 'Impacts of international timber procurement policies on Central Africa's forestry sector: The case of Cameroon', *Forest Policy and Economics*, **32** 40–8.

Equator Principles 2003, *Leading banks announce adoption of Equator Principles*. Viewed 14 April 2015, http://www.equator-principles.com/index.php/all-adoption/adoption-news-by-year/65-2003/167-leading-banks-announce-adoption-of-equator-principles.

EU FLEGT Facility 2015a, *Vietnam*. Viewed 14 April 2015, http://www.euflegt.efi.int/vietnam.

EU FLEGT Facility 2015b, *VPA countries*. Viewed 14 April 2015, http://www.euflegt.efi.int/vpa-countries.

EU FLEGT Facility 2015 'China–EU cooperation. Bilateral coordination mechanism'. Viewed 15 April 2015, http://www.euflegt.efi.int/china-eu.

European Commission 2003, 'Forest law enforcement, governance and trade (FLEGT). Proposal for an EU action plan', *Communication from the Commission to the Council and the European Parliament*. Viewed 12 April 2015, http://www.euflegt.efi.int/documents/10180/23398/FLEGT+Action+Plan/3c0cfca1-1503-458a-9d05-1717bf226e23.

European Commission 2007a, 'Control of the supply chain: Wood tracing systems and chain of custody', *FLEGT Briefing Note Number 04*. Viewed 14 April 2015, http://www.euflegt.efi.int/documents/10180/28299/FLEGT+Briefing+Notes+4+-+Control+of+the+supply+chain+-+Wood+tracing+systems+and+chain+of+custody/707452ca-4d0e-4fa1-b4c1-71d68888b51e.

European Commission 2007b, 'Guidelines for independent monitoring', *FLEGT Briefing Note Number 07*. Viewed 15 April 2015, http://www.euflegt.efi.int/documents/10180/28299/FLEGT+Briefing+Notes+7+-+Guidelines+for+independent+monitoring/8785cc01-fda3-46d3-ae2b-d9f79cfb57fa.

European Commission 2007c, 'Legality assurance systems: Requirements for verification', *FLEGT Briefing Note Number 05*. Viewed 14 April 2015, http://www.euflegt.efi.int/documents/10180/28299/FLEGT+Briefing+Notes+5+-+Legality+assurance+systems+-+requirements+for+verification/9f30f065-ff3d-41b0-9ea2-726e293e0231.

European Commission 2007d, 'What is FLEGT?' *FLEGT Briefing Note Number 01*. Viewed 13 April 2015, http://www.euflegt.efi.int/documents/10180/28299/FLEGT+Briefing+Notes+1+-+What+is+FLEGT/8e6155fe-6a0e-4606-98d1-2aaa74160e26.

European Commission 2007e, 'What is legal timber?' *FLEGT Briefing Note Number 02*. Viewed 5 May 2015, http://ec.europa.eu/europeaid/sites/devco/files/publication-flegt-briefing-note-series-2007-2-200703_en.pdf.
European Commission 2010, *Timber regulation*. Viewed 15 April 2015, http://ec.europa.eu/environment/forests/timber_regulation.htm.
European Commission 2015, *State of implementation of EU timber regulation in 28 member states*. Viewed 30 April 2015, http://ec.europa.eu/environment/forests/pdf/EUTR%20implementation%20scoreboard.pdf.
European Forest Institute 2009, 'What is a voluntary partnership agreement?' *EFI Policy Brief 3*. Viewed 13 April 2015, http://www.euflegt.efi.int/documents/10180/23013/EFI+Policy+Brief+3+-+What+is+a+Voluntary+Partnership +Agreement/076495d8-741e-49da-aeaf-b67e2d3d2239.
European Forest Institute 2015, 'EU timber regulation and FLEGT action plan: Lessons learned and policy implications', *Think Forest*. Viewed 30 April 2015, http://www.efi.int/files/attachments/thinkforest/efi_thinkforest-brief_eutr.pdf.
FAO 2004, 'Proceedings FAO Advisory Committee on Paper and Wood Products Forty-fifth Session', 16–17 April, Canberra, Australia.
Frydenberg, J. 2014, 'Time to cut down Labor's approach to logging control', *Australian Financial Review*, 11 December.
Global Forest Watch 2015, *Countries with greatest tree cover loss (2001–2013)*. Viewed 16 April 2015, http://www.globalforestwatch.org/countries/overview.
Global Witness 2013, *Three-quarters of Ghana's logging permits could break Europe's new timber law. Global Witness analysis of official Ghana logging permit lists*. Viewed 30 April 2015, https://www.globalwitness.org/sites/default/files/gw_ghana_logging_permits.pdf.
Goncalves, M., Panjer, M., Greenberg, T. and Magrath, W. 2012, 'Justice for forests. Improving criminal justice efforts to combat illegal logging', The World Bank. Viewed 12 April 2015, http://siteresources.worldbank.org/EXTFINANCIALSECTOR/Resources/Illegal_Logging.pdf.
Green, P., Ward, T. and McConnachie, K. 2007, 'Logging and legality: Environmental crime, civil society and the state', *Social Justice*, **34** (2) 94–110.
Greenpeace 2004, *The untouchables: Rimbunan Hijau's world of forest crime and political patronage*. Amsterdam: Greenpeace International. Viewed 26 April 2015, http://www.greenpeace.org/new-zealand/Global/new-zealand/report/2006/12/the-untouchables.pdf.
Greenpeace 2006, *Partners in crime: A Greenpeace investigation into Finland's illegal timber trade with Russia*. Viewed 9 May 2015, http://www.greenpeace.org/raw/content/international/press/reports/forest-crime-finland.pdf.
Greenpeace 2014b, *Licence to launder. How Herakles Farms' illegal timber trade threatens Cameroon's forests and VPA*. Viewed 30 April 2015, http://www.greenpeace.org/international/Global/international/publications/forests/2014/Licence-to-Launder.pdf.
Gupta, M., Davey, S., Townsend, P. and Cunningham, D. 2012, 'Illegal logging regulations: Analysis of Australia's timber imports in 2007 and 2010', ABARES. Viewed 12 May 2015, http://www.daff.gov.au/SiteCollectionDocuments/abares/publications/clientreports/Illegal_logging.pdf.
Halsey, M. and White, R. 2006, *Crime, Ecophilosophy and Environmental Harm*, Aldershot: Ashgate Publishing.

Hance, J. 2012, 'Asia Pulp & Paper loses another customer: Danone', Mongabay. Viewed 9 May 2015, http://news.mongabay.com/2012/0402-hance_danone_app.html.

Hoare, A. 2014, 'Europe's forest strategy in the next decade: options for the Voluntary Partnership Agreements', EER PP 2014/06 ed., London: Chatham House.

Hudson, J. and Paul, C. 2011, 'FLEGT action plan. Progress report 2003-2010', European Commission. Viewed 30 April 2015, https://ec.europa.eu/europeaid/sites/devco/files/report-progess-2003-2010-flegt-20110126_en.pdf.

Humphreys, D. 1996, *Forest politics: The evolution of international cooperation*, London: Earthscan.

Humphreys, D. 2006, *Logjam: Deforestation and the crisis of global governance*, London: Earthscan.

Interpol 2013a, 'Assessment of law enforcement capacity needs to tackle forest crime', *Interpol environmental crime programme*. Viewed 29 April 2015, http://www.fao.org/sustainable-forest-management/toolbox/tools/tool-detail/en/c/217847/.

Interpol 2014, 'Trade in illegal timber target of Interpol and WCO-supported operation in Peru'. Interpol. Viewed 29 April 2015, http://www.interpol.int/en/layout/set/print/News-and-media/News/2014/N2014-139.

Interpol and World Bank 2009, 'The Chainsaw Project: An Interpol perspective on law enforcement in illegal logging'. Interpol General Secretariat. Viewed 12 April 2015, http://www.illegal-logging.info/sites/default/files/uploads/WorldBankChainsawIllegalLoggingReport.pdf.

Kesperowicz, P. 2012, 'GOP plans vote to ease Lacey Act rules which led to raid on Gibson Guitar', *The Hill*. Viewed 10 May 2015, http://thehill.com/blogs/floor-action/house/238107-gop-plans-vote-to-ease-lacey-act-rules-on-imported-wood.

Khan, M. A. 2010, 'Timber mafia made floods worse', *Al Jazeera*. Viewed 24 April 2015, http://www.aljazeera.com/focus/floodofmisery/2010/08/201081614111704604.html.

Koyuncu, C. and Yilmaz, R. 2009, 'The impact of corruption on deforestation: A cross-country evidence', *The Journal of Developing Areas*, **42** (2).

Lawson, S. and MacFaul, L. 2010, *Illegal Logging and Related Trade. Indicators of the Global Response*, London: Chatham House.

Lesniewska, F. and McDermott, C. L. 2014, 'FLEGT VPAs: Laying a pathway to sustainability via legality lessons from Ghana and Indonesia', *Forest Policy and Economics*. Viewed 24 April 2015, http://www.sciencedirect.com/science/article/pii/S1389934114000185.

Lubis, A. M. 2013, 'APEC agrees to isolate the US, Australia over forestry trade bans', *Jakarta Post*. Viewed 10 May 2015, http://www.thejakartapost.com/news/2013/08/19/apec-agrees-isolate-us-australia-over-forestry-trade-bans.html.

Mason, C. 2012, 'PNG investigator claims Australia "Cayman Islands" of Pacific money-laundering', *Pacific Scoop*. Viewed 12 April 2015, http://pacific.scoop.co.nz/2012/11/png-investigator-claims-australia-cayman-is-of-pacific-money-laundering/print/.

McElwee, P. 2004, *You say illegal, I say legal: The relationship between 'illegal' logging and land tenure, poverty, and forest use rights in Vietnam*, Binghamton, NY: Haworth Press.

McIntyre, M., DeSantis, A. and Quealy, K. 2011, 'A hidden lobby for Indonesian paper', *The New York Times*. Viewed 8 May 2015, http://www.nytimes.com/interactive/2011/03/29/us/liberty-graphic.html?_r=0.

Milliken, R. 2013, 'Hug those trees', *Anne Summers Reports*. Viewed 4 May 2015, http://annesummers.com.au/wp-content/uploads/2014/11/hugthosetrees.pdf.

Narayanasamy, S. 2014, 'Banking on shaky ground: Australia's big four banks and land grabs', OXFAM Australia. Viewed 26 April 2015, https://www.oxfam.org.au/wp-content/uploads/site-media/pdf/2014-47australia%27sbig4banks andlandgrabs_fa_web.pdf.

Nellemann, C. and Interpol Environmental Crime Programme (eds) 2012, 'Green carbon, black trade', *United Nations Environment Programme*, Arendal: CRID. Viewed 6 May 2015, http://www.grida.no/publications/rr/green-carbon-black-trade/.

Neuman, W. and Zarate, A. 2013, 'Corruption in Peru aids cutting of rain forest', *The New York Times*. Viewed 8 May 2015, http://www.nytimes.com/2013/10/19/world/americas/corrruption-in-peru-aids-cutting-of-rainforest.html?r=0.

Ochieng, R. M., Visseren-Hamakers, I. J. and Nketiah, K. S. 2013, 'Interaction between the FLEGT-VPA and REDD+ in Ghana: Recommendations for interaction management', *Forest Policy and Economics*, **32** 32–9.

Oxley, A. 2013, 'A contender for Australia's worst law', *Quadrant*. Viewed 6 May 2015, https://quadrant.org.au/magazine/2013/10/contender-worst-law-australia/.

Ozinga, S. and Gerard, N. 2005, *Strategies to prevent illegal logging*, Cornwall: MPG Books.

PNGFIA 2011, *Harming PNG: Australia's illegal logging prohibition bill*, Papua New Guinea: Papua New Guinea Forest Industries Association, viewed 27 April 2015, http://www.fiapng.com/PDF_files/Aust%20Senate%20 Sub mission_Illegal%20Logging.pdf.

Poynton, S. 2013, 'Chain of custody nonsense from FSC & PEFC: Protecting income streams rather than the world's forests'. Viewed 23 November 2013, http://news.mongabay.com/2013/07/chain-of-custody-nonsense-from-fsc-pefc-protecting-income-streams-rather-than-the-worlds-forests/.

Ruggiero, V. and South, N. 2013, 'Green criminology and crimes of the economy: Theory, research and praxis', *Critical Criminology*, **21** 359–73.

Scheyvens, H. and López-Casero, F. 2010, 'Enhancing customs collaboration to combat the trade in illegal timber', *Policy Report*, Kanagawa, Japan: IGES.

Schloenhardt, A. 2008, 'The illegal trade in timber and timber products in the Asia-Pacific region', Canberra, ACT: Australian Institute of Criminology. Viewed 20 April 2015, http://aic.gov.au/media_library/publications/rpp/89/rpp089.pdf.

Setiono, B. 2007, *Fighting illegal logging and forest-related financial crimes: The anti-money laundering approach*, Canberra, ACT: Department of International Relations, Australian National University.

Setiono, B. and Husein, Y. 2005, *Fighting forest crime and promoting prudent banking for sustainable forest management: The anti-money laundering approach*. Bogor, Indonesia: Centre for International Forestry Research.

Tacconi, L. 2007, *Illegal logging: Law enforcement, livelihoods and the timber trade*, Sterling: Earthscan.

UNODC 2010, *The globalisation of crime, a transnational organized crime threat assessment*. Viewed 5 March 2015, http://www.unodc.org/unodc/en/data-and-analysis/tocta-2010.html.

Watson, A. 2006, *The proposed New Zealand approach towards addressing illegal logging and associated trade activities*, Ministry of Agriculture and Forestry Wellington. Viewed 2 April 2015, http://maxa.maf.govt.nz/forestry/illegal-logging/illegal-logging-discussion-paper/index.htm.

Wilson, C. 2014, 'Illegal logging wreaking havoc on impoverished rural communities', *Inter Press Service News Agency*. Viewed 10 April 2015, http://www.ipsnews.net/2014/12/illegal-loggin-wreaking-havoc-on-impoverished-rural-communities/.

Woods, K. and Canby, K. 2011, 'Baseline study 4, Myanmar: Overview of forest law enforcement, governance and trade', EU FLEGT. Viewed 10 July 2015, www.forest-trends.org/documents/files/doc_3159.pdf.

WWF 2015a, *Deforestation*. Viewed 18 April 2015, http://wwf.panda.org/about_our_earth/about_forests/deforestation/forest_illegal_logging.

WWF 2015b, *Review of the European Union Timber Regulation*. Viewed 30 April 2015, http://assets.wwf.org.uk/downloads/eutr_briefing_march_2015.pdf.

4. Conservation of biological diversity – PES and BOM

HISTORY AND DESCRIPTIVE BACKGROUND OF BIODIVERSITY CONSERVATION

As mentioned in previous chapters, the CBD was one of the three legally binding agreements adopted at the 1992 'Earth Summit' in Rio de Janeiro, Brazil. As was the case with the text for the Framework Convention on Climate Change, the text of the CBD had been generated through a series of meetings prior to the Rio meetings, so that very little negotiation at the actual UNCED meeting was necessary. The text of the agreement itself (including a preamble, 42 Articles and three annex segments) is predicated on expanding upon and further specifying the primary objectives of the Convention, which are 'the conservation of biological diversity, the sustainable use of its components and the fair and equitable sharing of the benefits arising out of the utilization of genetic resources' (Convention on Biological Diversity 1992). The Convention entered into force in 1993. Currently (2015) 195 nation states have committed to being Parties to the Convention, which means that they have not only signed on to the Convention, but their governments have ratified it. Parties to the Convention (in addition to observers and other officially recognised and accredited stakeholders) meet every two years at COP meetings, during which Meetings of Parties (MOP) of the various protocols also often simultaneously take place.

While the treaty sets goals and objectives, the responsibility of achieving those goals – the implementation of agreed-upon objectives – lies with the nation states (Parties to the Convention) themselves. This has been identified as being one of the problematic issues of the Convention in terms of lack of mechanisms to enforce implementation (Herrera Izaguirre 2008, Wold 1998). This dynamic, associated with all agreements negotiated under the auspices of the United Nations with the exception of those which can be associated with the International Court of Justice, speaks to the tension between the principle of state sovereignty that is codified in the UN Charter (and reiterated in all environmental agreements) and the need for nation states to come together to address global environmental challenges (Kuehls 1996, Paolini et al. 1998).

With the goal of specifying the fairly broad objectives of the Convention, three protocols have, to date, been adopted by Parties to the Convention. In 2000, the Cartagena Protocol on Biosafety was adopted at the 'Extraordinary Meeting of the COP' in Montreal, Canada. In 2010, both the Nagoya-Kuala Lumpur Supplementary Protocol on Liability and Redress to the Cartagena Protocol on Biosafety and the Nagoya Protocol on Access and Benefit Sharing were adopted (at COP10 in Nagoya, Japan). The Cartagena Protocol on Biosafety (known as 'the Cartagena Protocol'), the first of these protocols to be adopted, entered into force in 2003. It was designed to address living modified organisms (LMOs) that may impact biological diversity, particularly in relation to the transboundary movements of such LMOs. Related to the topic of this book, under the Cartagena Protocol, the Biosafety Clearinghouse (BCH) was established. The BCH contains provisions on financial resources and capacity-building particularly focused on countries of the global South and those with weak or non-existing regulatory frameworks. The Cartagena Protocol makes decisions through its governing body which meets under the 'COP/MOP' framework. At COP11/MOP5, which took place in Hyderabad, India in October of 2012, an Ad Hoc Technical Expert Group was established related to 'socio-economic considerations', many of which intersect with the primary topics addressed in this volume (Andree 2005, Gehring and Oberthur 2006).

In addition to regime frameworks related to the Convention protocols, and often with the objective of contributing to the negotiations surrounding the protocols, several 'work programmes' have been set up under the auspices of the CBD in order to focus on particular elements related to one or more articles of the Convention. Two of these work programmes in particular have specific relevance to both North/South dynamics and non-state actor engagement: the Working Group on Article 8(j) (WG8(j)), and the Ad Hoc Open-ended Working Group on Protected Areas (WGPA). These will be discussed below in relation to North/South relations and state/non-state actors.

The CBD's Subsidiary Body on Scientific, Technical, and Technological Advice (SBSTTA) meets regularly to address relevant issues in contribution to the work of the Convention. Additionally, the Intergovernmental Platform on Biodiversity and Ecosystem Services (IPBES) was recently established (2012) in order to 'synthesize, review, assess and critically evaluate relevant information and knowledge generated worldwide by governments, academia, scientific organizations, non-governmental organizations and indigenous communities' (IPBES 2015) in relation to 'the state of the planet's biodiversity, its ecosystems and the essential services they provide to society' (ibid.). Thus, in terms of market-based approaches that have been applied to the conservation of biological diversity, the IPBES represents not only a body related to scientific expertise, but also explicitly a key element of the regime related to ecosystem services. It therefore intersects in important ways with the discussion below regarding PES and BOM.

Michaelowa and Michaelowa note that, as a function of the OECD's (Organisation for Economic Co-operation and Development) Creditor Reporting System (CRS), donors may have an incentive to demonstrate financial support in reference to their Rio commitments (2011). However, the CRS is based on donor-reported figures, which, according to NGOs and other stakeholders engaged in environmental governance regimes, is therefore not a strong indicator of actual figures related to biodiversity conservation. In fact, Miller et al., through a systematic assessment of actual funding for biological diversity aid, determined that, while aid increased significantly in the 1990s, 'funding falls well short of amounts promised in Rio by wealthy nations and is significantly less than reported in previous studies' (Miller et al. 2013). EU national official 4 commented:

> We've been very good in the CBD to draft a work program on economic incentive measures in the early days. They are very general and all very nice, but when we reached a point where we became very concrete, then sometimes we stood up and said, 'Well, that's all very nice but we've been discussing perverse incentive, we look at the European common agriculture policy [CAP] has one perverse system. First get it out of the way and then we'll talk. Okay?'

> And – well, that's where the whole thing just got stuck. Of course we try to generate how we are reforming the CAP to be supportive of our biodiversity goals and ... there's this negotiation [shifting the payments away from production to environmental management] and ... I must say I'm not necessarily defending the European view here but I do feel that the current revision of the common agricultural policy is, for the first time, maybe really moving in the right direction. And we will be paying farmers for delivering on biodiversity, for delivering on environmental objectives for ecosystem services. And that's good.

> And the question is: would it be better if you don't pay them at all? In terms of biodiversity, I'm not so sure. So, well, let's see what comes out of the discussions that they are both ... finalised and that – but it was just an

example to show how ... different stakeholders run into each other and get all stuck in discussions on issues that are not so much CBD-oriented or biodiversity focused but – that come from an agriculture or trade perspective.

INGO representative 5 was optimistic, and commented:

> What we do in the Nagoya Protocol now [represents] the first time that we are obliged to pay something to the underdeveloped countries for their services to the world. [Up to now, developed countries] have paid nothing. Today there is a proper exchange and when we started the draft biodiversity [CBD] text, we had first been thinking to put a tax on all plantations – coffee, tea, tax money that could be used for the implementation of the biodiversity treaty. But this has not gone through. Today, you have at least compensation under the Nagoya Protocol.

The concept of applying economic incentives to biodiversity conservation and ecosystem services began to evolve in the late 1970s, when environmental economists sought to demonstrate that environmental policies could be strengthened by providing economic incentives. The first major document advocating economic incentives was the Project 88 report to the US Congress, which recommended cap-and-trade instruments and led to the creation of a market for SO_2 emissions allowances (Stavins 1988). An increasing number of studies followed suit advocating regulation through the market, or through forms of management relying on market mechanisms as the most effective way to conserve nature (e.g. Pearce 1991, Daily 1997, Heal 2000, Landell-Mills and Porras 2002, Pagiola et al. 2002). For instance, Daily developed the idea of applying economic incentives to biodiversity conservation (Daily 1997).

A number of stakeholders in international arenas took up the idea of applying economic incentives to biodiversity conservation and ecosystem services, including the International Union for Conservation of Nature (IUCN), the World Bank, the UNEP, the OECD, the CBD and the WTO. The CBD, which was adopted in 1992, called in its Article 11 on the Parties to adopt incentive measures for biodiversity conservation. However, it was not until 2000 that a special working group under the SBSTTA was set up to address the issue and collaboration commenced with other organisations working on the issue – IUCN, the OECD and the WTO. All argued for the need to measure the economic value of biodiversity and to develop positive incentives in favour of biodiversity conservation. The Millennium Ecosystem Assessment, which was carried out between 2001 and 2005 to assess the consequences of ecosystem change for human well-being and to establish the scientific basis for actions needed to enhance the conservation and sustainable use of ecosystems and their contributions to human well-being also promoted the shift from perverse incentives to market-based instruments (Millennium Ecosystem Assessment 2005: 21–2).

Ecosystem services (ES) can be defined as the benefits that people obtain from ecosystems (Millennium Ecosystem Assessment 2005: v). An article by Costanza el al. (1997) published in *Nature* advocated developing market approaches to ES by applying monetary valuation, and provided economic analogies and metaphors to describe the functioning of ecosystems. It led to the emergence of the ES concept as an opportunity to strengthen economic incentives for biodiversity conservation. This was also promoted under the CBD, for instance by the COP 9 Decision IX/6 on 'incentive measures', which could be harnessed in the service of conservation. However, this ES concept also provoked a number of highly critical publications (Brockington 2011, Peluso 2012), which followed Harvey in understanding the concept as one of 'the Trojan horses of global neoliberalism' (Harvey 2005: 177). In the debate that followed the publication of the above *Nature* article, critics argued that its characterisation of ES was simplistic (Herendeen 1998) and that the monetary valuation of ES would be a first step in their commercialisation (e.g. Vatn 2000, Kosoy and Corbera 2010, Gómez-Baggethun and Ruiz-Perez 2011).

In the past two decades the concept of ES has been developed as a framework to link economics and the environment, with ES defined as the benefits that the environment provides for people. Refined and mainstreamed in the 2005 Millennium Ecosystem Assessment, the concept involves a comprehensive categorisation of four types of ES, namely: (1) supporting services such as soil formation that underpin provision of other services, (2) regulating services like carbon sequestration in forests, (3) provisioning services, including the production of water, foods and fibres for people, and (4) cultural services, such as recreation and spiritual benefits from the environment. In this framework, biodiversity is both part of the natural capital from which services are generated, and in some instances, an ecosystems services, for example, in terms of crop genetic diversity. Proponents of ecosystems services see one advantage as establishing an evaluation framework to enable all benefits to be identified and valued (using market and non-market valuations) to inform decisions impacting on the environment.

Market-based instruments include two basic forms based on different rationales: PES, based on the 'beneficiary pays' principle, and BOM, based on the 'disturber pays' principle. These two distinct mechanisms, which are typically considered to be innovative and market-based, are the scope of the following analysis.

INGO representative 4 highlighted the need for use of ES in decision-making:

> I think we need to look at the economics of a healthy environment versus the economics of a totally destroyed environment, where we're headed now, and then convince government decision makers that they really have no choice. You know it's the same thing you see here in the US Congress, suggesting all sorts of bills to suspend environmental enforcement because of the economy – it's insane. Fortunately they haven't passed, but it's still insane even from an economic perspective. Put your resources into alternative energy, etcetera – things that will bring in a lot of money, but don't suspend environmental enforcement. You're going to have to clean it up later.

Another advantage in identifying generation of benefits may enable the establishment of payment systems to see beneficiaries pay ecosystem service providers, internalising within markets what have been environmental externalities. One example is payment of fees by water users to fund conservation of catchments to supply clean water by local landholders.

Interviewees were largely supportive of greater use of the ES concept. Developed country national official 4 said that ES were particularly helpful. They created:

> something that actually means something that is a little bit more tangible to people, too [which is important]. So one of the values of protected areas is to protect catchments and deliver water. There's some growing data around the world about what proportion of human water supply actually comes out of protected areas. That's a very obvious ecosystem service that has a tangible value. Fresh air, catchment stability, soil stability are other ones. What is starting to happen on disaster risk mitigation, natural ecosystems – again, … good data – you wonder why people don't take more heed of it. If you keep your mangrove systems intact, then you're less liable to coastal flooding.

> There's a real recognition of the importance of ecosystem services that natural systems provide, and it is very hard to talk to anyone who doesn't think that access to water is going to be just a massive problem this century. And so, debates that focus around water quality and quality of global supply are going to play out quite strongly, and there's a great opportunity for a more substantive body of work around how – similar to the carbon space – natural systems can play a role in actually delivering that. Like, natural systems store carbon. There are good arguments, and I think there are opportunities for better data and better communication around managing risk around those things. So, natural systems *do* buffer some of the current risks that come from natural variations. So, in delivering ecosystem services, you've got a more reliable supply, in natural systems, you've got a more reliable supply of carbon, sequestration of carbon, so the intergovernmental platform on biodiversity ecosystem services could play a really important role in delivering up the information and arguments around that.

However, the language describing the value of ecosystems to people could be important in generating political support. INGO official 3 declared:

> I hate the phrase 'ecosystem services'. Most people don't understand [and] think it's the garbage collection and sewage disposal which is *environmental* services. We're tending now to move back to the earlier language of 'the benefits people get from nature'. What is quite remarkable is in some of the conventions, you have the same countries, the same ministries, sometimes even the same people, taking quite different stances in different convention and processes. In the most recent CBD cycle, we have been working very hard to get some understanding into place amongst the CBD community that it's not just that you need water to maintain ecosystems but also the systems are providing you with your water and natural infrastructure. You start using language like 'natural infrastructure', 'water security', even 'ecosystems of water', rather than 'water for ecosystems', and they can't see the difference between the two and block it.

INGO official 3 outlined the difficulty in applying such a utilitarian concept within environmental institutions:

> I admit to not liking the phrase 'biodiversity conventions'. I think it's a hindrance and it is incorrect. If you look at actually what the text of these conventions cites, these are 'sustainable use' conventions. Ramsar [wetlands Convention] has *always* been about sustainable use. Many of our focal points still don't get that or are unwilling to recognise it because they're comfortable in their own nature-conservation protected areas, agencies and departments and don't understand particularly, and don't like going out to engage other sectors. Although we have a significant suite of cross-sectoral guidance of the issues, designed to help our people communicate and engage with those other sectors of government and society who are driving change, they [do not] use it. Amongst the least used of the Ramsar guidance that has been adopted has been water resource management. They love designating Ramsar sites. But in terms of utilizing cross-sectoral guidance or guidance on issues that are the major drivers of loss and deterioration of wetlands, then they don't use Ramsar guidance.

> The real dilemma is that, of course, if you have overpopulation that needs to survive tomorrow and resources are scarce, and then the decision will be made to feed that population. And what we say again with MEA is very clear on this: you can manage systems and sectors to get a reasonably good trade-off. Look at the Millennium Development Goals on poverty, on health, on sanitation, or whatever. With a bit of trade-off, you can maintain the systems to deliver those services for people, and deliver them more sustainably for a longer term.

Applying the concept, INGO official 3 added:

> The ecosystem approach or an ecosystem-based approach, landscape scale planning and management, not sectoral planning and management – most decision-making is still made within sectors. It's a hard one to do particularly when you have long-established, well-embedded governance, or legal frameworks and so on – breaking those into a more coherent trade-off approach, politically and practically, is incredibly hard because you basically, say with water governance, the more strongly and deeply embedded existing water governance mechanisms the legislation is, the harder it is to respond to the change. You are constrained to actually move with what you know you need to do because of existing governance and embedded governance structures.

EU national official 4 saw ecosystem services providing a framework for adding up environmental income streams:

> It's a challenge but it does not necessarily stand from or take place within the context of the international conventions. Of course, it stands from the international conventions and the discussions going on but I must say, we decided to back off and then let them do their job and we'll do ours.

PAYMENTS FOR ECOSYSTEM SERVICES

The instruments that are most often mentioned in the discussion of market-based instruments for ES are PES schemes. Wunder (2005: 3) defines payments for ES as voluntary, conditional transactions between at least one buyer and one seller for a well-defined environmental service. These transactions are based on economic and/or financial mechanisms that enable producers to give up practices harmful to ecosystems and/or adopt practices that favour the maintenance or supply of ES. Such payments can take the form of compensating communities for stopping poaching, compensating farmers for stopping pollution or incentives for practising extensive grazing among others. PES can also be viewed as a market-based approach to ecosystem conservation and management, which attaches an economic value to the provision of ES and aims to change incentives for land use in order to maintain or restore natural ecosystems so that they continue to provide the desired environmental service(s) (WWF 2006: 2).

In comparison to other environmental conservation instruments, PES schemes have particular economic features (Wunder 2005: 6), which can be considered innovative. They have the advantages of a contractual relationship between one or more beneficiaries and one or more suppliers/producers, especially when it is a direct, bilateral relationship (no dispersal of resources, application of measures suitable for the locality, involvement and responsibility of the people concerned, etc.). PES are designed as 'transactions', which can be sensitive towards the dynamics of local development, but in the end the primary intention is to sell and buy a service to achieve more rational, environmentally friendly ecosystem use (Wunder 2005: 6). In this sense, PES have the potential to make protecting the environment become a lucrative activity for local communities. Proponents of PES argue that these schemes will foster resource conservation as long as environmental service users are prepared to pay adequate compensation to secure services, and environmental service providers are incentivised to continue generating these services in return for compensation, rather than pursuing other income-generating activities that might degrade them (e.g. FAO 2011: 143–7, Pagiola et al. 2005a: 238). In this way, PES schemes seek to create market mechanisms to enable bargaining and transactions between environmental service users and providers that are in both parties' interests: in other words, internalising what would otherwise be an externality (Pagiola 2008: 14).

Muradian et al. (2010) distinguish three main criteria for market mechanisms, which are voluntariness, a high commodification and a high conditionality. Because PES is voluntary, it should lead to more effective action. A PES scheme should commit the parties to an explicit contractual relationship, for a specific purpose and for precise results. A more sustainable ecosystem use should be easier to achieve this way than with traditional command-and-control approaches such as imposing regulations or polluter-pays taxes. Conditionality – the business-like principle only to pay if the service is actually delivered – is viewed as the most innovative feature of PES vis-à-vis traditional conservation tools (Muradian et al. 2010: 1206). In the process of commodification, i.e. the transformation of goods or services into commodities, four stages can be distinguished: economic framing, monetisation, appropriation and commercialisation (Gómez-Baggethun and Ruiz-Perez 2011: 8). In the economic framing stage usually a simplification takes place, as only those aspects of ecosystems are selected which can be commercialised. Therefore, the spotlight is often put on regulation services (carbon, watershed, biodiversity or habitat) and recreational services (ecotourism). They represent fictitious commodities that have no tangible reality apart from the prospect of their potential for market transactions (Boisvert et al. 2013: 1126).

The next stage is valuation of the ES, which, as valuation of the environment in general, has been widely discussed in the economic literature. A study on The Economics of Ecosystems and Biodiversity

(TEEB) was a major step in the institutionalisation of ES monetary valuation (TEEB 2010). As an international initiative to highlight the global economic benefits of biodiversity, its objective was to draw together expertise from the fields of science, economics and policy to show how economic concepts and tools can help equip society with the means to incorporate the values of nature into decision-making at all levels (TEEB 2010: 3). The TEEB study revived criticism. Rather than a simple measure of ES, critics saw TEEB's aim in bringing investors and (the conservation of) nature closer together so that the former can see the latter as a legitimate target for the deployment of business acumen (Arsel and Büscher 2012: 57). MacDonald and Corson (2012: 180) conclude that the TEEB study underpins a larger political project that aligns capitalism with a new kind of ecological modernisation in which 'the market' and market devices serve as key mechanisms in practical efforts to conform the real and the virtual. Far from being a simple measure of ecosystem services, the critics see the monetary expression of ES values as a prelude to their appropriation, which in turn leads to their commercialisation as the final stage of commodification (Boisvert et al. 2013: 1126).

There is still some time before this description is realised, however. European Union national official 5 saw 'the importance of the TEEB study' was that it had in fact demonstrated that commercialising biodiversity was currently 'an economic failure'. To make it successful would 'take ten years or something like that, and practical proof'. INGO official 2 agreed, stressing that the work around TEEB was 'extremely important', and it needed 'to continue and get greater visibility'. Scholars are far more critical and question the viability of PES in its current form entirely. McAfee traces the evolution of PES from REDD+ and ultimately the CDM. She argues that neither of these mechanisms have demonstrated their effectiveness to date, and are based on the false premise that these mechanisms truly delivered emissions reductions, that would not otherwise have occurred (McAfee 2012: 112). She interprets these mechanisms as having a restricted understanding of economic value, based entirely on market efficiency (ibid.: 125). She concludes that 'genuinely sustainable development' needs to arise instead 'from recognition of the full, multiple, present and future values of ecosystems to local and national populations as well as to wider humanity' (ibid: 126).

Sources and Means of Delivery of Finance

There are some case studies on payments for environmental services. For example, Engel et al. (2008: 663) analysed some PES in both developing and developed countries in 2005. They suggested that PES programmes can also be seen as an environmental subsidy (to ES providers), combined in some cases with a user fee (on ES users), and warned that they may be misused for protectionist purposes and thus result in a potential source of inefficiency of outcomes for environmental subsidies. To find out the misuse of resources, the study included a questionnaire on accounting and leakages, and identified inefficiencies in resource use in many case studies.

A major challenge in PES is the land tenure system, which has been identified as a huge obstacle to implementation. In distributing benefits to the real poor, it is essential to declare the landowner and the value of alternative benefits. However, it is an injustice not to consider the poverty of PES non-participating poor (Pagiola et al. 2005b: 238). According to Pirard (2011: 382), 'if one wishes to involve substantially the poorest people of the targeted sites, then it seems necessary to provide upfront payments in order to cover the initial investment costs' (Pagiola et al. 2005b: 250). These upfront payments help in biodiversity conservation, and downstream service users are more likely to be better off.

Another problem in delivery of finance is transaction costs, which often create obstacles to participation of poor people because working with many small, dispersed farmers imposes high transaction costs on all concerned (Engel et al. 2008). However, Pagiola et al. (2005b: 238) argue that market-based PES has lowered the cost of benefit distribution in Latin America. High transaction costs could be avoided by differentiating the payment systems for different ecological services. The best example of this is in Costa Rica where Engel et al. (2008) experienced a need to be flexible and to adapt to lessons learnt and to changing circumstances. Another example of efficient distribution of benefits PES is in Colombia where this is not only paying opportunity cost but also lifting the economic status of poor people (Tacconi et al. 2010: 8). In the Amazon region of Brazil, there are financial rewards for smallholders for developing and implementing long-term sustainable land management practices. However, the misuse of PES benefits with excessive allocation to high political profile stakeholders, for example in the fire-bonus scheme of Philippines (Tacconi et al. 2010: 11), avoids the rules and regulations in order to pay to the sellers.

There are some empirical studies in biodiversity policy instruments. Miteva and Pattanayak (2012: 70) have reviewed a number of publications, making a comparison between those with and those without implications of conservation policies. They found that PES is benefitted by decentralisation and that protected areas could be owned by local stakeholders. Though it is most difficult to find a uniform conservation instrument in developing countries, the limited evidence suggests that protected areas cause modest reductions in deforestation, and thus affect the conservation of biodiversity (Miteva and Pattanayak 2012: 86). Therefore, it is difficult to finalise a single best instrument to be implemented in the developing countries. In this sense, a globally accepted set of guidelines is urgently required to implement PES agreements. With this motive, UNEP (2008: 2) developed some of the standard steps such as identifying ecosystem service prospects and potential buyers, assessing institutional and technical capacity, structuring agreements and implementing the agreements. Moreover, the guidelines preferred long-term incentive plans over short-term plans, as the latter result in unsustainability in forestry and farming practices, which draws down natural capital and limits options for future development.

A cost–benefit analysis will identify the cost of PES inaction as there are many examples of overlapping ecological functions and services (de Groot et al. 2002), leading to the possibilities of double-counting. Chiabai et al. (2011: 406) developed an evaluation framework, deriving a per hectare estimate by applying meta-analysis, value-transfer and scaling-up procedures, and depicted that North America, Europe, Japan and Korea, Australia and New Zealand and also some developing countries like China and other Asian countries will benefit from PES policy. Through this cost–benefit analysis an important figure was identified in 2050 world GDP, ranging from a benefit of +0.03 per cent to a loss of –0.13 per cent per year, the greatest negative impact being projected for Brazil, showing an annual loss of 2–6 per cent. This figure indicates that future research should go towards developing understandings about the use of renewable natural capital stocks in a sustainable way over the long term. The valuation of ecosystems and their services determines the amount of benefits to be delivered to the beneficiaries through these instruments. In this sense, according to Groot et al. (2012: 50), 'given that many of the positive externalities of ecosystems are lost or strongly reduced after land use conversion, better accounting for the public goods and services provided by ecosystems is crucial to improve decision making and institution for the biodiversity conservation and sustainable ecosystem management'. Therefore, it is essential to assess the ES, and to plan the mechanism of delivery of finance in order to achieve pro-poor growth in developing countries.

BIODIVERSITY OFFSET MECHANISMS

In discussions of market-based instruments for ES, the type of instrument most often cited after PES is 'biodiversity offsets'. These can be defined as 'measurable conservation outcomes resulting from actions designed to compensate for significant residual adverse biodiversity impacts arising from project development after appropriate prevention and mitigation measures have been taken' (Business and Biodiversity Offsets Programme (BBOP) 2009: 4). They are based on compensation schemes for impacts on – or the destruction of – endangered species' habitats. These two types of compensation and their corresponding institutional arrangements follow a more general approach to combatting ecosystem destruction, which is commonly called 'mitigation policies'. All policies include 'mitigation hierarchy', which means that compensation should only be a last resort for developers who plan a potentially environmentally destructive project. They first need to consider avoiding as far as possible any impact on sensitive ecosystems, for example by modifying the route or location of planned infrastructures. The impacts must then be mitigated by all technically usable means, to reduce the effect on the environment as much as possible. The residual damage must be offset. The goal of biodiversity offsets is to achieve no 'net loss' and preferably a 'net gain' of biodiversity on the ground with respect to species composition, habitat structure, ecosystem function and people's use and cultural values associated with biodiversity (BBOP 2009: 5).

Mitigation policies are usually provided for in the regulatory framework of a host of countries, particularly industrialised ones, but it has recently been rediscovered and reinterpreted. Notable examples are the 1973 Endangered Species Act and the Clean Water Act in the US, the 1976 *Loi relative à la protection de la nature* in France and the *Bundesnaturschutzgesetz* in Germany. Offsets are thus closely tied to regulations for authorising development projects, and cannot be implemented unless the developer has obtained a permit. While this would mean that offsets should be viewed as non-market-based instruments, since the late 1980s, with the introduction of environmental deregulation policies, and even more since the early 2000s, these compensation mechanisms have become increasingly market-based. This trend is clear in the US and Australia, where offset banks for damage to biodiversity were developed in the late 1990s in California and then expanded to all the US and, in 2006, in Australia (New South Wales). The schemes are usually called 'species banking', 'habitat banking', 'biodiversity banking' for impacts on habitats of endangered species and 'mitigation banking' for wetlands.

The purpose of these mechanisms is to pay compensation for impacts on ecosystems – wetland functions, habitats of endangered fauna and flora – but they do not work like PES systems. It is not the beneficiaries of the ecosystems who pay but those who destroy them. There are various forms in which the developers can make the compensation. They may undertake their own conservation or remediation project on the land they own or buy. They may call on a specialist supplier to carry out this work for them. The way the transaction is made can also vary: options include the operator making a direct payment of the sum agreed between the parties, or making an acquisition of credits equivalent to the damage attributed to the project. This latter possibility, also referred to as 'environmental credit exchange' was first developed for wetland compensation. The wetlands are considered in terms of a small number of functions so that they are comparable, and a common unit of measurement can be used to ensure that the area destroyed and the area to be restored or protected are ecologically equivalent (Robertson 2006: 368). For this to work, to develop credit exchange to ensure 'no net loss', ES had to be viewed in simplified, standardised terms, a first step towards their commodification (Robertson 2006: 368).

While the regulatory framework still strongly structures the definition and implementation of compensation and the mitigation hierarchy is not completely reversed, offset is considered more routinely from the start of a project, along with other measures. However, trading has not really expanded to the rest of the world. One of the few exceptions is Germany, where *Ökokonten* ('eco-accounts') have been set up at the municipal level in various states, but have also faced considerable legal challenges (Busse et al. 2013).

Researchers have investigated both the theoretical and practical aspects of implementing biodiversity offset schemes. A key theoretical issue is the definition and measurement of biodiversity, as there is no universal or unambiguous definition. While differing legislation has in common the notion of no net loss, the ability to measure losses and gains, and the concept of substitution or replacement to compensate for impacts on biodiversity caused by humans, biodiversity does not have a currency to measure it by. There is consequently a need to define concepts such as 'no net loss' and 'equivalence' – and to address issues of longevity, time lag, reversibility, uncertainty and thresholds. The major practical issues with offset projects meeting biodiversity objectives are those of ensuring compliance, effective monitoring and the results of conceptual flaws in the actual process. It is difficult to be specific about the actual outcomes of offset programmes worldwide due to lack of useful data. Although this is part of a larger general problem of the failure to evaluate conservation projects adequately, it is also an indication of both theoretical problems (such as the lack of currency to measure with) and practical concerns such as insufficient monitoring. As projects come on board in developing countries, these problems are likely to be compounded. Ways will need to be found to deal with the lack of (or differing) perspectives on environmental legislation, capability and resources for evaluation and enforcement (Bull et al. 2013: 369–77). Despite the difficulties, advantages to developing nations include 'promoting stakeholder engagement in conservation, leveraging funding to meet strategic conservation objectives and catalysing improvements in environmental legislation' (ibid.: 377).

But there are no fewer problems with compliance and uncertainty in developed countries. Studies have shown that only 30 per cent of US wetland banking schemes met all the criteria, and 74 per cent had no net loss. When it came to monitoring ecological outcomes, none of California's created wetlands were functionally successful. With Canada's fish habitat compensation only 12–13 per cent of offsets were implemented appropriately (Bull et al. 2013: 375). Monitoring was also a problem for preservation of Canada's fish habitat (Quigley and Harper 2006). Through its Fisheries Act, and Policy for the Management of Fish Habitat, Canada has a goal to have 'no net loss of the productive capacity of fish habitats' (Quigley and Harper 2006: 336). Legally binding post-construction monitoring was carried out less than 43 per cent of the time, and the monitoring that was done was found to be superficial, at times consisting of nothing more than a photograph and reports; the compensation was completed with no measurable outcomes. Government habitat management staff allocated little time to compliance monitoring (1.7 per cent of their workload). In addition to not complying with habitat requirements there were a large number of Fisheries Act violations. Despite the high amounts of non-compliance with habitat requirements, only 3 proponents out of 2529 authorisations had been charged in the five years leading up to the study. In Canada, there was clearly a need for institutional change if implementation was to lead to achievement of the no-net-loss goal, with a focus on improved monitoring and enforcement, along with compensation ratios. This was especially relevant, as the introduction of the policy regarding habitat had led to a proliferation of authorisations, with parties relying on this process as a key conservation measure for fish habitat (ibid.: 337–48).

In Australia a Senate inquiry was launched in 2014 to investigate offsetting with regard to five projects: the Abbot Point Coal Terminal; Waratah Coal's Galilee Coal Project; the Jundakot Airport in Perth; and Maules Creek coal mine in New South Wales. In the case of Maules Creek, the mining company Whitehaven Coal used offsets intended to protect the critically endangered white box gum, which now only exists in 0.1 per cent of its original range. According to ecologists, the offset properties do not contain white box, but are instead predominantly stringy bark. They have noted that up to 95 per cent of the company's mapping was wrong. Neither the federal nor state governments conducted on-ground surveys before granting approval (Australian Broadcasting Corporation (ABC) 2014). In the Australian Capital Territory (ACT) the government used already existing nature reserves (whose biodiversity had been enhanced through the work of volunteers) to offset the development of new suburbs. This contravened the principle that offsets must add to biodiversity in ways that would not have occurred otherwise. In the case of the ACT, most of the new urban development was removing nationally threatened box gum woodlands, native grasslands and threatened species such as the striped legless lizard (Gibbons and Zeil 2014).

In a study of Latin American countries, researchers found that while all the surveyed countries had environmental assessment laws and regulations, only Brazil, Colombia, Mexico and Peru required the implementation of offsets. They also found that the choice of sites should be part of an exercise in landscape ecology to maintain sight of overarching conservation objectives. This use of landscape ecology occurred in Colombia and Peru, but not other Latin American countries. When it came to monitoring, while adequate monitoring is needed for adaptive management and to increase transparency, there was a lack of post-implementation monitoring, and where monitoring did occur it tended to be short term, and therefore unable to detect offset implementation problems (Villarroya et al. 2014).

Sources and Means of Delivery of Finance

There is an ongoing debate about the consistency in biodiversity conservation when considering approaches, especially effective monitoring (Bull et al. 2013: 369). Some techniques, such as active restoration policy preferred by Curran et al. (2014: 617), are important to consider as an approach that helps to deliver the finance in a more efficient way. There are some studies on BOM: for example, Quintero and Mathur (2011) suggested that in Brazil, infrastructure projects are more amenable to financial support in order to compensate for net loss. The compensation amount could depend on the intensity of undesirable effects encountered. This directly demands some extra funds to overcome an already overstrained loss in the biodiversity. Therefore, it can be concluded from this study that even a fraction of the revenues generated by large infrastructure projects may greatly exceed the current annual operating budgets for conservation in most developing countries.

A no-net-loss policy is important in compensating for biodiversity loss. In this case, a benchmark is created to provide a measure to compare targets. This means that in order to help deliver a no net loss through biodiversity offsets, any biodiversity gains must be comparable to losses in addition to conservation gains that may have occurred in the absence of the offset, and be lasting and protected from risk of failure (Gardner et al. 2013: 1254). Such a framework can strengthen the potential for offsets to provide an ecologically defensible mechanism that can help reconcile conservation and development. Moreover, 'there is also a need for greater recognition that in some situations, and despite every attempt at mitigation, no net loss of biodiversity cannot be guaranteed; that is, through development by governments where there is a clear and overriding public interest in the project' (Gardner et al. 2013: 1263).

In this sense, a complete guideline for the development of biodiversity offsets policy is required. Biodiversity offsets hold much promise for helping to expand and strengthen the protected area networks in the developing world. To fulfil this promise, governments need to design and implement policies that direct compensation from development projects to temporarily fill the most important protected area funding gaps (Pilgrim and Bennun 2014). In this regard, conservation planners can assist governments and companies by refining methods for ensuring expansion potential, comparability and longevity of offsets in protected areas, and thus contributing to science-based plans and policy guiding offset investment. Furthermore, civil society can play an important role while implementing the guidelines particularly in ensuring that governments adopt protected area responsibilities. Therefore, in line with increasing revenues, and to ensure sound governance of offset funding schemes, offsets can contribute to saving, rather than sinking, protected areas (Pilgrim and Bennun 2014).

To have a complete biodiversity offsets mechanism, comparisons of the policy implementation need to be analysed. McKenney and Kiesecker (2010: 165) find some commonalities in substantial policies that may serve as a sound basis for the future development of biodiversity offsets policy. The comparison also identifies issues requiring further policy guidance, including how best to ensure conformity with the mitigation hierarchy; identifying the most environmentally preferable offsets within a landscape context; and determining appropriate mitigation replacement ratios. In this regard, McKenney and Kiesecker (2010: 175) recommend an accounting framework that incorporates expansion potential, probability of success and time to conservation maturity.

In this sense, quantification of net value of loss or benefit is important. Overton et al. (2013) proposed an approach of net present biodiversity value (NPBV) to assess the benefits that could overcome the net loss. This approach claims that 'a particular advantage of the NPBV framework is that it provides a general approach for the design of out-of-kind offsets, and the prospect of achieving better biodiversity outcomes by allowing the relative amounts of different biodiversity to change across the conservation landscape'. Therefore, this approach should be studied using simulated biodiversity exchanges and also trialled in the field to better understand the expected impacts on biodiversity of implementing such an approach (Overton et al. 2013: 109).

The above discussion clearly points out an immediate need for appropriate biodiversity value mechanism before proceeding to compensation. Moreover, the offsets are inadequate to achieve no net loss of biodiversity alone (Gardner et al. 2013). Therefore, the development of a mechanism assessing what extra benefit should be given to protect biodiversity to avoid net loss condition is urgently required. In this sense, delivery of finance remains a key component in the field of biodiversity conservation. A solid foundation for restoration offsets to tackle the situation can increase the efficiency of such mechanisms.

NORTH/SOUTH RELATIONS AND STATE AND NON-STATE ACTORS

Under the CBD, and as a result of the inherent issues contained within each of the topics for which the working groups were organised, both WGPA and WG8(j) have been marked by considerable participation of Indigenous peoples along with environmental and research-based (scientific) non-governmental organisations. In the case of protected areas, concerns quickly arose related to the tension between biodiversity preservation and Indigenous people's access to traditional resources. For the WG8(j), which makes specific reference to Indigenous and local communities, traditional ecological knowledge (TEK) was implicated. Article 8(j) reads as follows:

Each Contracting Party shall, as far as possible and as appropriate:

(j) Subject to its national legislation, respect, preserve and maintain knowledge, innovations and practices of indigenous and local communities embodying traditional lifestyles relevant for the conservation and sustainable use of biological diversity and promote their wider application with the approval and involvement of the holders of such knowledge, innovations and practices and encourage the equitable sharing of the benefits arising from the utilization of such knowledge, innovations and practices. (CBD Decision X/1 2011)

As the work of the WG8(j) developed, it became increasingly clear that there was much to contribute to the negotiations surrounding Access and Benefit Sharing (ABS), which ultimately culminated in the Nagoya Protocol on Access and Benefit Sharing (the Nagoya Protocol), as was mentioned above. Negotiations surrounding ABS were contentious for many stakeholders, in part due to concerns about intellectual property; concerns that arose both from government participants as well as non-governmental stakeholders (Suiseeya 2014).

Transformations in the economies of particular nation states (such as the BRIC countries) have resulted in a variety of different interests emanating from countries that were defined at Rio as being part of the global South. Brazil's interest in the negotiations related to biotechnology at CBD COP10 in Nagoya, for example, were highly related to soybean production (along with other biofuels and agricultural products) that comprises a significant contribution to Brazil's growing economy. The interests that were encapsulated in Brazil's contributions to the COP10 and COP11 negotiations related to biotechnology stood in stark contrast to the position taken by governments such as the Philippines, who argued to uphold the 'precautionary principle' elements enshrined in the CBD, as those pertain to biotechnology (Aksoy 2014, Brody 2010).

NGOs have expressed concern that offsets may not lead to preservation of biodiversity, but in fact create the opposite. In the UK, rather than using a 'mitigation hierarchy' when impacts cannot be avoided or reduced, offsets are being used as a way to fast-track development applications through planning systems with no attempt to utilise avoidance or mitigation. In France offsets have been used to re-invigorate an environmentally damaging proposal for an airport. In short, offsets can be a key factor in a development gaining approval to go ahead even when there are alternative mitigation options (FERN 2014: 5–6).

Despite such concerns, offset legislation has been developed in 45 countries, and is under development in another 27. This has led researchers to recommend the creation of better governance systems and to make use of the practical science that already exists to meet challenges faced in implementing such schemes (Bull et al. 2013: 369).

QUALITY OF GOVERNANCE – PES

Table 4.1   PES – quality of governance by region (February 2015)

Principle	1. Meaningful participation Maximum score: 25 Minimum: 5							
Criterion	1. Interest representation Maximum score: 15 Minimum: 3				2. Organisational responsibility Maximum score: 10 Minimum: 2			Principle Score
Indicator	**Inclusiveness**	**Equality**	**Resources**	Criterion Score	**Accountability**	**Transparency**	Criterion Score	
North (34)	3.7	3.0	1.7	8.3	2.6	2.7	5.4	13.6
South (47)	3.1	3.1	2.5	8.6	3.3	3.2	6.4	15.0
Principle	2. Productive deliberation Maximum score: 30 Minimum: 6							
Criterion	3. Decision-making Maximum score: 15 Minimum: 3				4. Implementation Maximum score: 15 Minimum: 3			Principle Score
Indicator	**Democracy**	**Agreement**	**Dispute settlement**	Criterion Score	**Behavioural change**	**Problem-solving**	**Durability**	Criterion Score
North	2.8	2.5	2.7	8.0	3.1	3.1	3.0	9.2	17.2
South	3.0	3.1	3.1	9.2	3.4	3.1	3.3	9.9	19.1
Total (out of 55)								
North				30.8				
South				34.1				

Note: Light grey represents the highest scoring indicator by region; dark grey the lowest; numbers in **bold** are below the threshold value of 50 per cent.

Table 4.2 PES – quality of governance by sector (February 2015)

Principle	1. Meaningful participation Maximum score: 25 Minimum: 5							
Criterion	1. Interest representation Maximum score: 15 Minimum: 3				2. Organisational responsibility Maximum score: 10 Minimum: 2			Principle Score
Indicator	**Inclusiveness**	**Equality**	**Resources**	Criterion Score	**Accountability**	**Transparency**	Criterion Score	
Environment	3.6	2.8	2.2	8.6	2.8	2.9	5.7	14.3
Social	3.0	2.8	2.0	7.8	2.0	1.5	3.5	11.3
Economic	4.0	3.0	1.0	8.0	3.3	3.7	7.0	15.0
Government	4.1	3.4	2.3	9.8	3.5	3.4	6.9	16.7
Academic	3.8	3.2	2.1	9.1	3.2	3.1	6.3	15.4
Other	3.4	2.6	2.3	8.3	2.5	2.3	4.8	13.1
Principle	2. Productive deliberation Maximum score: 30 Minimum: 6							
Criterion	3. Decision-making Maximum score: 15 Minimum: 3				4. Implementation Maximum score: 15 Minimum: 3			Principle Score
Indicator	**Democracy**	**Agreement**	**Dispute settlement**	Criterion Score	**Behavioural change**	**Problem-solving**	**Durability**	Criterion Score
Environment	2.9	2.8	2.9	8.6	3.5	3.0	3.2	9.7	18.3
Social	1.5	1.8	2.0	5.3	3.0	3.0	3.0	9.0	14.3
Economic	2.7	3.0	3.0	8.7	3.3	3.3	3.7	10.3	19.0
Government	3.2	3.5	3.3	10.0	3.2	3.0	3.3	9.5	19.5
Academic	3.2	3.0	3.0	9.2	3.3	3.3	3.2	9.8	19.0
Other	2.3	2.5	2.0	6.8	2.5	2.3	2.0	6.8	13.6

Total (out of 55)	
Environment	32.6
Social	25.6
Economic	34.0
Government	36.2
Academic	34.4
Other	26.7

Note: Light grey represents the highest scoring indicator by sector; dark grey the lowest; numbers in **bold** are below the threshold value of 50 per cent.

Commentary on the Results

Eighty-one respondents answered in relation to PES, with the preponderance from the South. There was some discrepancy in the results between regions. The South awarded a relatively high 'pass' compared to a more modest 'satisfactory' result from the North. These results were repeated at the principle and criterion levels. Resources was the lowest scoring indicator for both regions: in the case of the North it was an outright 'fail' (and the lowest indicator overall); for the South, the indicator just reached the threshold 'pass' level of 50 per cent. The highest scoring indicator was inclusiveness (North), followed by behaviour change (South). Ratings from the North varied more than those from the South (ranging between 1.7 and 3.7 *cf.* 2.5 and 3.3).

On a sectoral basis, government provided the highest score, followed by academic, economic and environment. 'Other' and the social sector awarded PES a 'fail', but in the case of 'other' this was almost a 'pass'. These results were reflected at the principle and criterion levels, with some exceptions. At the criterion level for example, 'other' gave PES a 'fail' for organisational responsibility, decision-making and implementation, but a 'pass' for interest representation. Inclusiveness was universally the highest indicator across all sectors, with the highest overall rating from government; the social sector awarded the same rating (3.0) to behaviour change, problem-solving and durability. Resources was the lowest scoring indicator for environment, economic, government and academic respondents, with a 'fail' rating from all sectors. 'Other' selected durability as the lowest indicator; for the social respondents, transparency and democracy.

Commentary from Survey Respondents

Survey respondents made a number of observations regarding PES. Two commented on the degree to which PES could be seen as being inclusive. One Southern academic believed that PES still needed to 'demonstrate its contribution to the rural poor' as it 'promises much more than it delivers'. Another Southern environmental respondent believed that PES was inclusive because it was largely a national-level initiative, generally executed at the 'local level'. However, they thought there were 'several lacunae' that needed to be addressed to make PES 'more inclusive from a pro-poor, gender and Indigenous people's rights perspective'. One of the 'other' Northern respondents commenting on equality suggested that 'the problem is one of design', which had rendered some PES projects 'unsustainable'. This was because:

The logical connection of design to objective is at best slim. The effort to be even-handed turns into an effort to find a 'patch' that eliminates some discriminatory impact. But these patches are even less logical than the original design, and they sometimes actually work against the objective.

Another Northern academic thought that issues of inequality could be addressed. They were of the opinion that PES stood a 'strong chance' of treating 'all participants equally, if contracts are under fair conditions'. So too did another Southern environmental sector respondent. PES had the potential to 'address the concerns of participants equally', because it was designed at the local and national level to facilitate 'interaction between service providers and recipients'. However, 'elites among the service providers' were able to 'dominate the interest and concerns of poor, women and resource-dependent groups'.

One Southern academic commented on the quality of decision-making within PES projects. Agreements that were made 'usually' resulted in 'concrete actions', but they added that 'no mechanisms are in place to actually measure how much additional environmental services' were generated. They were also of the view that PES had 'clearer mechanisms for dispute settlement' than some other initiatives, because procedures were specified 'usually within a national legal framework, or through contractual arrangements'.

Two respondents provided positive assessments of the implementation capacity of PES. One Southern environmental respondent thought that both 'local or national level PES can change behaviour' because there was a 'high chance' that the payments 'for the contribution of conservation of ecosystem services' would reach project participants. Echoing previous views regarding equality, one Northern academic thought that PES worked best if it was based on 'independent contracts where participants have a free decision, and all partners really benefit from investments in ecological, social and economic improvements'. Another Southern environmental respondent believed that 'PES could be long lasting if the pricing is good'.

QUALITY OF GOVERNANCE – BOM

Table 4.3   BOM – quality of governance by region (February 2015)

Principle	1. Meaningful participation Maximum score: 25 Minimum: 5							
Criterion	1. Interest representation Maximum score: 15 Minimum: 3				2. Organisational responsibility Maximum score: 10 Minimum: 2			Principle Score
Indicator	**Inclusiveness**	**Equality**	**Resources**	Criterion Score	**Accountability**	**Transparency**	Criterion Score	
North (35)	3.2	2.8	1.5	7.5	**2.4**	2.5	4.9	12.5
South (51)	3.0	3.0	2.4	8.5	3.1	3.0	6.1	14.6
Principle	2. Productive deliberation Maximum score: 30 Minimum: 6							
Criterion	3. Decision-making Maximum score: 15 Minimum: 3				4. Implementation Maximum score: 15 Minimum: 3			Principle Score
Indicator	Democracy	Agreement	**Dispute settlement**	Criterion Score	**Behavioural change**	**Problem-solving**	**Durability**	Criterion Score	
North	2.6	**2.4**	**2.4**	**7.4**	2.7	2.6	2.7	8.0	15.3
South	2.9	3.0	2.9	8.7	3.1	3.0	3.1	9.2	17.9
Total (out of 55)								
North				27.8				
South				32.5				

Note: Light grey represents the highest scoring indicator by region; dark grey the lowest; numbers in **bold** are below the threshold value of 50 per cent.

Table 4.4   BOM – quality of governance by sector (February 2015)

Principle	1. Meaningful participation Maximum score: 25 Minimum: 5							
Criterion	1. Interest representation Maximum score: 15 Minimum: 3				2. Organisational responsibility Maximum score: 10 Minimum: 2			Principle Score
Indicator	Inclusiveness	Equality	Resources	Criterion Score	Accountability	Transparency	Criterion Score	
Environment	3.0	2.9	2.2	8.1	2.7	2.8	5.5	13.6
Social	2.3	2.0	1.5	5.8	1.8	1.3	3.1	**8.9**
Economic	3.3	3.3	1.3	7.9	3.0	3.7	6.7	14.6
Government	3.4	3.3	2.0	8.7	3.2	3.2	6.4	15.1
Academic	3.3	3.0	2.0	8.3	2.9	2.8	5.7	14.0
Other	3.2	2.8	2.3	8.3	2.5	2.3	4.8	13.1

Principle	2. Productive deliberation Maximum score: 30 Minimum: 6							
Criterion	3. Decision-making Maximum score: 15 Minimum: 3				4. Implementation Maximum score: 15 Minimum: 3			Principle Score
Indicator	Democracy	Agreement	Dispute settlement	Criterion Score	Behavioural change	Problem solving	Durability	Criterion Score	
Environment	2.6	2.7	2.7	8.0	3.1	2.7	3.0	8.8	16.8
Social	1.5	1.5	1.8	4.8	2.5	2.0	2.3	6.8	**11.6**
Economic	2.7	3.3	3.0	9.0	3.3	3.3	2.7	9.3	18.3
Government	3.2	3.2	3.1	9.5	3.2	3.1	3.0	9.3	18.8
Academic	3.0	2.7	2.7	8.4	2.8	2.9	3.1	8.8	17.2
Other	2.3	2.7	2.0	7.0	2.3	2.3	2.0	6.6	13.6

Total (out of 55)	
Environment	30.4
Social	**20.5**
Economic	32.9
Government	33.9
Academic	31.2
Other	26.7

Note: Light grey represents the highest scoring indicator by sector; dark grey the lowest; numbers in **bold** are below the threshold value of 50 per cent.

Commentary on Results

Although 86 respondents answered questions regarding BOM, there was a considerable difference in the numbers between South and North (51 *cf.* 35). The mechanism received only a very low 'pass' from Northern respondents, compared to a moderate 'pass' from the South. These results were reflected at the principle, criterion and indicator levels for the North: the mechanism received only a threshold 'pass' for participation, and failed the criteria of organisational responsibility and dispute settlement as well as several indicators (resources, accountability, agreement and dispute settlement). Resources was the weakest indicator, receiving a 'fail' from both North (1.5) and South (2.4) – the only indicator to be 'failed' by the South. Inclusiveness was the highest rated indicator overall, awarded by the North; for the South it was durability. The variability in ratings for the North was greater than the South (1.5–3.2 *cf.* 2.4–3.1).

Government provided the highest score overall, followed by academics, and the economic and environmental sectors. Both social and 'other' respondents gave a 'fail' score. For the social respondents, this 'fail' was for both of the principles, three of the criteria (organisational responsibility, decision-making and implementation, but not interest representation) and all of the indicators (with the exception of behavioural change). For 'other' respondents, BOM 'failed' the principle of deliberation and the same criteria as the social sector, as well as several indicators. Resources was the weakest performing indicator. It was 'failed' by all respondents and was the lowest rated indicator for four sectors (environment, government, academic and economic). The social sector gave its lowest rating to transparency. 'Other' gave their lowest ratings to both dispute settlement and durability. Inclusiveness received the highest rating from three sectors (government, academic and other). Environmental and social respondents selected behavioural change. The highest rating awarded overall was for transparency (3.7), by the economic sector.

Commentary from Survey Respondents

One developing country government respondent from Africa provided a detailed governance analysis of their country's approach to managing offsets. These were nested within a broader national biodiversity initiative. The respondent began by explaining that the 'programme aims to establish sustainable land management in productive landscapes and expand the protected areas estate on private land'. Although the intention of the programme 'was not to establish a mechanism for offsets, the structure of the programme lends itself to this, as the requirements of the programme ensures that the offset happens the way it should'. They explained further that the broader programme:

> was designed to give a level of security to private protected areas that are equal to that of government-owned and managed protected areas, both in terms of quality and time-span. This applies to areas secured in the offset process, as well as the other private protected areas.

They continued by noting that 'in practice offsets are a minefield with different requirements for biodiversity offsets, wetland offsets and forest offsets'. When the programme came to dealing with offsets, it tried to standardise 'offset arrangements'. But what was 'problematic' was that due to the 'resource constraints that the programme operates under', it was 'difficult to address everything it needs to'. They felt that 'standards should be applied across the board, if not, it could be contested', but this has not yet happened.

The respondent thought that the accountability of the programme was high, and pointed to the fact that there was an 'annual evaluation of the implementation of the approved management plan' which was undertaken by the provincial-level programme implementer. Interestingly, the broader initiative was 'initiated through the EIA [environmental impact assessment] process', and if it was determined that an offset was required, 'both the declaration process and the management plan needs to be publicly consulted'. They thought the process was very highly transparent, and pointed to the fact that 'NGOs that have a particular interest in the process are sometimes more closely involved, particularly in the biodiversity assessment and the development of the management plan'.

In relation to decision-making, the respondent was of the view that the democratic aspects of the programme were also very high. This was because both the EIA legislation and national protected areas laws had 'very strict requirements for public participation'. They noted that the 'programme is too young to really evaluate the strength of the agreements', but they were of the view that it had 'by far the strictest agreements in the country in terms of the establishment of private protected areas'. The programme was also 'supported by legally binding contracts and title deed restrictions'. Only time would tell 'the true effectiveness'. Concerning dispute settlement, the programme was too new for the respondent to comment definitively, but they did observe that implementing offsets was an 'unknown requirement, and there is a huge amount of opposition to establishing the mechanism, particularly from the developers'. But it was part of the EIA process that if an offset was required, this 'informs developers' participation'. Once the details for a particular site were 'established, and the contracts and management plan developed, what is in there will guide dispute resolution'. The respondent also added that they would 'expect very little dispute'.

The respondent also offered some detailed perspectives on implementation of the programme, which, in the case of offsets, was still 'in the initial stages', and offsets were not at a level to 'contribute significantly to the programme yet, but once established should form a bigger part'. They explained in some detail the process of implementing the offset. The developer was required 'to acquire the land, develop a management plan that needs to be approved by the conservation author-ity, declare the Nature Reserve and manage it'. The programme itself also participated 'in the assessment process of the proposed site, the develop-ment of the management plan' and made the declaration. Annual evalu-ations were then conducted in the context of the national protected areas legislation. 'If implemented correctly', the respondent believed that biodiversity offsets had:

> A huge potential to change behaviour in certain sectors: you can choose to develop in a critical biodiversity area, and offset, and be responsible for the offset financially, or move the development out of the CBA and not need to face an offset. Or choose a type of land use that does not require an offset. This is however not very effective with regards to industries such as coalmines. The coal beds are almost always associated with wetlands and water catchment areas, and very rarely occur in areas that are not critical for ecological infrastructure.

This person saw offsets as 'one of the few ways in which we can ensure that at least some of these ecosystems are permanently protected', but they were keen to stress that rehabilitation did not constitute an offset, 'as rehabilitation does not lead to anything near what a pristine ecosystem is. We see offsets as securing pristine ecosystems legally against transform-ation.' They also believed that 'if the offset is secured correctly' the durability of the programme would be very high. This was because 'the contract includes a power of attorney agreement that allows for the registration of a title deed restriction that is mostly valid in perpetuity'. There was also 'an income tax incentive coupled to the declaration of nature reserves' that was available to owners of offset sites. But if they withdrew 'from this agreement, apart from the legal implication of breaking an EIA requirement', they were also obliged to 'pay back the tax reduction'.

ANALYSIS AND CONCLUSIONS

Most PES schemes and BOMs, presented as examples of market-based instruments, are not truly market-based. To be market-based they would need to fulfil essential characteristics of an economic incentive. One is to provide a signal that will influence individual choices, in this case steering them towards sustainable management of ES. Another is that they would require the virtues of efficiency and effectiveness that standard economic analysis attributes to the market. However, most institutional arrangements that are typically considered as PES schemes or biodiversity offsets can be voluntary or mandatory, and influenced or controlled by the authorities to varying degrees, and take different forms. The only common factor of this wide range of diverse instruments can be seen in their contrasting features compared to the government command-and-control measures that many authors criticised for their supposed ineffectiveness during the 1980s.

The term 'market-based instruments' therefore stands for a new way of considering and grouping together existing environmental policy tools. The concept of PES and biodiversity offsets may even encompass instruments that until the 1980s were regarded as government intervention, including environmental taxes and subsidies. Rather than a completely new type of instrument, a market-based instrument reflects the fact that new institutional arrangements and aspirations have developed in relation to existing tools. In the case of market-based instruments for environmental service provision we can see two redefinitions: conventional policy instruments are modified in a way that they comprise, at least in formal terms, market transactions, and their goals (catchment protection, biodiversity conservation, carbon capture, etc.) are adapted to match the concept of ES.

BIBLIOGRAPHY

Aksoy, Z. 2014, 'Local–global linkages in environmental governance: The case of crop genetic resources', *Global Environmental Politics*, **14** (2) 26–44.
Andree, P. 2005, 'The Cartagena Protocol on biosafety and shifts in the discourse of precaution', *Global Environmental Politics*, **5** (4) 25–46.
Arsel, M. & Büscher, B. 2012, 'NatureTM Inc.: Changes and continuities in neoliberal conservation and market-based environmental policy', *Development and Change*, **43** (1) 53–78.
Australian Broadcasting Corporation (ABC) 2014, 'The trouble with offsets', *Background Briefing*. Viewed 16 May 2015, http://www.abc.net.au/radionational/programs/backgroundbriefing/2014-03-16/5312944.

BBOP 2009, *Business, biodiversity offsets and BBOP: An overview.* Washington, DC: Business and Biodiversity Offsets Programme. Viewed 10 May 2015, http://www.forest-trends.org/biodiversityoffsetprogram/guidelines/overview.pdf.

Boisvert, V., Méral, P. P. and Froger, G. 2013, 'Market-based instruments for ecosystem services: Institutional innovation or renovation?' *Society and Natural Resources: An International Journal*, **26** (10) 1122–36.

Brockington, D. 2011, 'Ecosystem services and fictitious commodities', *Environmental Conservation*, **38** (4) 367–9.

Brody, B. A. 2010, 'Intellectual property, state sovereignty, and biotechnology', *Kennedy Institute of Ethics Journal*, **20** (1) 51–73.

Bull, J. W., Suttle, K. B., Gordon, A., Singh, N. J. and Milner-Gulland, E. J. 2013, 'Biodiversity offsets in theory and practice', *Oryx*, **47** (3) 369.

Busse, J., Dirnberger, F., Pröbstl-Haider, U. and Schmid, W. 2013, *Die Umweltprüfung in der Gemeinde: mit Ökokonto, Umweltbericht, Artenschutzrecht, Energieplanung und Refinanzierung*, Munich: Hüthig Jehle Rehm Verlag.

CBD 2011, 'Decision X/1 Access to genetic resources and the fair and equitable sharing of benefits arising from their utilization', *Report of the Tenth Meeting of the Conference of the Parties to the Convention on Biological Diversity (UNEP/CBD/COP/10/27*, 20 January 2011) Annex.* Viewed 10 July 2015, https://www.cbd.int/decision/cop/default.shtml?id=12267.

Chiabai, A., Travisi, C. M., Markandya, A., Ding, H. and Nunes, P. A. L. D. 2011, 'Economic assessment of forest ecosystem services losses: cost of policy inaction', *Environmental & Resource Economics*, **50** (3) 405–45.

Convention on Biological Diversity 1992, 'Convention on biological diversity: Text and annexes'. Secretariat of the Convention on Biological Diversity and the United Nations Environment Programme. Viewed 10 July 2015, https://www.cbd.int/doc/legal/cbd-en.pdf.

Costanza, R., d'Arge, R., de Groot, R., Farber, S., Grasso, M., Hannon, B., Limburg, K., Naeem, S., O'Neill, R. V., Paruelo, J., Raskin, G. R., Sutton, P. and van der Belt, M. 1997, 'The value of the world's ecosystem services and natural capital', *Nature*, **387** (6630) 251–60.

Curran, M., Hellweg, S. and Beck, J. 2014, 'Is there any empirical support for biodiversity offset policy?', *Ecological Applications*, **24** (4) 617–32.

Daily, G. C. 1997, *Nature's services: Societal dependence on natural ecosystems*, Washington, DC: Island Press.

de Groot, R. S., Wilson, M. A. and Boumans, R. M. J. 2002, 'A typology for the classification, description and valuation of ecosystem functions, goods and services', *Ecological Economics*, **41** (3) 393–408.

Engel, S., Pagiola, S. and Wunder, S. 2008, 'Designing payments for environmental services in theory and practice: An overview of the issues', *Ecological Economics*, **65** (4) 663–74.

FAO 2011, *Payment for ecosystem services and food security*, Rome: FAO. Viewed 12 May 2015, http://www.fao.org/docrep/014/i2100e/i2100e.PDF.

FERN 2014, *Briefing note 3: Biodiversity offsetting in practice.* Viewed 17 May 2015, http://www.fern.org/sites/fern.org/files/Biodiversity3_EN.pdf.

Gardner, T. A., Hase, A., Brownlie, S., Ekstrom, J. M. M., Pilgrim, J. D., Savy, C. E., Stephens, R. T. T., Treweek, J. O., Ussher, G. T., Ward, G. and Ten

Kate, K. 2013, 'Biodiversity Offsets and the Challenge of Achieving No Net Loss', *Conservation Biology*, **27** (6) 1254–64.

Gehring, T. and Oberthur, S. 2006, 'Institutional interaction in global environmental governance: The case of the Cartagena protocol and the world trade organization', *Global Environmental Politics*, **6** (2) 1–31.

Gibbons, P. and Zeil, J. 2014, 'It's becoming harder to see the trees for the revenue', *The Age*. Viewed 16 May 2015, http://www.theage.com.au/comment/ its-becoming-harder-to-see-the-trees-for-the-revenue-20140128-31l2b.html.

Gómez-Baggethun, E. and Ruiz-Perez, M. 2011, 'Economic valuation and the commodification of ecosystem services', *Progress in Physical Geography*, **35** (5) 613–28.

Groot, R. S. d., Brander, L., Ploeg, S. v. d., Costanza, R., Bernard, F., Braat, L. C., Christie, M., Crossman, N., Ghermandi, A., Hein, L. G., Hussain, S., Kumar, P., McVittie, A., Portela, R., Rodriguez, L. C., Brink, P. t. and Beukering, P. J. H. v. 2012, 'Global estimates of the value of ecosystems and their services in monetary units', *Ecosystem Services*, **1** (1).

Harvey, D. 2005, *A brief history of neoliberalism*, New York: Oxford University Press.

Heal, G. 2000, 'Valuing ecosystem services', *Ecosystems*, **3** (2000) 24–30.

Herendeen, R. A. 1998, 'Monetary-costing environmental services: Nothing is lost, something is gained', *Ecology Economics*, **25** (1) 29–30.

Herrera Izaguirre, J. A. 2008, 'The 1992 United Nations Convention on Biological Diversity', *Boletín Mexicano de Derecho Comparado*, **XLI** (122) 1023–40.

IPBES 2015, *About IPBES*. Intergovernmental Platform on Biodiversity and Ecosystem Services. Viewed 10 July 2015, http://www.ipbes.net/about-ipbes.html.

Kosoy, N. and Corbera, E. 2010, 'Payments for ecosystem services as commodity fetishism', *Ecological Economics*, **69** (6) 1228–36.

Kuehls, T. 1996, *Beyond sovereign territory: The space of ecopolitics*, Minneapolis, MN: University of Minnesota Press.

Landell-Mills, N. and Porras, I. 2002, *Silver bullet or fools' gold: Developing markets for forest environmental services and the poor*, London, UK: IIED.

MacDonald, K. I. and Corson, C. 2012, '"TEEB begins now": A virtual moment in the production of natural capital', *Development and Change*, **43** (1) 159–84.

McAfee, K. 2012, 'The contradictory logic of global ecosystem services markets', *Development and Change*, **43** (1) 105–31.

McKenney, B. A. and Kiesecker, J. M. 2010, 'Policy Development for Biodiversity Offsets: A Review of Offset Frameworks', *Environmental Management*, **45** (1) 165–76.

Michaelowa, A. and Michaelowa, K. 2011, 'Climate business for poverty reduction? The role of the World Bank', The Review of International Organizations, 6 (3–4), 259–86.

Millennium Ecosystem Assessment 2005, *Ecosystems and human well-being: Synthesis*, Washington, DC: Island Press.

Miller, D. C., Agrawal, A. and Roberts, J. T. 2013, 'Biodiversity, governance, and the allocation of international aid for conservation', *Conservation Letters*, **6** (1) 12–20.

Miteva, D. A. and Pattanayak, S. K. 2012, 'Evaluation of biodiversity policy instruments: what works and what doesn't?' *Oxford Review of Economic Policy*, **28** (1) 69–92.

Muradian, R., Corbera, E., Pascual, U., Kosoy, N. and May, P. H. 2010, 'Reconciling theory and practice: An alternative conceptual framework for understanding payments for environmental services', *Ecological Economics*, **69** (6) 1202–8.

Overton, J. M., Stephens, R. T. T. and Ferrier, S. 2013, 'Net present biodiversity value and the design of biodiversity offsets', *Ambio*, **42** (1) 100–10.

Pagiola, S. 2008, 'Can payments for environmental services help protect coastal and marine areas?' Viewed 12 May 2015, http://siteresources.worldbank.org/INTENVMAT/Resources/3011340-1238620444756/5980735-1238620476358/8CanPayments.pdf.

Pagiola, S., Arcenas, A. and Platais, G. 2005a, 'Can payment for environmental services help reduce poverty?', *World Development*, **33** (2) 237–53.

Pagiola, S., Arcenas, A. and Platais, G. 2005b, 'Can payments for environmental services help reduce poverty? An exploration of the issues and the evidence to date from Latin America', *World Development*, **33** (2) 237–53.

Pagiola, S., Bishop, J. and Landell-Mills, N. 2002, *Selling forest environmental services: Market-based mechanisms for conservation and development*, Sterling, VA: Earthscan.

Paolini, A. J., Jarvis, A. P. and Reus-Smit, C. 1998, *Between sovereignty and global governance: The United Nations, the state and civil society*, Basingstoke, London: Macmillan.

Pearce, D. (ed.) 1991, *New environmental policies: The recent experience of OECD countries and its relevance to developing countries*.

Peluso, N. 2012, 'What's nature got to do with it? A situated historical perspective on socio-natural commodities', *Development Change*, **43** (1) 79–104.

Pilgrim, J. D. and Bennun, L. 2014, 'Will biodiversity offsets save or sink protected areas?' *Conservation Letters*, **7** (5) 423–4.

Pirard, R. 2011, 'Luca Tacconi, Sango Mahanty and Helen Suich (eds): Payments for environmental services, forest conservation and climate change: livelihoods in the REDD?' *International Environmental Agreements: Politics, Law and Economics*, **11** (4) 381.

Quigley, J. T. and Harper, D. J. 2006, 'Compliance with Canada's Fisheries Act: A field audit of habitat compensation projects', *Environmental Management*, **37** (3) 334–50.

Quintero, J. D. and Mathur, A. 2011, 'Biodiversity offsets and infrastructure', *Conservation Biology*, **25** (6) 1121–3.

Robertson, M. 2006, 'The nature that capital can see: Science, state, and market in the commodification of ecosystem services', *Environment and Planning D: Society and Space*, **24** (3) 367–87.

Stavins, R. N. e. 1988, *Project 88: Harnessing market forces to protect our environment*, sponsored by Senator Timothy E. Wirth, Colorado, and Senator John Heinz, Pennsylvania, Washington, DC: Environmental Policy Institute.

Suiseeya, K. R. M. 2014, 'Negotiating the Nagoya protocol: Indigenous demands for justice', *Global Environmental Politics*, **14** (3) 102–24.

Tacconi, L., Mahanty, S. and Suich, H. 2010, *Payments for environmental services, forest conservation and climate change: Livelihoods in the REDD*, Cheltenham, UK: Edward Elgar Publishing.

TEEB 2010, *The economics of ecosystems and biodiversity: Ecological and economic foundations*, London: Earthscan.

UNEP 2008, 'Payments for Ecosystem Services: Getting Started. A Primer'. Viewed 10 July 2015, http://www.unep.org/pdf/PaymentsForEcosystem Services_en.pdf

Vatn, A. 2000, 'The environment as a commodity', *Environmental Values*, **9** 493–509.

Villarroya, A., Barros, A. C. and Kiesecker, J. 2014, 'Policy development for environmental licensing and biodiversity offsets in Latin America', PLOS. Viewed 18 May 2015, http://journals.plos.org/plosone/article?id=10.1371/journal.pone.0107144.

Wold, C. 1998, 'The futility, utility, and future of the biodiversity convention', *Colorado Journal of International Environmental Law and Policy*, **9** (1) 1–42.

Wunder, S. 2005, 'Payments for environmental services: Some nuts and bolts'. CIFOR Occasional Paper. Bogor, Indonesia: CIFOR. Viewed 15 May 2015, http://www.cifor.org/publications/pdf_files/OccPapers/OP-42.pdf.

WWF 2006, 'Payments for Environmental Services – An Equitable Approach for Reducing Poverty and Conserving Nature', Gland, Switzerland: WWF. Viewed November 2008, http://assets.panda.org/downloads/pes_report_2006.pdf.

5. Comparative analysis

RESULTS OF THE GOVERNANCE ANALYSIS

Table 5.1   Comparative quality of governance by mechanism

Principle	1. Meaningful participation Maximum score: 25 Minimum: 5							
Criterion	1. Interest representation Maximum score: 15 Minimum: 3				2. Organisational responsibility Maximum score: 10 Minimum: 2			Principle Score
Indicator	Inclusiveness	Equality	Resources	Criterion Score	Accountability	Transparency	Criterion Score	
CDM(90)	2.8	2.7	2	7.6	3.0	2.9	5.9	13.5
PEFC (89)	3.4	3.0	2.2	8.6	3.2	3.0	6.1	14.7
BOM (86)	3.2	2.9	2.1	8.2	3.0	2.9	5.9	14.1
FLEGT (86)	3.1	2.9	1.9	8	2.9	2.9	5.7	13.7
FSC (93)	3.2	2.9	2.1	8.2	3.0	2.9	5.9	14
REDD+ (90)	3.3	3.0	2.2	8.5	3.0	3.0	6	14.5
PES (81)	3.1	3.0	2.1	8.1	2.8	2.8	5.6	13.7

Principle	2. Productive deliberation Maximum score: 30 Minimum: 6							
Criterion	3. Decision-making Maximum score: 15 Minimum: 3				4. Implementation Maximum score: 15 Minimum: 3			Principle Score
Indicator	Democracy	Agreement	Dispute settlement	Criterion Score	Behavioural change	Problem-solving	Durability	Criterion Score	
CDM	2.7	2.9	2.7	8.3	2.8	2.7	2.8	8.2	16.5
PEFC	2.7	2.8	2.6	8.1	2.9	2.9	2.9	8.8	16.9
BOM	2.8	2.7	2.7	8.2	3.0	2.8	2.9	8.7	16.9
FLEGT	2.8	3.0	2.7	8.4	3.1	3.0	3.1	9.1	17.6
FSC	2.9	3.0	2.8	8.6	3.0	3.0	3.2	9.2	17.8
REDD+	2.8	3.0	2.8	8.6	3.1	3.1	3.2	9.3	17.9
PES	2.9	2.9	2.9	8.7	3.3	3.1	3.2	9.6	18.3

Total (out of 55)	
CDM	29.9
PEFC	30.6
BOM	30.6
FLEGT	31.6
FSC	31.9
REDD+	32.6
PES	32.7

Note: Light grey represents the highest scoring indicator by mechanism; dark grey the lowest; numbers in **bold** are below the threshold value of 50 per cent.

Table 5.2 Comparative quality of governance by mechanism and region

Mechanism	North	Mechanism	South	Mechanism	Average
CDM	27.8	PEFC	30.7	CDM	29.9
BOM	27.8	CDM	31.5	PEFC	30.6
FLEGT	29	BOM	32.5	BOM	30.6
FSC	0.2	FSC	33.4	FLEGT	31.6
PEFC	30.4	FLEGT	33.6	FSC	31.9
REDD+	30.5	PES	34.1	REDD+	32.6
PES	30.8	REDD+	34.4	PES	32.7

Note: Light grey represents the highest score; dark grey the lowest.

Table 5.3 Comparative quality of governance by mechanism and sector

Sector	Mechanism							
	CDM	REDD+	FSC	PEFC	FLEGT	PES	BOM	Average
Social	21.2	23.2	20.3	19	18.1	25.6	20.5	21.1
Other	24.1	30	30.8	27.6	28.7	26.7	26.7	27.8
Environment	30.4	32.6	32	30	31.5	32.6	30.4	31.4
Academic	30.7	33.1	32.1	32	32.7	34.4	31.2	32.3
Economic	32.7	35	39	33.7	35.4	34	32.9	34.7
Government	34	38	34.5	33.4	34.2	36.2	33.9	34.9

Note: Light grey represents the highest score; dark grey the lowest.

COMMENTARY ON RESULTS

Looking at the total results for all mechanisms, CDM was the weakest performer overall, followed by PEFC and BOM (with equal scores). FLEGT and FSC were in the middle range (with very close scores). The highest performers were REDD+ and PES with very close scores (32.6 *cf.* 32.7). It should be noted that the difference between the highest and lowest scoring mechanisms was relatively small, at 5 per cent, and that while all mechanisms 'passed', there were no stellar performers: the best that could be said was that all mechanisms were 'satisfactory'; some more so than others. When respondents' scores were analysed as a single cohort, it was evident that there were no mechanisms that failed to reach the threshold levels for a 'pass' at either the principle or criterion levels. The results at the indicator level are more revealing. Resources was the weakest indicator across all mechanisms – and the only indicator to fail –

with little variation in ratings. Inclusiveness was the highest rating indicator across five mechanisms, and the highest rated indicator overall. For CDM transparency was the highest rated indicator, but at 2.9 still only in the 'medium' range. For PES the highest rating was awarded to behaviour change, which was also awarded an equally high rating to inclusiveness in the case of FLEGT. Respondents evaluating FSC gave durability the same rating as inclusiveness.

When evaluated on a regional level, PES and REDD+ were the highest performing mechanisms. PES slightly outperformed REDD+ among Northern respondents, and vice versa for the South. For Northern respondents, CDM and BOM were the weakest performers, sharing the same score. For the South, PEFC was the weakest performer, followed by CDM. The difference between PEFC and FSC was far less marked in the scores provided by Northern respondents. BOM received a higher rating from Southern respondents, as did FLEGT. In the case of FLEGT the difference in scores was quite marked; for the North, it was ranked in the bottom three mechanisms, for the South in the top three. BOM on the other hand was in the bottom three mechanisms for both regions. Overall, all scores provided by the South were higher than those from the North.

Social sector respondents consistently provided the lowest scores for all mechanisms, 'failing' them all, and awarding the lowest average score. The sector's highest scoring mechanism was PES and the lowest was FLEGT, which also received the weakest score overall (21.1). 'Other' followed suit, and 'failed' three (CDM, PES, BOM); CDM received the lowest score, FSC the highest. The environmental sector identified PEFC as the lowest performer, and REDD+ as the highest. Academics gave their lowest score to CDM, and the highest to PES. Government provided the highest score for four mechanisms (CDM, REDD+, PES and BOM) as well as the highest average score (34.9). The economic sector provided the highest score overall for FSC (39); its lowest score was for CDM. PES was seen as the best performer by three sectors (social, environmental, academic), while CDM received the lowest ratings from three sectors as well (other, academic, economic).

COMMENTARY FROM SURVEY RESPONDENTS

Respondents provided wide-ranging comments. Two summary responses are worth looking at in their entirety. On an optimistic note, one Southern economic respondent believed that: 'in the overall span of human history the idea of global multilateral environmental governance is so recent and starts off from such a low base that its consensus-building achievements to date are nothing short of astonishing.' However, from an economic perspective, 'the question of cost-effectiveness is moot, since there are no credible alternative models'. Another environmental respondent from the South was not so complimentary. For them 'the programmes seem to take a one fits all approach'. As a consequence they had not been able 'to take into account technical capacity differentials'. This was because:

> The process to access resources is too complex, especially for developing countries, mainly due to the failure by the programmes to seriously consider capacity gaps, which raises questions as to what extent developing countries' views are integrated in the conceptualization and programming.

In terms of the mechanisms' ability to represent the interests of multi-stakeholders, one Northern academic thought 'overall few of these governance processes are well understood at the local level'. This made it 'difficult to support policy-makers who contribute to and apply these frameworks, if they appear to run at a high international level'. For another Southern environmental respondent, the mechanisms were 'too cumbersome, and very expensive for developing countries to manage'. They concluded that: 'these programmes are mainly geared towards benefiting developed countries.' One Southern academic expanded on this perspective. They saw the problem less as a developing/developed country issue, but as a 'sectorial' one, which meant that in most initiatives participants ended up 'looking too much towards inside the sector, and too little to their relation with other sectors'. Another environmental respondent from the South thought that the 'awareness about the actual provisions of most of the international initiatives is very low at the grassroots, which does not enable poor to participate in these'. According to a social respondent from the South, the solution to improving these initiatives was by bringing together 'the rural settlers and farmers of each area'. One developing country respondent from 'other', who identified as 'private sector', was of the view that 'more representation is needed from the South'. Another government respondent from the South further stressed that 'community inclusiveness must be enhanced through participation in all stages, right from conceptualisation to planning, implementation and monitoring.' According to another Southern governmental respondent, inclusiveness was brought about by the 'harmonisation of existing forest laws with multilateral laws, awareness raising, community involvement in decision making' and by providing 'training to forestry professionals and concerned communities'.

In relation to issues of equality, one Northern academic noted that 'little states are not able to attend in same intensity like bigger states' in

UN conferences. One Southern environmental provided a potential solution recommending that all these programmes 'improve their outreach', and asserting that they 'must involve local governments, CSOs and NGOs'. One Northern academic thought that:

> All of these initiatives make some attempt to engage stakeholders equally. But I also think that it is impossible. Stakeholders differ in their capacity to be engaged and in the appropriate mode of engagement. Thus some are always functionally excluded.

Another Southern respondent from the environmental sector was of the opinion, 'all countries do not need to be treated equally'. To another environmental respondent from the South, it depended 'on the country's interest'. The implication in these two responses may be that the respondents thought Southern countries should have a greater role, but this is not explicit. Commenting on the same issue, another Southern respondent from 'other' noted that while 'both north and south have equal participation', it was a matter of the 'power balance', and the South 'could not communicate' their needs. For them, 'that's why more representation is needed from the South'. For one Southern government respondent, the problem was that inequality arose from the fact that the 'masses are not aware about these environmental conventions'; it was only 'the concerned' who got involved.

Several respondents made a link between equality and provision of resources. One Northern academic asked, 'How can you treat all participants equally when the range of variation, or resources and economic roles, et al. are so large?' Commenting on 'capacity-building' one Northern government respondent thought that those to 'benefit from these opportunities currently' were 'mainly' the 'most vocal/knowledged (developing) countries'. But the reality, according to one Southern academic was that

> Most initiatives require more private investment (time, human and financial resources) in accessing the initiatives than all potential participants can spare. Only few have mechanisms to support interested participants to access the initiatives.

Another Northern academic observed that 'for most initiatives financing is problematic'. An environmental respondent from the North was more critical. They thought that the programmes 'do not provide, but rather demand resources'. As one Northern academic put it: 'if financial resources were available I would be much more engaged.'

Two respondents commented generally on issues of accountability and transparency, and both were from the North. The first, from the 'other' sector, made a connection between accountability and transparency, suggesting that all mechanisms 'would benefit from publicly available monitoring and evaluation'. This respondent wanted the programmes to agree to 'make continuous monitoring publically available'. The other, an academic, was overtly critical, observing that in most mechanisms participants themselves 'largely' determined the 'measures of account-ability'. This led the respondent to conclude: 'since there is little accountability, I translate that to mean something similar to low trans-parency.'

Southern and Northern respondents also provided their views on democracy. From the South, one 'other' respondent saw 'room for improvement in practicing democracy'. Another, from the environmental sector made the point that 'science and democracy are not good bedfellows most of the time'. A second environmental wanted to see that democracy was 'determined not so much by the initiatives, as [by] local orders and specific performers'. One Northern academic questioned the level at which democracy should apply: 'the countries or participants in the initiatives?' In view of the 'selective process for representation' in these initiatives they felt that the 'democratic metric applied to partici-pants' should be 'much higher than the metric applied to the countries'. One Northern academic questioned the democratic legitimacy of 'these initiatives'. They had been designed by and for developed countries, not developing countries, despite the fact that developed countries were well endowed with 'natural resources including forest resources'. When it came to the making of agreements, one Northern respondent from the 'other' sector, who indicated they had 'personal experience' stated:

> In general, I have found that agreements between or with this type of international initiative are nearly meaningless, if you are speaking of agree-ments to work together, memoranda of understanding, etc. In all of the above, I have found their agreements on project funding to be adequate and fully implemented.

Another Northern academic echoed this, saying that 'the process of coming to agreement can be effective even when the objectives are not effective'. However, one Southern academic, also commenting on agree-ment, provided an alternative viewpoint, insisting that 'as long as these programs did not involve developing countries actively', they would be 'useless'.

Respondents were from the North were quite negative about the ability of any of the initiatives to change behaviour. One Northern academic said that he thought 'the initiatives are generally so ineffective that they will not likely change behaviour that much'. Another Northern academic suggested that to be more effective, all of the programmes needed 'some form of sanctions – or at least shaming for not implementing'. One final respondent from 'other' North revealed:

> I have worked on negotiation and implementation in all of these. The problem with all of them is basically the same. It is not enough to state objectives and say a program or national legislation must meet them. There must be a functional approach stated, and it must be logically designed to achieve the goal.

Respondents also questioned the initiatives' problem-solving capacity. One 'other' respondent from the South felt that 'most of the initiatives are expensive' and consequently had 'less access to local people' to be effective. One Northern environmental respondent did not think that 'any of these initiatives have been effective in addressing climate change or biodiversity loss'. The main impediment, according to one 'other' Northern respondent was that 'all have their own closed circles', and there was 'no cross-governance mechanism'. Finally, as far as durability was concerned, one Southern academic believed that in the absence of any better alternatives to 'save the Earth', these programmes would be 'everlasting'.

Respondents also commented more broadly about the various policy instruments. Some observations were made regarding the various approaches to combatting deforestation, notably forest certification. On the subject of the provision of resources for participation, one Northern economic respondent noted that neither FSC nor PEFC provided any resources for them to participate. In fact it was 'rather the opposite'. Usually it was the businesses themselves that ended up 'financing standards'. One Northern academic contrasted the 'efforts' made by 'some' certification schemes to address issues of accountability. By contrast, another Northern academic thought that the 'political or market power' exercised by FSC and PEFC could 'lead to corruption'. They pointed to the fact there was 'no real independent control' in either of the schemes. A third Northern academic was of the view that certification, as well as the payments-based approach, were 'much more transparent' than other policy instruments. Transparency meant that the 'objectives for certification are more specific' but it needed to be borne in mind that certification was 'not always effective'. One reason for certification's lack of effectiveness, according to a further Northern academic, was that environmental labelling initiatives at the local level were 'poorly understood'. As a consequence, 'the impact on behaviour' was 'minimal'. A fourth Northern academic provided a different viewpoint:

> Certification can change behavior since it will have a direct and indirect impact on the participant. A problem with certification is the variation in cost to the participant. Small owners can't afford it. A much better measurement of impact on behavior would be that compliance with local laws (such as best management practices) be considered sufficient certification. That would also enhance local support.

A fifth Northern academic acknowledged the contribution that 'certification on sustainability' could make to combat climate change. Certification was 'specific enough and measureable enough' to 'solve the narrow problem for the first stage of the process in using wood, i.e. growing the forest'. But it did not relate to 'the other linked stages of processing and use which are actually much more important'. Another Northern academic made the point that the daily loss of forest coverage was 'due to the lack of legislation'. This led them to conclude that none of initiatives were 'of any great help.' What was required, in their opinion were 'practical projects', and these were delivered by CDM, REDD and PES. This was because projects around 'afforestation or protection' were 'long-lasting' and provided payments 'continuously'.

The responses provided regarding the broader climate regime were not especially complimentary. For one Northern academic UNFCCC was not inclusive and provided 'a good example of a process that is distanced from the local discourse, even though there is a lot of local discourse on the issues that fall within the scope of the UNFCCC'. One 'other' respondent from the North explained that they had 'participated in an ad hoc project which involved Annex 1 and non annex countries', and they believed it had done so 'equitably'. However, another Northern academic questioned the necessity for equality, because the 'goal' of the climate regime was 'effective reduction in emissions, not equality of treatment'. For what mattered was 'individual participant and their ability [to] evaluate the impacts'.

Some respondents found a lack of resources to perform their tasks very difficult. One government representative explained that they worked in a department that claimed climate change was 'a highest priority for research, yet there is virtually no funding provided'. They complained that there had been '$0 in discretionary funding to scientists over the past several years'. Another Southern environmental respondent made the point that 'UNFCCC doesn't provide resource itself. It just develops the enabling conditions and frames the policy/rules for climate change mitigation and adaptation activities.' For them, the responsibility for allocating resources lay with the COP, which was 'fundamental' for framing mechanisms that ensured that resources reached 'resource managers, the poor and women'.

In relation to accountability, one Northern academic thought that accountability was 'lacking' on account of the failure of the Convention to stick to its objectives. One 'other' sector respondent (also Northern) believed that 'many institutions, especially UNEP and its direct responsibilities, as well as the UNFCCC, are relatively poor at accountability', and were also lacking in transparency because they treated their 'financial and other operational decision-making as confidential'.

The difficulty associated with reaching agreements within the regime was also the subject of several comments. One Northern government respondent 'very familiar with UNFCCC and REDD+' stated that 'current climate change agreements' were 'not working'. A Southern academic conceded: 'UNFCCC takes time to make decisions, but once made these influence policies, although not necessarily taking us all the way to the final objective: reducing climate change through reducing emissions.' Another academic from the North shared this perspective. In terms of their effectiveness, agreements could only 'be judged in their impact on carbon mitigation and/or adaptation'. For one Northern environmental respondent the regime had been 'effective in implementing policy' but 'not in addressing climate change'. One Southern environmental respondent thought 'carbon financing … could be long lasting' as a model for combatting climate change, but this was dependent 'on price'. Finally, one Northern academic was pessimistic about the regime, and made some suggestions for improvement:

> UNFCCC has been around for years yet there is no evidence of improved climate mitigation … It will be necessary to get to a simpler structure such as an income neutral carbon tax that actually is effective and supported by some international leaders begging the rest to come along as it is proven to be effective. Most current support is both sporadic and aimed at options with the least scientific basis.

A few responses were also offered in relation to the CBD, and its mechanisms. One Southern environmental respondent noted that the CBD had been around 'for quite some time and now includes a significant number of stakeholders, whilst the issue of Payment for Ecosystem Services is just starting to be in public domain in developing countries'. They considered the CBD to be very inclusive, largely on account of the fact that it had 'many aspects that can be practised at the very local level'. In a contrasting view, one Northern academic believed that the CBD did not treat agricultural interests at all equally, pointing to 'traditional farmers, when rights to use seeds are patented by monopolistic companies and non-patented seeds are not available'. One 'other' sectoral respondent (South) observed that the CBD treated all signatory countries equally at the 'international level', but:

> Meanwhile at national and sub-national levels, CBD-related documents and implementation are most likely implemented by a top-down approach, rather than a bottom-up one. There are too many different communities in the country, which make the country impossible to treat all equally.

Finally, one Southern environmental respondent questioned the CBD's effectiveness because it did not have a 'compensation mechanism'. Respective country members strove to 'conserve biodiversity to meet international commitments' and used 'controlled' approaches 'like protected areas'. But this approach was not likely to work because it did not 'motivate local communities'.

COMMENTARY FROM INTERVIEWEES

Interview subjects provided a wide-ranging number of observations, which are collected under a series of thematic headings below.

Changing the Economic System is Essential for Sustainable Development

According to EU national official 3, there was an urgent need to appreciate the 'deep interconnections' between politics, economics and environmental issues. The view was expressed that the public and some institutions (the Chinese government was named) understood that something had gone 'fundamentally wrong with the growth model'. Further, the current political economy did not know 'how to manage for resilience', and had no ability to 'understand thresholds', which had led to a 'convergence of resource stresses'. This had resulted in a 'theory of prosperity' that was 'broken' and institutions that had locked in 'unsustainable patterns of production'. Relabelling sustainability to communicate more effectively with uninterested or sceptical decision-makers was a common tactic, including with treasury and finance departments that effectively controlled government agendas. For instance, this official tried 'not to use the word "environment"', as it did not help communicate the change required within government. Instead it was better to focus on 'security, prosperity and equity' to motivate change.

This view was shared among many developing and developed country interviewees. Developing country national official 1 saw the need to better engage 'the economic ministries'. This would help them 'realise the consequences of global growth without the proper protection of natural resources'. But it could not be 'done in isolation'; there were many other institutions focusing on other issues that still needed to be maintained. But there was still a lack of insight of the larger problems. IGO official 5 believed that the biggest problem was that most inter-governmental processes and conventions were simply 'dealing with the symptoms of a problem', and not the 'root cause', which was consumption. NGO representative 7 agreed, observing that despite the fact that sustainable development was 'market-oriented', the understanding in the 'world of economics on environmental issues' was 'very little and only symbolic'. They hoped that the emergence of the 'green economy' discourse would lead to 'an interest and a desire among economists and economic thinkers' to look at how economies were connected to environmental and social issues. They thought this posed an opportunity to 'now start understanding how we can integrate these issues'. INGO representative 7 provided some startling statistics. They observed that: 'from 1960 to 1970 the world's gross product went from 3000 billion dollars to 4000. From 1970 to 1980 it went from 4000 to 29 000 and today it stays at 61 trillion dollars'. This had led to such an increase in volume of production that they thought humanity was 'now teetering on the edge of destruction'. The current model was a 'self-destructing system'. They also identified 'a unique opportunity to set the course straight', which did not happen every day.

However, developed country national official 5 was sceptical. The broader policy reality was 'more development, more competition'. This was not environment-friendly. They identified this as 'a contradiction in our world' arising from nineteenth-century 'positivist philosophy' which was 'still the remaining ideology now'. There was a lot of discussion about ecology, but nobody really wanted to 'change things'. They considered that sustainable development could 'only be a priority' if it accepted two fundamental requirements: 'biodiversity and the role of ecosystems to resist climate change' and the need to 'challenge the economical system'. These were currently in contradiction. It was important to have an economic 'model where we have prosperity where people live well', but the current emphasis on 'growing, growing, growing in a system' that was finite was 'limited':

People consider that the environment is something for when we have time and money. But they don't understand that it is a fundamental condition of prosperity. I usually say that we pretend to be a rational society but if rationality would govern our thinking then we would all be environmentalists. But it's so evident that we need a safe environment to do everything we do because everything totally depends on nature. And the fact that we do not consider that shows that we are not rational, we are totally emotional, and we obey ideology. And this ideology is 'ideology of growth' which is totally absurd, in the long term ...

We have no chance to change the process, if we do not challenge the dominating economic thinking with this growth ideology. And I tried once. I was part of the group who wrote the annual report of UNEP. And I tried to bring in the issue of growth – demography and economic growth. And they did not accept that. They said, 'Oh, UNEP cannot do that' ... So it's really an issue that is rejected even by UNEP – not because of them, but because of the situation in the system. And as long as we are not doing that [taking the imperative of economic growth into account], we will not succeed. We will just do small things, very good things, but not sufficient.

The Increase in the Role of Business Compared to Governments

Many interviewees considered that the role of business in implementing sustainable development had grown and that of governments had diminished. EU national official 5 speculated whether it was time to question if international treaties were the right kinds of 'vehicle' or whether private companies were 'better positioned to bring about these kinds of changes'. They thought that 'a lot' of people in government administrations believed that the private sector had 'far more opportunities' and were 'far more advanced in taking these opportunities to go for ... sustainable resourcing and sustainable production than governments can do through the UN system'. This was also partly because national governments had the ability to block decisions, especially about climate change. But it was also 'because a number of countries like Venezuela didn't want a private financed mechanism for climate change' and wanted 'government to control'. INGO representative 2 expressed a similar view. They thought everything had 'shifted away from government' post-1992. In the 1970s and 1980s, government was delivering public goods. In 1990s business started to deliver public goods, in the belief that 'government should not be in the business of governing'. They were of the opinion that this had 'split the environmental reality into: pre-cold war; and/or during cold war; and post-cold war'. It had created a situation of 'interstate relations but the state is missing'.

INGO representative 1 reflected on the changing role of business in the sustainable development debate. One of the most interesting aspects was 'the shift in corporate engagement between Rio and now … In Rio the corporations who showed up were largely there to say no, particularly in the climate context.' They were not really in evidence at Rio+10, but they did go to Rio+20, arguing, 'We're here, we're stakeholders and we think we can make a contribution.' This respondent pointed to US forestry company, Weyerhaeuser, reporting that it had investigated 'the eco-systems services' implications' of its operations in Uruguay and South Carolina. And there were more companies doing the same, including Coca-Cola, admitting that it needed to 'think about paying for water' and the 'long-term protection of the watershed' to make sure it continued to have access to its 'principle ingredient'. This respondent reflected that:

> It's no longer just assumed that something's going to come out of the pipe when we turn it on. We need to be concerned about what's happening upstream. So, it's sort of a shift of consciousness in a number of companies – big companies – about their reliance on various ecosystem services and their impact on those services coming out the other end. That's a shift. Now it's still a small subset of the companies, but for the big ones that have big global footprints they're starting to think about it. The challenge will be to go from a small group of leaders toward where this is much more mainstreamed.

This interviewee also observed that there were 'two other sets of actors out there': companies such as Exxon who would 'fight this tooth and nail', who would never be won over; and the 'major companies coming out of the emerging economies' in countries like China and Russia who simply did not care, because they had not yet reached the stage of embracing corporate social responsibility. But this interviewee did note a 'shift in the corporate consciousness and understanding of the importance of ecosystems services and the impacts that the corporate activities have on nature'. The challenge was to reach the '80% in the middle who are open to being convinced', but this required creating 'the business case as to why they need to do that'. They thought that the shift in the 'corporate mentality' was more important than the 'government mentality' at this point. Intergovernmental agencies were not the right actors to 'sell the green economy in the US in the domestic political context right now'. It needed to be the corporate CEOs and environmental groups. Environment groups had the 'credibility', and if the 'CEO of Walmart' were to announce a greening of its supply chain to enhance competitiveness, the bottom line and job creation, 'suddenly environment becomes a political winner.'

The interviewee went on to speculate as to whether global environmental governance and international institutions needed further reform, or if the focus should move to the private sector. They thought that global institutions were 'not up-to-date' on where the private sector had got to, principally because they were 'not open enough to private sector engagement'. They had attended a UNEP/World Economic Forum meeting on environmental governance and had spoken to an African government diplomat and permanent representative to UNEP. The representative had accused the governing council in New York of being made up of 'professional bureaucrats' who were operating on the basis of negotiating instructions 'the way the world worked ten or twenty years ago'. They were not 'up to speed' with developments in their own countries, which were 'far more advanced'.

The perspective of the African UNEP representative resonated with the interviewee, who went on to describe what it had been like when they were a national government negotiator on forest issues. The Brazilians had also resisted ES 'tooth and nail'. But this interviewee had attended a meeting at the GEF Council only the week before, where the Brazilian government had put forward 'a proposal to the GEF on funding for ecosystem services in Brazil'. But 'the foreign ministry guy' attending the discussions 'didn't have the instructions that said "We're doing ecosystem services in Sao Paulo, so let's support this for everyone else"'. This led the interviewee to conclude that:

> The reform effort for the institutions needs to be about broadening the conversation to bring in more perspectives on what's actually happening in the world and what some of the solutions are that are being developed out there – and breaking out of the mentality of the traditional UN negotiators who sit in those conference rooms in the UN basement.

The Business Case for Sustainability is Unproven

A repeated theme from interviewees was that the economic case for conservation of the environment and for sustainability was unproven, hindering efforts for greater sustainability. But interviewees also stressed the importance of valuing biodiversity economically. INGO official 2 thought the CBD needed to have a presence in the economic domain, because:

> The threats and the forces that damage, undermine and erode biodiversity are the forestry sector, the agricultural sector, the fisheries sector, the mining sector, the transportation sector, all those sectors where the economic power is – and that's where biodiversity is going to be protected or degraded, and so

we can't afford to be outside those domains. We have to be in the heart of those, and that's why the economic argument is so important because ministers need to be able to make the case to their constituencies and their peers why they're taking one decision or another.

Developed country national official 3 expanded on these ideas. They did not think the issue lay with environmentally sustainable development, which they considered to be 'sensible'. The problem was that it was 'shockingly and undeniably clear' that the general perception about sustainable development was that it was all 'about just continued economic development', which they considered 'unbelievable in this current age'. They hoped that the UN High Level Panel on Global Sustainability (or Global Sustainability Panel – GSP) would have a 'big impact'. They wanted it to address issues around the governance of markets in the global economic system to ensure at least a 'bare understanding of sustainability as a central component in the future economy'. They were looking for a 'very visionary long-term agenda' that resulted in a 'gradual alignment' of markets to sustainability concerns and conflicts, in order to prevent 'the short-term economic benefit as being the only thing that noticed'.

In order to achieve such a vision, EU national official 3 considered that real environmental progress required governments to see that reform of the economic system was 'attractive enough to go with a low carbon economy' and should represent 'an opportunity, not a risk'. China was an example of a government that saw the economic opportunity 'in moving up the value chain' with low-carbon growth, in developing 'better infrastructure', and was staring to embed such measures in their national five-year social and economic development plans. In China, 'the real economy' was 'doing more than most' for low-carbon development. They identified two key changes necessary to accelerate progress to sustainable development: a new model for green growth, and ensuring that these were reflected 'in international structures', particularly macroeconomic structures like the Bretton Woods institutions. Developing country national official 5 added that there were, however, 'little core elements where proof' of the green economy concept was 'starting to have an impact'. They were unsure whether developments would be fast enough to 'turn things around'. They agreed that China had 'the right idea around this'. But the US, which was 'just so damn influential' was a stranded 'whale', and the 'missed opportunities in the US' to take action were 'just extraordinary'.

INGO official 2 stressed the importance of making 'the economic case'. They had attended WSSD on behalf of the UN, which had tried at that time to emphasise to governments that they should not adopt 'a narrow development agenda', and that 'without investment' it was not possible to have 'sound environmental management', if they wanted to achieve sustainable development goals. The official knew it was not possible to 'make that case without the economic case' and had been involved in 'some cutting-edge work at the time that even caught the attention of *The Economist*'. This was because it had stressed 'the economic value of investing in environmental management for development' and that investing in biodiversity ES was 'economically viable'. They were keen to acknowledge 'issues of aesthetics and so on, and spiritual values' but reiterated the importance of making the economic argument in 'many ways'. But the economic data and case studies were still insufficient, and more research was needed before it was 'too late'.

Supporting this view, developed country national official 3 suggested that in order to 'generate positive feedback to negotiation processes and diplomacy', it was necessary to demonstrate that 'those countries that embrace the green economy will grow quickly'. They were involved in Global Green Growth Institute in Seoul, which they considered to be an institution that was 'doing something new'. But the odds remained 'stacked against the success', because of the 'difficulty of finding sufficient projects', to demonstrate the proposition that 'green growth is not an oxymoron'. The difficulty, according to INGO representative 6, was that despite the 'eco-reform' in industry, people still had need of material goods, which meant production and manufacturing, mining, agriculture, fishing, and so forth. People still needed jobs to secure wages, to spend on those products. Without 'consumerism' there was no common understanding 'of the systems that we use'. Introducing any kind of constraint on that system was seen as being a 'problem' that government had to tackle, because of the 'short-term political cycles' that required 'an immediate political and financial benefit'. They understood but questioned the merits of incontrovertibly proving the business case for sustainable development:

> That suits loads of people because then you don't need to change. You're not changing business processes and you're not retooling in manufacturing at great cost and not putting people out of work in places where it's just going to cost too much to change. So yes, it's a very useful political argument – and a very common political argument. Do we need to wait to prove it, or what changes things? … Sometimes change happens with enlightened decision-makers that carry people with them. Sometimes change happens as a consequence of problems building up, over a period of time. I don't know the answer to the question. Do we have to wait until the green economy is proved for decision-makers to take it up?

The Importance of the Green Economy

In the Introduction of this volume, the notion of the 'green economy' was identified as a new way of rebranding and promoting sustainable development. Many interviewees emphasised the power of the concept. EU national official 1 believed that the green economy and green growth were 'a fundamental part' of the future. Post-Rio, such approaches were important on account of the ongoing 'depletion of natural resources'. It was not enough to focus on international environmental governance, or the creation of a UN environment organisation. The international community would 'soon come unstuck'. The green economy was the 'basis for action across the international system'. This environment was 'a very important component' and the 'driver of a lot of this', but it was 'politically naïve' to consider moving forward by 'looking at it through the environment prism alone'.

A common view was that green growth in the private sector was an increasingly essential part of the solution for greater sustainability. This was expressed by European Union national official 1, who thought that 'real financing' had to come from the private sector because it was the private sector that opened up markets to growth, and consequently 'public sector interests'. Individual companies could benefit by operating 'in an environmentally responsible manner, without degradation of resources' but in institutional terms the challenge was how to 'marry' public and private sector finance, and connect it to the 'policy formulation side, and indeed, delivery'. The next 20 years needed to be looked at with that frame in mind, as opposed to the 'fairly traditional' intergovernmental processes and agreements, or multilateral frameworks and international obligations. That was 'fine in '92', but things were 'somewhat different now'. They identified the need for 'an international system', that was 'applicable to all countries, as opposed to the adoption of higher standards by individual countries, that's then applied on a fairly individual basis'.

But the problem was that this could fall foul of the WTO, which led to the issue of 'environment versus trade' and how to manage the two 'coherently':

> One might argue that trade has the upper hand at the moment in terms of those particular constraints, so it needs to be looked at together and those standards adopted, perhaps through some international system that can then be applied universally or can be seen as being mutually supporting of WTO.

However, INGO representative 3 warned that in Europe the green economy would only bring prosperity if it did not contribute to 'land and water grabs' which had the potential to destroy 'people's livelihoods in developing countries because in these countries, we also often don't have the legal base to protect such communities'. They argued that there would need to be more 'corporate accountability', which was something that was resisted by the US, Canada and Australia and countries who were dependent on them, and were 'afraid' business 'might relocate their headquarters'. The issue of accountability was consequently a 'major issue we have to deal with' because if it was not dealt with, 'we'll have more and more social movements who will stand up against this'. They were doubtful as to whether corporate responsibility could be advanced through voluntary market-based approaches such as certification, because there was no certainty the market would deliver. If all that the markets did was to 'oblige companies to publish their financial reports and to have them audited', they argued that 'we might as well make a legal rule that they also have to report on their social and environmental impact'.

Despite the lack of clarity on which direction the green economy would take, there was little doubt that it needed political support. EU national official 4 stressed the need to 'show some really good examples'. This was because support did not 'just fall from the sky'. In order 'to trigger a green economy' it was essential 'to establish the value, for example, of biodiversity, which is often now neglected or not recognised'. If that recognition of the value of biodiversity was not 'captured' and reflected 'in decision-making or in investing', then there would be little likelihood that the green economy would get off the ground. Government support was needed to 'set the scene' and 'lay out the ambitions'. Then they needed to invite 'entrepreneurships, and all their creativity, to come up with all kinds of solution'. This might require 'allowing several solutions to go side by side' and deciding in ten years' time which was the most successful. But in order to create green markets it was also important for governments to get the 'incentives right' and when necessary 'regulate markets where they currently do not function well'.

EU national official 5 was of the view that political support was increasing. They pointed to the 'good work' the OECD was doing in this area, notably the development of 'green growth strategies', such as the one that had been adopted in the Netherlands. They also pointed to the OECD's work on including sustainability in national accounting systems. They saw this as the 'interface between science and policy'. Such efforts had put the green economy 'on the agenda', but this now meant that governments had to come up with 'sensible decisions' on what constituted a green economy, and how it was constructed and put into operation. They concluded that if 'economy and economics have any place in our environmental discussions' it was essential to 'fit these two and apparently impossible things together'. That required 'separate thinking spaces' and 'some wise heads to come together and kick around some really sensible ideas'.

INGO official 1 argued that by working at a greater scale, green economy initiatives would succeed. They considered that while there was presently a 'good suite of instruments' around, there were 'certainly gaps'. This was why there was still a need for 'cross-cutting green economy initiatives' that were 'much wider than a convention'. Conventions could be understood as a legislative framework, but the green economy represented policy. Legislation, policy and financing were required to 'bind things together'. But it was unrealistic to think that the green economy would generate 'a convention or any hard negotiations' in and of itself. What was more likely was that 'soft language' would be 'catalytic' and 'encourage people down this track, to do the right thing and share basic knowledge'. INGO official 2 indicated that 'in terms of where biodiversity fits in the agenda' they could see 'a reframing of the issues' on account of the increasing attention being paid to green economic issues. They believed this had helped in 'shifting the debate a little bit'. But the issue was 'to make sure the green stays in the greening of the economy and it isn't just a kind of a brown agenda that we're talking about', particularly in the case of 'biodiversity ecosystem services'. This meant that 'advocacy' was 'needed to define terms in a way that the green really stays in there', as there was 'a risk that it could fall out'. Despite the dangers, INGO official 6 thought that 'green economy' discussions were generally positive. They had allowed people to 'make connections', but a 'perception problem' remained, meaning that 'people did not always understand what it means, which then creates some confusion leading to less-than-productive outcomes.' INGO representative 7 agreed on the virtues of the green economy, but pointed to the existence of an 'economic problem', which they interpreted to be 'the masterminds – or the "experts" – of the world banks and the regional banks or the International Finance Institutions'. There was no integration between these institutions and other institutions that understood and dealt with 'social issues'. They believed that the best way to ensure integration was to have 'sustainable development governance' that could 'challenge economic governance as well as social governance'. Sustainable development governance needed 'political parity' and then it could do the 'right thing'.

INGO representative 8 provided a historical perspective on the growth of understanding what a genuinely green economy might like look. They thought that Johannesburg (i.e. Rio+10) had been 'too early for that conversation to have ensued'. With the increasing rise of globalisation it was now better understood that it was 'necessary to find mechanisms to try and address' its impacts. They believed that the dialogue around sustainability was reaching a point where the philosophy of 'core growth' was being replaced by a 'trans-boundary' approach that was moving towards a 'global regulatory framework, which supports the kind of economies we want created'. INGO representative 7 summarised the situation:

> On to the scene comes the green economy. And for the first time in history, let me be that bold, there is an interest and a desire among economists and economic thinkers to say, 'Okay, how do we look at the economics and the economy?' So there is a unique opportunity now more so than ever before, to say – seriously – that we can actually start understanding how we can integrate these issues.

Criticism of the green economy concept

A number of interviewees were uncertain that the green economy concept would contribute anything new, valuable or significant to existing efforts to encourage sustainable development. EU national official 2 thought the world was facing some 'hard issues' that were occurring 'here and now', and that 'looking for another process to help magically' was 'wishful thinking'. They were of the view that ES would become the 'next jargon-laden buzzword', which encouraged the belief that everything was going to 'come all right' once the green economy arrived.

INGO representative 1 stated that the green economy discussion enabled governments to avoid their responsibilities. They had 'been playing with the Clinton Global Initiative model', which they much preferred. Looking back and reflecting on Johannesburg they thought that the 'outcomes of the partnerships' had been 'kind of cool at the time'. But they remembered looking at them at the time and wondering:

> So, this is national governments abdicating responsibility and saying 'everyone else will take care of it', which kind of went along with the era of globalisation and also went along with the ideology of the Bush administration. The problem with them was there was no accountability, so you look back ten years later and ask which ones are still around, and [what] have they accomplished? And even if they had accomplished their goals, would they have added up to anything? One of the things I liked about the Clinton Global Initiative Model is even though it's a pain in the neck – and we just had to do this two weeks ago – you have to report back on what you did, or you don't get invited again. So we're trying to look at a model of getting a bunch of countries' and a bunch of companies' commitments to demonstrate the green economy and practice and say, 'This is what we're going to do,' and then hold themselves accountable so that we can come back in two or three years and

report on progress and lessons learned. The optimistic scenario is that you demonstrate success and you create a constituency for that and encourage others to replicate it, and then you'll have confidence in these solutions by the time you have to negotiate the post-MDG framework.

They thought this was a good approach, but it assumed that people were 'willing to come back and have the conversation again and be held accountable to what they said they were doing'. The problem was that it was necessary to have a 'body' that was 'going to hold them accountable to report to, and in the UN context right now that's the CSD'. But they would rather be killed than 'have to go to another one'. This led them to wonder whether it was possible for those entities that had made commitments to simply 'self-organise'. If they had formed partnerships and made commitments they could simply agree to 'come back in three years, and report back on it and say, "this worked, this didn't, we're going to continue it, we encourage others to do it."' They were of the opinion that it was 'almost easier to get that from some of the corporate and NGO partners', but that it was 'probably more difficult for some of the government partners', especially if there was a change of government.

INGO representative 2 was particularly critical of the green economy concept. They admitted it had 'gained traction' but that was because it had been one of the 'core topics for Rio+20' and had become an 'indicator' of success. As one of the top topics of conference, that meant there was 'some political capital behind it'. But at the time of the conference, it was possible to 'see the differences in opinion', and that 'a lot of developing countries' had challenged the concept. These countries had questioned its value, observing 'we have the green, give us the economy'. This interviewee thought that it was 'just a repackaging of sustainable development'. It had become 'controversial' and as a consequence had not 'gained the traction, but it should have because maybe, so for some it's too ambitious, for others, for many, it's not ambitious enough'. Environmentalists especially saw that environment and development had simply been rebranded, and wrapped in 'the new clothes of the emperor'. But it had not resolved the 'fundamental tension' that existed between GDP and the Gross Happiness Index (GHI) – 'between material wealth and growth versus human security and social wellbeing'. Taking all this into consideration, they were uncertain as to whether the green economy would ever function as 'a good indicator'. They had gone through the transcripts of the government responses at Rio+20 and had evaluated how governments had reacted to it. They had concluded that there were 'many different opinions'.

Developed country national official 5 neatly summed up the opposition to the concept: 'it's good about green technologies. But if it is just to produce more, then we won't save anything.'

The Changing Nature of North/South–South/North Dynamics

A number of interviewees identified the changing nature of developed and developing country relations. EU national official 1 observed that humanity was 'now in an era where things have changed since 1992. We have middle-income countries, we have emerging economies – it's not quite the developed/developing divide, as existed then.' INGO representative 7 argued that if the global community had agreed to 'fight poverty' and had identified 'some success', there was no need to have 'the kind of development outlook' that had existed 'in the 1970s'. They had listened to many of their 'friends in the G77 camp', and it had become obvious that they were using the 'North/South divide to promote their own interest'. The world was different now. In the 1970s there really was a 'North/South economy', based on 'the North investing in the South'. But today, there were examples of countries like Nigeria, India, Brazil, South Africa, China that were 'investing everywhere'. The world was no longer 'bipolar', but 'multipolar'. Another change that had occurred was that in the 1970s it had been possible to identify specific localities of poverty. Now poverty was 'everywhere'. They provided examples:

> Twelve per cent of the EU population, which amounts to sixty, seventy million people, live on or below the poverty line. The same thing in the United States, it's even worse here. So poverty is global, environmental issues are global, societal re-creation is global. You cannot look at this in the North/South divide anymore.

From their perspective, developing country government official 2 explained that developing countries came to the discussion around the North/South divide 'from a development angle': UNHCE in 1972 was 'more environment' in comparison to UNCED in 1992. In UNCED it was 'development' that 'became a central piece with sustainable development'. Developing country government official 2 explained:

> I think within the green economy there is a big divide between developed and developing countries and particularly the OECD countries that are pushing for green economy. Developing countries want green economy in the context of sustainable development, so there is a big difference ... Green economy is not just about markets, it is not just about economy, that's where sustainable development comes in: where you talk about social and economic and poverty, and those development issues.

This interviewee went on to clarify that developing countries did not want any trade barriers, or 'any issue that can derail development'. The issue on the other hand was that developed nations did not want to 'change their behaviours'. They were worried about the change in the discourse from sustainable development to green economy:

> There are scholars and there are practitioners that are thinking that sustainable development has failed and we should push a new concept, and a green economy came out of that. Now that's a very dangerous territory to get into because sustainable development as a new concept has taken 20 years – it has matured significantly and what we should be doing is to promote it further [and] realise its implementation. They are now narrowing it down to just the economy. Green economy is just about economy. We're getting down into old battles of North/South. When we defined sustainable development all key pillars were there: social, economic, environmental. Through the green economy they are actually trying to promote the businesses of those developed countries' companies.

INGO representative 1 had a slightly different viewpoint. They considered that the green economy was 'primarily a conversation about what's going on for developing countries'. But the challenge was to frame it 'so the green economy isn't seen as something the North is imposing on the South'. At present, this was the way conversations were 'being perceived'. To change this, it was necessary to also persuade developed countries to buy into the green economy. They thought that there would be a few that would be willing to do so, and pointed to Germany and South Korea, and believed there were others. Consequently, the UN had to ask what this all meant in the 'development context'. It was 'not enough to stir up low-carbon development'; issues such as energy access in developing countries and 'framing the development conversation' as the precursor to the 'post-MDG framework' was what was required.

ANALYSIS AND CONCLUSIONS

A number of interesting conclusions can be drawn from the perspectives of survey respondents. As a general observation, it appears that intergovernmentalism as an approach to addressing environmental problems appears to be more favoured than more purely market-based initiatives built around commodity trading (timber and carbon), and payments rather than offsets may be the preferred approach. In regard to the power relations between North and South, and state and non-state actors, the favour shown to all the case studies by developing countries demonstrates that sustainable development with its related policy instruments and market mechanisms seems to be more favourably received in 'recipient' countries of the South than the 'donor' countries of the North. The high level of confidence expressed by governmental and economic respondents, to be contrasted with the social (and to a lesser extent, environmental) sectors, reveals that civil society has less confidence in its role in the political economy of sustainable development than governmental and economic interests. Finally, while all the case studies produced positive results concerning inclusiveness, demonstrating that non-state actors at least feel they have a role to play, a chronic lack of resources undermines everybody's ability to participate meaningfully in the institutional structures created to deliver sustainable development.

From the interviews, one of the clearest messages is that in order for sustainable development to work, *the current economic system has to be changed*. The problem with sustainable development as it is currently expressed is that it effectively occurs as an 'economy within an economy'. Those seeking to engage in sustainable development must internalise their costs, in a competitive economic environment where everyone else engages in burden-shifting and cost-externalisation. This makes 'green' business uneconomic. Rio, and the years immediately afterwards, represented a point in history where capitalism, to coin an ecological term, underwent speciation. The single bottom line business, built exclusively to generate profit, was challenged by a new business model. The triple bottom line enterprise, emerging from the economy–environment–society policy discourse, began to reshape the way in which certain parts of the global economy functioned. A new emphasis on concepts such as 'benefit-sharing' and 'poverty alleviation' began to emerge, whereby the wealth generated by business was in part returned to the communities where the income was generated, thereby stimulating further activity and supply. Commodities began to be available in the market place, seeking to demonstrate their commitment to sustainability, and were adopted by retailers, which in turn stimulated demand. Whole new standards for businesses were created, based on demonstrating their environmental and social credentials.

For a while things looked promising. But at present the *business case for sustainability is unproven*. The fundamental economic drivers remain unchanged. Global commodities such as timber, already providing essential ES, like clean air and water, continue to be sourced illegally, with no or few environmental controls. In addition, other businesses began to spring up, promoting themselves as sustainable but with little real commitment to fundamental change, resulting in a new word in the English lexicon, 'greenwash'. This placed enormous pressure on the triple bottom line businesses to stay true to the cause. They have begun to seek ways to make themselves more competitive with the single bottom liners, and make changes to the standards they were operating under, or lose market share. This model of 'growth at any cost' has been adopted by many 'green' commodity sectors.

But it is unfair to lay the blame entirely at the feet of those enterprises that are trying to demonstrate sustainability. There continues to be an *increase in the role of business compared to governments* in sustainable development. At present, governments wield a significant amount of power and control. They can pick and choose which business sectors to favour, and which to oppose. In the climate negotiations for example, those countries (such as Australia) that are heavily dependent on non-renewables such as coal for income generation, introduce domestic policies hostile to sustainable development, and align themselves with other similarly inclined governments. Conversely, where governments support sustainable development, the very act of providing domestic subsidies and international aid creates an uneven playing field, where the private sector reliant on venture capital and start-up investment is unable to compete with the 'soft' public sector money that is being poured into climate finance. Similarly, the pro- and anti-government camps in the climate negotiations have created uncertainty over the future of offset markets. Excessive interventions in EU offset markets by governments, in the form of 'free' credits, have also created confusing price signals. Allowing business to generate its own projects and programmes, subject to consistent standards agreed to by governments but free from further interference, would go a long way to demonstrating the viability of the sustainability business case for sustainable development.

Despite its challenges, the *importance of the green economy* should not be underestimated. In the case of timber for example, nearly 10 per cent of the world's forests are now certified, but over 90 per cent of these are in the Northern hemisphere, and less than 2 per cent is from the tropical regions (UNECE 2012: 1). Global capital also has a significant stream of assets managed with a view to taking environmental, social and governance issues into consideration – approximately USD 31.2 billion in 2012 (GSIA 2012: 2). But again, it should be borne in mind that the total amount of assets under management in the US alone for the same period amounted to almost USD 30 trillion (Statista n.d.). Whatever the value of sustainable markets, it also needs to be noted that there is a significant level of *criticism of the green economy concept.* There is more to the rise of the 'green' discourse than the fact that sustainable development has come to be seen as a tired and outmoded concept in need of replacement with fresh terminology to keep the policymakers interested. Green growth is an economic model that promotes consumption, not improving social and environment conditions in an era when, for some, there should be an end to growth (Rubin 2012). For some commentators and practitioners, it represents a backward step from the compromise of sustainable development, which sought to reconcile two previously irreconcilable concepts through poverty alleviation and access to benefit sharing. These objectives appear to be missing in the green economy.

BIBLIOGRAPHY

Global Sustainable Investment Alliance (GSIA) 2012, *Global sustainable investment review*. Viewed 16 May 2015, http://gsiareview2012.gsi-alliance.org/pubData/source/Global%20Sustainable%20Investement%20Alliance.pdf.
Rubin, J. 2012, *The end of growth*, Toronto, Canada: Random House.
Statista n.d., 'Global assets under management from 2007 to 2013, by region (in trillion U.S. dollars)'. Viewed 16 May 2015, http://www.statista.com/statistics/264907/asset-under-management-worldwide-by-region/.
United Nations Economic Commission for Europe (UNECE) 2012, *Forest products: annual market review 2011–2012*. Viewed 16 May 2015, http://www.unece.org/fileadmin/DAM/timber/publications/FPAMR_2012.pdf.

Conclusion

Environmental policy has evolved from being a largely local or national affair to one that encompasses the whole planet, and environmental problems are now recognised as having a global dimension. The international community has effectively redefined the environment as an issue, which can be addressed through the norm of sustainable development. States have been in the business of environmental management for some time, and have developed a series of policy instruments. However, this process is evolving, affected by the globalised nature of the contemporary era. This book has looked in some detail at how the market and sustainable development have come to play a crucial role in the evolution of a new generation of policy instruments. The 'politics' behind these instruments is more about which sectors (business, society and government) favour which model, and how the competition between these instruments is being played out in the market. Consequently, *The Political Economy of Sustainable Development: Policy Instruments and Market Mechanisms* seemed a timely investigation into the analytical and normative aspects of this, the Age of Sustainable Development (Sachs 2015: 1).

Policy scholars now emphasise the increasing role being played by private actors in global environmental politics, and conclude that 'private governance' has become a reality that few can deny. This is intricately linked to the process of economic globalisation and a concurrent restructure of state functions; although companies are still lobbying governments via existing structures such as multilateral environmental agreements (MEAs), they are also interacting one with another, with non-state interests such as environmental NGOs and IPOs, and with the state. Together, all these actors are co-creating institutions in which the relations between the private sector, the state and civil society have engendered governance systems that look and feel like public bodies, and intergovernmental organisations (IGOs). These arrangements go beyond simple short-term or self-interested cooperation that is transitory in nature, because the kinds of collaboration that are occurring are both durable and established. In the environmental policy domain, the research has identified various categories and subcategories of policy instrument, from voluntary arrangements to legally binding agreements. Within this domain, the move from traditional command-control regulatory approaches towards newer market-based instruments has been pronounced. State authority has been eroded (or ceded), and legitimacy has been conferred on many different types of mechanism. One of the foremost of these is the market-based instrument, which is worthy of examination in its own right – hence this volume. The state is by no means the sole arbiter of power in market-driven governance systems. A broad spectrum of actors determines the value of one mechanism over another, and shapes its institutional design and objectives. Although the players are those who are also involved in conventional public policy-making they have become the proxy representatives for a non-present public, which has granted them the right to act on their behalf on the basis of shared values. In this mix, government is merely another interest group, albeit a powerful one. This has radically transformed what constitutes authority, and non-state or 'hybrid' forms of institution sit alongside the conventional 'regimes' described in international relations theory.

The challenge confronting these 'new' environmental policy instruments is how to deliver the kinds of democratic safeguards, previously provided by the nation state. In the case of market mechanisms, to demonstrate their bona fides, many have adopted a corporate discourse that emphasises corporate social responsibility and voluntary standards. The numbers of programmes and approaches, combined with a plethora of competing and conflicting standards, have created a great deal of confusion. Despite a general consensus that these mechanisms should demonstrate such values as accountability, responsibility, transparency and sustainability, there is little else in common. While accountability and transparency are acknowledged as the place to begin the development of stakeholder relations, the end point is not yet clear. The primary accountability of the board of a corporation is to its shareowners, and it is asserted that taking a wider view of stakeholders creates value and wealth for a company, reduces risk, yields opportunities for innovation and heads emergent problems off at the pass. This sort of collaborative model generates new partnerships between businesses, NGOs and governments, and creates new services and products.

The norm of global environmental governance, established at the UNCED, was for voluntary self-regulated approaches to corporate accountability, responsibility and implementation. The work of the Strategic Advisory Group on the Environment (SAGE) on environmental management provided the technical content of the subsequent lobbying and content development that occurred during the UNCED preparatory conference in January 1992. The group's recommendations ultimately became some of the core principles underlying the substantive documents of UNCED, and contributed to the comprehensive policy guidance contained in *Agenda 21* as well as the Rio Declaration itself. Corporate responsibility in this context was complementary to the existing environmental regulatory and legislative arrangements of the state. Operational standards did not specify absolute environmental performance requirements; rather, they were based on a more limited set of obligations. Under those obligations, a company's environmental commitments were confined to providing a framework under which a company determined its own internal environmental management priorities, and systematised them accordingly.

The Earth Summit helped entrench the concept of sustainable development, and created government and multistakeholder support for market-based systems for tackling environmental problems. The creation of the UNFCCC provided a global agreement for tackling climate change, and encouraged discussions that eventually resulted in the KP, a policy instrument aimed at developing and implementing market mechanisms to reduce greenhouse gas emissions. The KP created a market for carbon and, since signatory countries had to reduce emissions, companies who reduced their emissions were able to sell their carbon savings to other companies (e.g. heavy polluters). Although these were 'licences to pollute', emissions were being reduced overall as greenhouse gases became a tradable commodity (like coal or steel). The 5 per cent reduction agreed to in 1997 put a 'cap' on emission levels (95 per cent of 1990 levels), meaning that heavy polluters had to offset their emissions by purchasing carbon credits in some form or other via an ETS. However, ETSs are only a partial solution. If the market does not rise to the challenge and the climate does not stabilise, a ban on fossil fuel-based energy production and consumption will be necessary. In this case, more interventionist systems such as direct carbon taxation or other measures may be more effective. Zero emissions and even below-zero reductions to deal with background levels may also be necessary.

In 2013 the KP commitment period ended and new arrangements are being put in place on the basis of the outcomes at the 2015 21st Conference of the Parties (COP 21) in Paris. As a minimum, a 60-40 per cent reduction in greenhouse gas emissions is required to stabilise the climate. Will the CDM survive into the future? If it does, the examples of poor CDM projects reviewed in this volume clearly demonstrate that extra policy is required in market-based carbon financing to avoid perverse incentives – such as offsetting refrigerants, or converting old growth forests to plantations – and generate legitimate sources of emissions reductions. Mainstreaming a pro-poor growth agenda in CDM decision-making is a visible challenge in developing countries. This is because such countries do not have adequate access to knowledge platforms and planned strategies, and already experience the burdensome impacts of climate change, which forces them to focus on such impacts rather than addressing poverty. This situation can be resolved by implementing pro-poor growth CDM add-on projects alongside regular CDMs. Here, there is some clear potential for 'co-benefits' between projects in capturing (or enhancing?) local market potential. Indian-based CDM biomass projects provide one such example: in these projects, there was a strong demand by carbon market participants for a CDM mechanism with pro-poor growth benefits attached, and the uptake was good.

Whatever happens to the CDM over the longer term, and indeed, whatever market mechanisms replace it, it is vital that the robust MRV methodologies developed in recent years are not abandoned. MRV – along with the actual, demonstrable and additional reductions in global emissions – is the centrepiece of the CDM legacy. However, the fact that CDM was identified as the weakest performing mechanism in this study should serve to warn those who wish to keep it alive that much more effort is required across the mechanism as a whole, even if its MRV provisions are to be commended.

Despite being a 'next generation' model of market mechanism, and avoiding the carbon 'sinks' controversies of early CDM forest projects, REDD+ is nevertheless also confronting significant issues as to how it is regulated, under what guidelines it operates, and how benefits can be efficiently and effectively delivered on the ground. These issues illustrate that consistent, community-focused policies for financing are required across countries. The development of sustainable supply chains for REDD+ 'products' as well as the distribution of 'compensation' credits would create conducive environments for financing pro-poor growth. To ensure the accountability of and to communities in emerging supply chains and payment mechanisms, it is essential to prepare consistent legislative guidelines and governance standards for REDD+ across countries, rather than piecemeal 'safeguards'. These would also help in national negotiations with the private sector. Part of such frameworks is locally informed monitoring and reporting systems, which should be managed in part by those local communities. Here, local academic networks are another possible means where links could be formed with global knowledge networks to mainstream the REDD+ education, form knowledge platforms and train local people (UNEP 2014: 111). The comparatively high performance of REDD+ contra CDM may show that some lessons have been learned, although it needs to be remembered that the mechanism is only just emerging from its pilot 'REDD Readiness' phase, and 'results-based' payments have yet to be formalised on a long-term basis. In other words, its contribution to reducing emissions is as yet untried. It is also still unclear whether REDD+ will become a generator of offsets, or payments, or both. The relatively high performance of this mechanism in the governance quality survey therefore needs to be viewed with caution, as it indicates an aspirational set of expectations among the policy and stakeholder communities.

Forest certification has had a powerful influence on the sustainability of forest management above and beyond the UNFCCC, especially in terms of commodity trading. As a form of private governance linked to government regulations, it has the potential to complement, rather than replace, public instruments, particularly since governments remain a key actor. Certification plays an important role in terms of government policy implementation, because it affects not only the behaviour of certified business, but also larger numbers of other enterprises. It represents a new institutional form of sustainable development beyond existing governmental processes.

Such private governance systems may improve environmental performance in ways that traditional public, command and compliance models have not. Voluntary-compliance market mechanisms coincide with increased civil society demands at a time of reduced government spending, and have created a form of international 'liberal environmentalism' that seeks to avoid command-and-control responses and the traditional 'business versus environment' dilemma. Nevertheless, certification still requires compliance with government regulation. Governments can also act as stakeholders, procurers and users of certification, and can provide resources to assist those seeking certification, as well as participate in standards development.

As the case studies of the FSC and the PEFC demonstrated, meeting the needs of the diverse stakeholder groups inherent in such systems can create internal tensions and affect notions of legitimacy among stakeholders. Different strategies have been undertaken to achieve legitimacy. The rivalry between NGOs and industry visions of forest certification demonstrates nicely the tensions that exist in this form of market-based instrument. The FSC, created initially as a means of providing tropical timber from well-managed small-scale forest operations, became a victim of its own success, and could not supply demand. Timber of 'mixed' origins began to be blended into products, resulting in 'percentage-based' claims on labels, with the proviso that the non-FSC wood had come from 'controlled' sources. Instead of maintaining its market differentiation – of using its 'premium' environmental and social status – FSC economic stakeholders chose volumes of sales instead, unleashing a whole series of internal controversies among social and environmental stakeholders that have not been resolved.

In an interesting contrast, PEFC emerged as a rival to FSC, as a consequence of fears of small-scale producers in Europe that they would lose market share to industrial forest enterprises certified under the FSC brand. In creating a competitive programme, much of the philosophy of independent, third party certification rubbed off on those schemes brought into the stable. While it may be true to say that PEFC remains industry-dominated, it is also true to say that the actual degree of difference in management on the ground between the two schemes has reduced over the years. Previous studies have emphasised the difference in quality of governance between the schemes (Cadman 2011). This difference was reflected in the online survey results, especially concerning the lack of regard for PEFC in the global South. However, the difference is narrowing. This should ring alarm bells in the FSC camp, and encourage PEFC to perform better in terms of multistakeholder governance than at present. Without broader requirements about stakeholder participation in decision-making, the market will inevitably choose the easiest scheme to comply with, in exchange for market access. The inconsistencies across schemes, and the fragmentation of the forest regime complex may go some way towards explaining the lack of success in combatting deforestation, which is on the increase despite the existence of these programmes.

There is growing awareness of the problems associated with illegal logging, partly due to the loss of revenue by governments as a result of the undermining of domestic markets, but also in response to a focus on good governance in international forums and the increasing role of consumer countries (Ozinga and Gerard 2005: 440). Despite this, there is widespread acceptance that not enough attention and resources are being focused on addressing the problems. Forest law enforcement, governance and trade have become the focus of international processes that operate collaboratively with a number of stakeholders, and represent another type of market-based instrument, aimed specifically at illegal logging. Yet many of the initiatives are voluntary, with few resources to ensure compliance.

In the EU region, negotiations around VPAs have certainly enhanced the capacity of domestic CSOs to participate in forest governance, and initiated a far-reaching process of legal reform. FLEGT had resulted in increased transparency requirements, and created an impressive array of institutional mechanisms for auditing, monitoring and reviewing the operations of the national timber legality assurance regime. As with many of the mechanisms studied in this volume, compliance is essential, yet it is missing from the acronym, despite its clear association with enforcement. Concern has been expressed about the FLEGT Action Plan, and the pertinent observation has been made that 'even the best forest management policies will be ineffective unless complemented by robust enforcement mechanisms' (Interpol 2013b). However, governments that have introduced legislation outside this mechanism should not be free from criticism. The significant watering-down of Australian legislation has left the potential for illegal timber to continue to enter the supply stream. Consumer countries consequently have an obligation to ensure that their compliance mechanisms are robust and enforced. It is also a reminder that regulatory market mechanisms, such as those that are focused on trade, are no more or less effective than 'pure' market mechanisms. Both can (and do) fall victim to compliance and enforcement provisions that lack stringency.

Producer countries in Africa, Asia and Latin America also have obligations to ensure that the measures they put in place to meet VPA obligations are effective. Consistency, clarity and coherence are essential between all forest-related laws and regulations, and other legal and regulatory instruments. National government reviews of the measures in place in many source countries to address corruption are required, and these need to be linked to recommendations that can be implemented. All forest agencies and forestry enterprises, large and small, also need to develop benefit-sharing arrangements with affected local communities; also, FPIC around tenure and use rights must be sought, and approval documented and published. This applies as much to forest certification and emissions reduction as to legality verification. Sanctions should be in place (such as revocation of concessions) if this is not provided. Systems to reconcile timber volumes at different points in domestic supply chains also need to be incorporated into timber management systems. Announcements and results of allocation processes, and general information on the location of concessions and data on timber seizures, also need to be available to the public. In addition, it is important that data are accurate, and subject to MRV. Finally, forest management certification and legality verification must be separated from inherently unsustainable activities, otherwise they will become drivers for deforestation and forest degradation.

Processor countries also have obligations, notably those in Asia. Implementation of a range of aspects of high-level policy needs to be improved if illegal logging is to be successfully combatted in the future. Legislative or regulatory arrangements to enforce existing policies (in addition to procurement policies) are required if recent gains that have been made are to be consolidated. Enforcement mechanisms as part of a broader enforcement regime are required, otherwise processor countries (particularly China) will continue to drive illegal logging globally. Formalised trade or customs arrangements with major trading partners should be developed, otherwise the trend for increasing illegal logging identified in this study will continue. Legality and sustainability definitions are required in the form of national legislation, and provisions should be enforced, otherwise procurement policies will not have the desired effect of preventing illegal logging. There is a positive trend for companies adopting voluntary initiatives to address the illegality of raw materials. Even so, these companies are still not complying even with these codes, and sanctions must be in place to enforce non-compliance. Without these, the processor industries' contribution to preventing illegal logging will be tokenistic at best, and at worst, an active encouragement in source regions to continue illegal activities. Finally, certification schemes and legality verification programmes must not issue certificates to companies that do not handle sustainability certified or verified timber. Otherwise, both will become drivers of unsustainable and illegal logging.

With no global forestry convention, the interaction between different state and non-state approaches is occurring in a fragmented system. Methods of addressing unsustainable forest management have been characterised as 'experimentalist' (Overdevest and Zeitlin 2014b: 43). Different policy instruments (such as certification and legality verification) have been combined with various aspects of the voluntary standards-based approaches (such as performance monitoring, and revision and review). There is clearly a need for increased capacity to coordinate across this particular 'regime complex'. Of particular importance here is the need for benchmarking and transparent comparison of the successes and failures of its components (Overdevest and Zeitlin 2014a); at the moment, there is very little of this. One of the problems here, again, is the lack of consistent standards. Both sustainability certification (in the forms of FSC and PEFC) and legality verification have confused their operational standards (what they prescribe and measure on the ground), with their own 'good' forest governance. As the case studies have shown, all schemes are fraught with their own governance challenges, and market-based instruments should not make claims about quality of governance on the basis of their own proprietorial standards. Of further concern are the differences in sustainability requirements between the FSC and PEFC, and between forest certification and legality verification. These have the real potential to create a race to the bottom. In this regard, it needs to be remembered that *legal* does not equate to *sustainable*.

Under the aegis of the CBD, the evolving ecosystem services concept has contributed significantly to the adoption of economic discourses and economic reference frames in biodiversity conservation. It is interesting to note how these services have bifurcated between the PES 'beneficiary pays' and the BOM 'disturber pays' models. It is also significant, in the light of these divergent approaches that PES performed so much better than BOM in the eyes of survey participants. The problems confronting BOM, notably the extent to which it is exposed to unscrupulous developers exploiting it as mechanism *for* habitat destruction rather than *against* habitat destruction, and the weak regulatory environments in which it operates, are of extreme concern. The observation might be made that BOM is facilitating an unjust approach to the valuation of nature (Matulis 2014). It certainly seems antithetical to the basic tenet of sustainability (i.e. that it 'meets the needs of the present without compromising the ability of future generations to meet their own needs' (UN 1987: 41)). It would appear to be difficult for future generations to meet their own needs, when freeways or skyscrapers have replaced the basis of those needs.

Although such a broad accusation may have some value, it is important to be able to differentiate between different types of market mechanism with more precision before allocating blame indiscriminately and dismissing market-based approaches altogether (Corbera 2015). In this instance the perspectives of survey respondents contra BOM may provide some anecdotal evidence to support at least the contention that some models of ecosystem service are preferred over others.

However, even the extent to which existing biodiversity schemes are truly market-based is questionable. Due to the inherent complexities of socio-ecological systems and the existence of considerable transaction costs, they do not meet all the criteria for market mechanisms: voluntariness, a high commodification and a high conditionality. The fact that PES comprise such a wide range of instruments suggests that their only common factor is that they stand in contrast to the government command-and-control measures that had been criticised for their supposed ineffectiveness during the 1980s. Voluntary offsets might be innovative funding mechanisms for conservation policies; all the same, BOMs cannot be characterised as market-based instruments because they do not necessarily imply market-like transactions. Mandatory offsets are simply a way to provide developers with flexibility in how they comply with environmental protection regulation. There is therefore no clear-cut evidence that offset mechanisms are market-based incentives and can be fairly considered market-based instruments for ecosystem service provision. This may be one of the explanations as to why they are both somewhat problematic to monetise, and why they are preferred in Latin American countries with anti-neoliberal sentiments.

Looking at sources and means of delivery and finance for sustainable development, there are two important issues to be addressed. First, the details of the targets need to be agreed by the national and international stakeholders. Further, any possible disputes among communities should be studied before making policies to resolve national and subnational political deadlocks. The instruments would therefore equip the financial mechanisms with a proper identification of opportunities in the specific ecological zone. To avoid excessively imposing top-down decisions on a local level, some mandatory guidelines are vital to ensure the integrity of mechanisms. Guidelines would bind the global objectives to the local benefits. The instrumental pros and cons should allow for a regular review of the benefits provided in exchange for the environmental services, to ensure that opportunity costs are covered over the life of the project (Tacconi et al. 2010: 255). If the policy comprises many local guidelines, it would require an intervention mechanism to assess the cost and ascertain the exploitation of resources in the specified communities.

Second, how to proceed towards a continued delivery of benefits is another issue that the instruments at hand often distort, because of the negative external influences related to finance, land tenure conflicts and governance. Undoubtedly, land tenure disputes need to be resolved in order to provide benefits to the communities in an equitable way. The land tenure conflicts are not necessarily an instrumental obstacle (Tacconi et al. 2010: 254); instead they represent socioeconomic disputes that increase social and sustainability risks and transaction costs. Transaction costs can be a major hurdle to the equal participation of poor people in developing communities. Smallholders in particular would face higher transaction cost compared to the benefits that they would achieve from the schemes. To avoid the impact of such costs, it is essential to combine carbon sequestration on individual land holdings with those in the community, thereby providing extra benefits to poor communities (ibid.: 255). Here, the concept of 'bundling' various market-based initiatives together would provide sufficient co-benefits to reduce transaction costs. All the same, the lessons from the global financial crisis need to be borne in mind, and it is important not to mix in 'toxic' products, such as those that engender perverse outcomes and negative social, environmental and economic impacts on the communities themselves. The last thing that the 'green' economy can afford is a loss of credibility.

Market mechanisms are both an exciting and worrying development in international environmental policy. They provide an opportunity for governments, business and civil society to come together to solve global environmental problems in ways that are more relevant to the contemporary era than traditional nation-state models of democratic decision-making. Nowhere are the transformative powers of market mechanisms clearer than in the changing nature of developed and developing nations, and state and non-state actors. Several of the case studies in this book have demonstrated how developing countries have been able to use 'under-privilege' as a means of leveraging the advantages to be gained from sustainable development. India and China exploited the CDM to a spectacular degree, crowding out almost all other countries in an explosion of projects. REDD+ has provided considerable amounts of funding to developing countries for capacity-building under the programme. In this regard, therefore, it is perhaps not surprising to see that the South consistently favoured the case studies in this book over their Northern colleagues. This transformative power has also had a knock-on effect of considerably empowering non-state actors in the high-level policy-making associated with climate change, biodiversity conservation and the sustainable management of forests. In each of these arenas, the role of non-state actors as both watchdogs and service providers made their support central to the success or failure of the case studies investigated. This is what made the tensions in each of the mechanisms so interesting from an analytical perspective.

It is also important to reinforce the point that many of the democratic safeguards that exist in parliamentary-style national systems are not always present in the sustainable development arena. Nobody 'votes' for Greenpeace when its behind-the-scenes lobbying results in a significant textual amendment in the climate negotiations, for example. The notion of global environmental governance (GEG) should therefore be seen in part as a response to this deficit. Its conception of 'good' governance should further be understood as an attempt to insert ideas such as participation, deliberation and 'multi-stakeholderism' into the sustainable development arena, to avoid some of the excesses of rampant free market-based capitalism. Viewing the mechanisms in this study through the lens of quality of governance was also designed to highlight their strengths and weaknesses in this regard.

Given the limited effectiveness of all the approaches to solving the problems identified in *Agenda 21*, the long-term viability of the mechanisms investigated in this book remains questionable. Without consistent standards for stakeholder participation in policy development and implementation, genuinely 'sustainable' development still seems a long way off. This is particularly pronounced at this current stage of environmental governance. Non-governmental and government participants in policy processes alike are questioning the shifting nature of inter-governmental policy making (such as that undertaken under the auspices of the UN). There are increasingly blurred boundaries between the nation state and transnational corporations, public and private partnerships for sustainable development. There are also concomitant questions about the nature and meaning of participation and deliberation in the context of neoliberal deregulation and privatisation on the one hand, and planetary survival on the other.

The introduction to this book promised to investigate what was right and wrong with sustainable development and to identify the best model to advance it. These are topical, timely and important questions with complex and often context-specific answers. This volume has certainly highlighted the strengths and weaknesses of the case studies investigated. The answer to the second question is less certain. But it is clear that if sustainable development wishes to survive and thrive, it must come out of the shadow of the single bottom line, and confront it head on. It is both an economic and evolutionary maxim that 'only the fittest survive'. The single bottom line economy is an old-world model, no longer fit for purpose in this contemporary era of global environmental crisis. If the 'green economy' merely reproduces what it sees in the old world, it too will pass. For those market mechanisms that seek to generate environmental and social capital in the 'new' economy, they must make quality, not quantity, their objective. Otherwise, it will be impossible to differentiate between the good, the bad and the ugly.

BIBLIOGRAPHY

Cadman, T. 2011, *Quality and legitimacy of global governance: case lessons from forestry*, Basingstoke, London: Palgrave Macmillan.

Corbera, E. 2015, 'Valuing nature, paying for ecosystem services and realizing social justice: A response to Matulis', *Ecological Economics*, **110** 154–7.

Interpol 2013b, *Combating illegal logging key to saving our forests and preventing climate change*. Viewed 15 May 2015, http://www.interpol.int/en/layout/set/print/News-and-media/News/2013/N20130321.

Matulis, B. S. 2014, 'The economic valuation of nature: A question of justice?' *Ecological Economics*, **104** 155–7.

Overdevest, C. and Zeitlin, J. 2014a, 'Assembling an experimentalist regime: Transnational governance interactions in the forest sector', *Regulation and Governance*, **8** (1) 22–48.

Overdevest, C. and Zeitlin, J. 2014b, 'Constructing a transnational timber legality assurance regime: Architecture, accomplishments, challenges', *Forest Policy and Economics*, **48** 6–15.

Ozinga, S. and Gerard, N. 2005, *Strategies to prevent illegal logging,* Cornwall: MPG Books,.

Sachs, J. 2015, *The age of sustainable development*, New York: Columbia University Press.

Tacconi, L., Mahanty, S. and Suich, H. 2010, *Payments for environmental services, forest conservation and climate change: livelihoods in the REDD*, Cheltenham: Edward Elgar Publishing.

UN 1987, *Report of the World Commission on Environment and Development: Our common future*, New York: United Nations Publications Department of Public Information. Viewed 15 July 2015, http://www.un-documents.net/wced-ocf.htm.

UNEP 2014, *Forests in a Changing Climate: A Sourcebook for Integrating REDD+ into Academic Programmes*. Nairobi, Kenya. Viewed 15 July 2015, http://www.unep.org/Training/docs/Forest_in_a_Changing_Climate.pdf.

Recommendations

Recommendation: Governments Should Establish Multi-stakeholder Platforms to Engage Businesses, Community Groups and Government Agencies in the Establishment and Implementation of Policy Instruments and Models for Sustainable Development

Stakeholders have much to contribute to the establishment of effective mechanisms for sustainable development. Considering how to get a green growth strategy rolled out equally well across the different national ministries with different perspectives, EU national official 5 said: 'That's the challenge we are facing in this moment and I don't have a blueprint for that.' One recommended process was 'to have a platform between the NGOs and the business community to develop pilots [in key industries] to achieve "no net loss" of biodiversity. So as company strategy, they'll have no net loss. We'll also see there's a competitive advantage.' A number of examples were given of multinational companies engaging in this process in Europe, including Unilever, Shell, AkzoNobel, DSM and Nutreco.

According to EU national official 5, a European nation had a task force for a green economy:

> [The task force] recognises three phases in fact. So in the first phase you stimulate the preparedness. In the second phase, you enable the mid-group and then in the last phase, you have to cut off the free riders. But we have economically difficult times. So what you see is that even this government says, 'Okay – as a long term strategy, we agree with it, but in the short term we chose direct economic growth.' ... that's the issue, that you have a dilemma between economic gain on the short term and sustainable economic growth on the long term. We believe that sustainable growth on the long term is the better way forward. The one thing government and business agree on is that resourcing, the ability to get your resources, is the main challenge for the Western world in the next 20 years. Look at what China does. Look at the political position of Brazil, which is changing very rapidly.

INGO official 2 added: 'One of the things that I've put a lot of attention on is investing in local communities [including with] the Equator

Initiative, which is designed to put attention on and recognise communities that are protecting biodiversity and eradicating poverty.' They intended to work with:

> a consortium of lots of other organisations to try to keep the green in that issue but also to get attention at the local level and its mantra might be something like 'no green economies without green communities'. I think evidence [shows] that investments in local communities is also money well spent, and I think if there's a prioritisation of the whole communities then oftentimes the biodiversity and the agenda – the ecosystem agenda – comes in with it.

Recommendation: Government Environmental Agencies Should Support but not Lead the Establishment and Implementation of Policy Instruments and Models for Sustainable Development

Environmental agencies in governments typically lack the political authority, skills and other resources to succeed in establishing and implementing effective policy instruments, and models for sustainable development. A range of interviewees highlighted this issue. INGO official 3 was blunt:

> When you look at the core of Ramsar, and indeed of CBD, it's all about sustainable use. It's about people. The fundamental role of wetlands in supporting people is in the preambular text of Ramsar. If you haven't read that preambular text, it is powerful stuff. It hits every nail way ahead of the game in the late 1960s and early 1970s, it is about connections between people and environment: the role the environment plays in supporting people's lives and livelihoods; and the role that people play in maintaining that environment. If you look at CMS [the Convention on Migratory Species], it's essentially the same issue. It's the sustainable use of Migratory Species. CITES [the Convention on International Trade in Endangered Species] is all about sustainable use in relation to international trade. The problem Ramsar faces, is that we still have the legacy of the focal points being in the wrong parts of the government. They are in the later conversation, 'put a fence around it and protect it'. Species conservation seems to me to be very powerful public relations, but it ends up focusing on individual species rather than the whole system.

INGO organisation representative 6 observed:

> Government see environment as a cost. They see trade negotiations as a potential benefit or then defending a financial interest. Environment comes with condition on cost and change of state and change of behaviour. So, that's environment. Ministers that are sent there are usually on the way up or on the way down, but they're not usually players in more heavy sectors of

government portfolio areas, like economic security or trade – they're not the heavy hitters.

Commenting on the problems of a few countries blocking agreements on more ambitious sustainable development goals, INGO representative 8 expressed frustration:

> I think ultimately it's about how to change the nay votes. We didn't discuss that in Rio. We didn't discuss that in Johannesburg. We didn't discuss it in San Francisco. So then, is everything on the table as it should be? Absolutely not. To some extent the reason for that is that the developed countries sent their environment divisions. This is clearly meant to be a conference focusing on the economy and the developed countries send their environment ministries; I mean – it's ridiculous.

Recommendation: Government Economic Agencies Should be Supported to Lead the Establishment and Implementation of Policy Instruments and Models for Sustainable Development

By contrast with the environmental departments, economic agencies in governments tend to have the political authority, skills and other resources to succeed in establishing and implementing effective policy instruments and models for sustainable development. A range of interviewees gave examples of how the economic agencies are currently part of the problem, but can, when engaged on their terms and supported, become leaders for sustainable development.

Highlighting how economic agencies are a key part of the problem, INGO representative 6 explained:

> I certainly see them [conflicts] between environment treaties but I also see them more in terms of other treaties or processes. So, for example there are parts of the way we do trade [such as] agricultural subsidies … fishery subsidies, fossil fuel subsidies, that have a significant impact on … the aspirations of environmental treaties.

Not engaging economic agencies can increase the challenge of gaining support for reform. As an example, INGO representative 8 said:

> So some people in UNEP made a strategic mistake with its [The Economics of Ecosystems and Biodiversity] report because it should have done it in a system wide report with bank, UNDP, then it would've [been] taken into consideration by the economic industries by trying to make itself the center of the conversation. It, to some extent, did exactly the opposite of what it was trying to achieve. It added to the worries that it was just creating bits of the economy. I don't think that's what most people wanted.

INGO representative 6 saw considerable opportunities in constructive engagement with economic agencies for reform:

> What I've been looking for lately is … as an environmentalist, how do I make my problem the decision-maker's problem, and how do we work together for a solution? What's in the decision-maker's interest, what's in my interest? Which is why some of this is suddenly getting political momentum. Finance departments are desperate for money. And if you can find them 1 billion, 2 billion, 5 billion, 20 billion, then from subsidy reform or from a financial transaction text, well, they're interested. But then our job is never done because then you have to say, 'now we really want you to mark this for renewable energy, reform renewal energy efficiencies or protecting biodiversity.' So we look at the players and their political interests, what's their policy platform or their political platform, what do they want to achieve? How can the objectives that we want [be] discussed in a way that helps them achieve what they want? … we're not trying to be either Cassandra or Pollyanna or Madame Lash. We're trying to sort of say, okay, well you want this; we want *this*, what's our journey together so that it works for both of us?

Recommendation: New Financial Mechanisms to Fund Sustainable Development Should Continue to be Developed, Drawing on the Lessons from Existing Mechanisms Described in this Volume

Many interviewees pointed to the need for new financial mechanisms beyond those assessed in this volume, to fund sustainable development. Building on the need to engage economic agencies, INGO representative 3 called for resources to be refocussed from the brown to the green economies:

> We know that there are no fair playing fields in the brown economy as we have it currently. It has so many benefits, tax breaks here and there and subsidies here and there that the green economy can never have paid for itself unless we address the unfair distribution at the moment of subsidies and then tax codes and independence, etcetera. I could understand that it's anti-current established brown economy and in some economic factors like asbestos, like uranium, like fossil fuels feel threatened by the concept of the green economy. One of the key ideas is to move public resources from the brown to the green area economy. And that would mean a loss of about 7 billion [euros] in subsidies to fossil fuels a year, or so. So, it's clear that this is an area of concern and so they [companies that are being subsidised] don't try to move.

Considering the need for some sort of independent technology assessment agency and regulations to increase scrutiny of new technologies, like unconventional gas extraction, INGO representative 3 continued:

The main problem is that even if we would like to have a technology assessment body based at UNEP, UNEP has gotten less funding than they have ever gotten. And they have this thing, they have to share commitments for 200 million Euros which compared to most of the big UN, well, this is very little compared to WHO's four billion and UNEP was five billion ... So, what we see is that we cannot have global governance if we don't have global taxes. We need to move to a system where we have a global contribution to protect our global environment and also, increase social equity ... If you want to move to global responsibility ... you can start doing it voluntarily. It's very nice if people start paying some extra cents on what they buy in supermarkets with green purchasing cards, or that if they spend some extra money when they buy plane tickets, but we have seen that that is really only a very small group who does it voluntarily. And so, after they moved to another way, we have to have a global system of governance and it needs a global source of income [like a] financial transaction tax.

Recommendation: Identify and Support Leadership from Particular Countries and Industry Sectors

A broader suite of leaders is required to lead the development and implementation of instruments and models for sustainable development. In terms of which governments may be the instigators of a change, a common perception was that the EU and China were key. For instance, EU national official 5 said:

I think in the European Union, yes. But it most depends on what is happening with the resource efficiency directive ordinance or the directive paper. The [European] Commission has announced that it will work on a resource efficiency white paper. And if China and Europe are common [agreement] that way, okay, then they'll have impacts.

There are a number of industry sectors that may hinder or help a more sustainable society; for instance, the view of INGO representative 8 was:

I mean, how [can] the American system have as a candidate [for President] someone from the banking industry standing for one of the parties, considering the damage that [the global financial crisis] ... did to everyone and to normal people's lives. So I think there's a clear narrative, and I'm sure that they're thinking about it. Yeah, there's a huge amount of infrastructure jobs in America. I mean, bridges are falling there. You know if you don't get some people to start to rebuild your infrastructure, it's going to be a serious problem. So I think there's a good green argument for some of these things. The construction industry is a huge opportunity. If you want to retrofit places, it's going to be the construction industry. It's going to bring jobs. It's going to bring American jobs.

Recommendation: Ensure National and International Level Interactions between Governments

Developing country national official 6 explained that linking rules at national and international scales was what really mattered. The 'fine print' needed to be written 'into some of the national rules, and the national laws and policy, now'. These elements needed to be inserted in water laws, energy plans and climate provisions domestically, because trying to 'negotiate compliance internationally' only ever occurred 'in-effectively'. But in the case of 'national compliance, everybody under-stands – right?' In terms of regulatory requirements, companies knew that they had to report on their compliance, and if they were in breach they would 'go to jail'. The 'enforcement capabilities' at the global level were 'different'. Global negotiations around all of the sustainability agree-ments, but notably climate change, had reached an 'unfortunate situation' where there was no consensus on what needed to be done. This had led them to conclude that everyone needed 'to work at the national level', which is where the important action could be taken. But they still accepted that nobody 'would have done anything … if you hadn't had the international part'. They did not agree that it was correct to 'just forget about the international stuff', but it was essential to get action at the national level, to get countries like 'China to do what it needs to do'. This interviewee stressed that the targets in their national energy plan would not have been as high if they had solely relied on national negotiations, rather than participating in the international climate negoti-ations. They saw 'an interaction between the national and international', and if there were not, they would otherwise 'give up on all the UNFCCC process'. They could see that 'international influence' and 'vice versa' strengthened the position of their country, and other BASIC members (Brazil, South Africa, India and China).

Bibliography

Abreu Mejía, D. 2010, 'The evolution of the climate change regime: Beyond a north-south divide?', *International Catalan Institute for Peace, Working Paper*, (2010/6).

ACF 2006, *NGOs lodge complaint against ANZ Bank for PNG illegal logging ties*, Australian Conservation Foundation. Viewed 28 April 2015, http://www.acfonline.org.au/news-media/media-release/ngos-lodge-complaint-against-anz-bank-png-illegal-logging-ties.

Aksoy, Z. 2014, 'Local–global linkages in environmental governance: The case of crop genetic resources', *Global Environmental Politics*, **14** (2) 26–44.

Andree, P. 2005, 'The Cartagena Protocol on biosafety and shifts in the discourse of precaution', *Global Environmental Politics*, **5** (4) 25–46.

Angelsen, A., Brockhaus, M., Kanninen, M., Sills, E., Sunderlin, W. D. and Wertz-Kanounnikoff, S. 2009, *Realising REDD+: National strategy and policy options*, Bogor Barat 16115, Indonesia: Center for International Forestry Research (CIFOR).

Angelsen, A., Brockhaus, M., Sunderlin, W. D. and Verchot, L. V. 2012, *Analysing REDD+: Challenges and choices*, Bogor, Indonesia: CIFOR.

Anonymous 2005a, 'Sustainable timber grows in popularity', *Contract Journal*, **428** (6523) 21.

Anonymous 2005b, 'Two new forestry schemes gain government approval (brief article)', *Contract Journal*, **429** (6538) 13.

Ares, E. 2014, 'Carbon Price Floor', *Science and Environment Section*, London: HM Treasury. Viewed 22 April 2015, http://www.astraresources.co.uk/wp-content/themes/Astra%20Resources/Astra%20Resources/2015/CarbonPriceFloor.pdf.

Arsel, M. and Büscher, B. 2012, 'NatureTM Inc.: Changes and continuities in neoliberal conservation and market-based environmental policy', *Development and Change*, **43** (1) 53–78.

ASI 2014, *ASI presents findings from the ISEAL peer review*. Viewed 2 May 2015, http://www.accreditation-services.com/archives/asi-presents-findings-from-the-iseal-peer-review.

Auld, G., Gulbrandsen, L. H. and McDermott, C. L. 2008, 'Certification schemes and the impacts on forests and forestry', *Annual Review of Environment and Resources*, **33** (1) 187–211.

Australian Broadcasting Corporation (ABC) 2014, 'The trouble with offsets', *Background Briefing*. Viewed 16 May 2015, http://www.abc.net.au/radionational/programs/backgroundbriefing/2014-03-16/5312944.

Australian Government 2012, *Illegal logging prohibition act 2012: Explanatory memorandum*. Viewed 28 April 2015, www.aph.gov.au.

Auty, R. 2002, *Sustaining development in mineral economies: the resource curse thesis*, London: Routledge.

Bäckstrand, K. 2006, 'Multi-stakeholder partnerships for sustainable development: Rethinking legitimacy, accountability and effectiveness', *European Environment*, **16** (5) 290–306.

Bäckstrand, K. 2008, 'Accountability of networked climate governance: The rise of transnational climate partnerships', *Global Environmental Politics*, **8** (3) 74–102.

Bäckstrand, K. and Lövbrand, E. (eds) 2007, *Climate governance beyond 2012: Competing discourses of green governmentality, ecological modernization and civic environmentalism*, Aldershot and Burlington: Ashgate.

Bäckstrand, K. and Lövbrand, E. 2006, 'Planting trees to mitigate climate change: Contested discourses of ecological modernization, green governmentality and civic environmentalism', *Global Environmental Politics,* **6** (1) 51–75.

BBOP 2009, *Business, biodiversity offsets and BBOP: An overview*. Washington, DC: Business and Biodiversity Offsets Programme. Viewed 10 May 2015, http://www.forest-trends.org/biodiversityoffset program/guidelines/overview.pdf.

Bernard, F., McFatridge, S. and Minang, P. A. 2012, 'The Private Sector in the REDD+ Supply Chain: Trends, challenges and opportunities', Manitoba, Canada: The International Institute for Sustainable Development (IISD).

Bernstein, S. and Cashore, B. 2004, 'Non-state global governance: Is forest certification a legitimate alternative to a global forest convention', *Hard choices, soft law: Voluntary standards in global trade, environment and social governance*, 33–63.

Birnie, P. 2000, 'The UN and the environment', in Roberts, A. and Kingsbury, B. (eds) *United Nations, Divided World: The UN's Roles in International Relations*, Oxford: Oxford University Press.

Boisvert, V., Méral, P. P. and Froger, G. 2013, 'Market-based instruments for ecosystem services: Institutional innovation or renovation?' *Society and Natural Resources: An International Journal*, **26** (10) 1122–36.

Bollen, A. and Ozinga, S. 2013, *Improving Forest Governance: A Comparison of FLEGT VPAs and their Impact*, Brussels: FERN.

Bouriaud, L. 2005, 'Causes of illegal logging in Central and Eastern Europe', *Small-scale Forests Economics, Management and Policy*, **4** (3) 269–92.

Boyer, B. 2005, 'Multilateral negotiation simulation exercise: The sustainable management and conservation of forests', in Berglund, M. (ed.) *International Environmental Lawmaking and Diplomacy Review 2005*, Joensuu: University of Joensuu Press.

Bricknell, S. 2010, 'Environmental crime in Australia', Australian Institute of Criminology. Viewed 2 April 2015, http://www.aic.gov.au.

Brockington, D. 2011, 'Ecosystem services and fictitious commodities', *Environmental Conservation*, **38** (4) 367–9.

Brody, B. A. 2010, 'Intellectual property, state sovereignty, and biotechnology', *Kennedy Institute of Ethics Journal*, **20** (1) 51–73.

Bull, J. W., Suttle, K. B., Gordon, A., Singh, N. J. and Milner-Gulland, E. J. 2013, 'Biodiversity offsets in theory and practice', *Oryx*, **47** (3) 369.

Bumpus, A. G. and Cole, J. C. 2010, 'How can the current CDM deliver sustainable development?', *Wiley Interdisciplinary Reviews: Climate Change*, **1** (4) 541–7.

Busse, J., Dirnberger, F., Pröbstl-Haider, U. and Schmid, W. 2013, *Die Umweltprüfung in der Gemeinde: mit Ökokonto, Umweltbericht, Artenschutzrecht, Energieplanung und Refinanzierung*, Munich: Hüthig Jehle Rehm Verlag.

Cadman, T. 2000, 'The Clearcut Case: How the Kyoto Protocol could become a driver for deforestation', Amsterdam: Greenpeace International. Viewed 20 April 2015, http://www.greenpeace.org/norway/Global/norway/p2/other/report/2000/the-clearcut-case-how-the-kyo.pdf.

Cadman, T. 2009, *Quality, legitimacy and global governance: A comparative analysis of four forest institutions*, PhD thesis, University of Tasmania.

Cadman, T. 2011, *Quality and legitimacy of global governance: case lessons from forestry*, Basingstoke, London: Palgrave Macmillan.

Cadman, T. 2013a, *Climate change and global policy regimes: towards institutional legitimacy*, Basingstoke, London: Palgrave Macmillan.

Cadman, T. (ed.) 2013b, *Introduction: Global governance and climate change*, Basingstoke, London: Palgrave Macmillan.

Cadman, T. 2014, 'Climate finance in an age of uncertainty', *Journal of Sustainable Finance and Investment*, **4** (4) 351–6.

Cadman, T. and Maraseni, T. N. 2012, 'The governance of REDD+: an institutional analysis in the Asia Pacific region and beyond', *Journal of Environmental Planning and Management*, **18** (1) 145–70.

Capistrano, D., Kanninen, M., Guariguata, M., Barr, C., Sunderland, T. and Raitzer, D., 2007, 'Revitalizing the UNFF: Critical Issues and Ways Forward, Country-led Initiative on Multi-year Programme of

Work of the United Nations Forum on Forests: Charting the Way Forward to 2015', February, Bali, Indonesia, 13–16.

Carbon Market Watch 2013, *Local realities of CDM projects: A compilation of case studies*. Viewed 20 April 2015, http://carbonmarket watch.org/wp-content/uploads/2015/02/CDM-Cases-Studies.pdf.

Carbon Market Watch n.d., *Plantar – Pig iron project, Brazil*. Viewed 20 April 2015, http://carbonmarketwatch.org/campaigns-issues/plantar-pig-iron-project-brazil.

Carbonweb 2001, *Lobbyists harvest the fruits of their labour at COP-6bis*. Viewed 20 April 2015, http://www.carbonweb.org/documents/corporateeurope.pdf.

Carodenuto, S. and Cerutti, P. O. 2014, 'Forest Law Enforcement, Governance and Trade (FLEGT) in Cameroon: Perceived private sector benefits from VPA implementation', *Forest Policy and Economics*, **48** 55–62.

Cashore, B., Auld, G. and Newsom, D. 2004, *Governing through markets: Forest certification and the emergence of non-state authority*, New Haven, London: Yale University Press.

Cashore, B., Egan, E., Auld, G. and Newsom, D. 2007, 'Revising theories of nonstate market-driven (nsmd) governance: Lessons from the Finnish Forest Certification Experience', *Global Environmental Politics*, **7** (1) 1–44.

CBD 2000, *Progress Report on the Implementation of the Programme of Work on the Biological Diversity of Inland Water Ecosystems (Implementation of Decision IV/4)*. Viewed 14 May 2015, https://www.cbd.int/kb/record/decision/7144.

CBD 2003, 'Interlinkages between biological diversity and climate change. In Advice on the integration of biodiversity considerations into the implementation of the United Nations Framework Convention on Climate Change and its Kyoto Protocol', *CBD Technical Series (No. 10)*. Viewed 14 May 2015, https://www.cbd.int/doc/publications/cbd-ts-10.pdf.

CBD 2004, *Decision adopted by the Conference of the Parties to the Convention on Biological Diversity at its seventh meeting*. Viewed 14 May 2015, https://www.cbd.int/doc/decisions/cop-07/cop-07-dec-04-en.pdf.

CBD 2011, 'Decision X/1 Access to genetic resources and the fair and equitable sharing of benefits arising from their utilization', *Report of the Tenth Meeting of the Conference of the Parties to the Convention on Biological Diversity (UNEP/CBD/COP/10/27*, 20 January 2011) Annex*. Viewed 10 July 2015, https://www.cbd.int/decision/cop/default.shtml?id=12267.

CDM 2014, 'CDM Board agrees improvements to stakeholder consultation', *Highlights – 80th meeting of the CDM Executive Board*. Viewed 20 April 2015, https://cdm.unfccc.int/press/newsroom/latestnews/releases/2014/0718_index.html.

CDM 2015a, 'Aviation emissions projects soon clear for take-off under the Kyoto Protocol's Clean Development Mechanism', *Press highlights – 82nd meeting of the CDM Executive Board*. Viewed 22 April 2015, http://cdm.unfccc.int/press/newsroom/latestnews/releases/2014/0213_index.html.

CDM 2015b, *CDM Statistics*. Viewed 8 May 2015, http://cdm.unfccc.int/Statistics/index.html.

CDM 2015c, 'Stakeholder communication form'. Viewed 3 July 2015, http://cdm.unfccc.int/filestorage/e/x/t/extfile-20150311160356170-EB_form05.pdf/EB_form05.pdf?t=bEF8bnF3YTVyfDAWn7hzn8ujAyOjZzbhgNCa.

CDM EB 2008, *Guidelines for Completing the Project Design Document (CDM-PDD) and the Proposed New Baseline and Monitoring Methodologies (CDM-NM)*. Viewed 14 May 2015, http://cdm.unfccc.int/Reference/Guidclarif/pdd/PDD_guid04.pdf.

CDM Executive Board (CDM EB) 2009, *Approved consolidated baseline and monitoring methodology ACM0002. Consolidated baseline methodology for grid-connected electricity generation from renewable sources*. Viewed 14 May 2015, http://cdm.unfccc.int/EB/045/eb45_repan10.pdf.

CDM Policy Dialogue 2012, *Climate change, carbon markets and the CDM: A call to action*. Luxembourg: CDM Policy Dialogue, viewed 22 April 2015, http://www.cdmpolicydialogue.org/report/rpt110912.pdf.

CDMWatch 2002, *Action Alert*. Viewed 20 April 2015, https://web.archive.org/web/20020921054723/http://www.cdmwatch.org/alert_list.php.

CDP 2014, 'Deforestation-free supply chains: From commitments to action', *Carbon Disclosure Project*. Viewed 10 May 2015, https://www.cdp.net/CDPResults/CDP-global-forests-report-2014.pdf.

Chiabai, A., Travisi, C. M., Markandya, A., Ding, H. and Nunes, P. A. L. D. 2011, 'Economic assessment of forest ecosystem services losses: cost of policy inaction', *Environmental & Resource Economics*, **50** (3) 405–45.

Chiew, T. H., Hewitt, J. and Keong, C. H. 2012, *Timor Leste: Scoping Baseline Information for Forest Law Enforcement, Governance and Trade*. Kuala Lumpur: EU FLEGT Action Plan in Asia.

Chiroleu-Assouline, M., Poudou, J.-C. and Roussel, S. 2012, 'North/South Contractual Design through the REDD+ Scheme'. Viewed 20

April 2015, http://www.feem.it/getpage.aspx?id=5223&sez=Publications &padre=73.

Clapp, J. 1999, 'Standard inequities', in Gibson, R. B. (ed.) *Voluntary initiatives: The new politics of corporate greening*, Peterborough: Broadview Press.

Clapp, J. 2005, 'Global environmental governance for corporate responsibility and accountability', *Global Environmental Politics*, **5** (3) 23–34.

Coglianese, C. 2001, *Is consensus an appropriate basis for regulatory policy?* Cambridge, MA: Harvard University Press.

Commonwealth of Australia 1997, *Australia's first approximation report for the Montreal Process*, Canberra: Montreal Implementation Group.

Convention on Biological Diversity 1992, 'Convention on biological diversity: Text and annexes'. Secretariat of the Convention on Biological Diversity and the United Nations Environment Programme. Viewed 10 July 2015, https://www.cbd.int/doc/legal/cbd-en.pdf.

Corbera, E. 2015, 'Valuing nature, paying for ecosystem services and realizing social justice: A response to Matulis', *Ecological Economics*, **110** 154–7.

Corbera, E. and Schroeder, H. 2011, 'Governing and implementing REDD', *Environmental Science and Policy*, **14** (2) 89–99.

Costanza, R., d'Arge, R., de Groot, R., Farber, S., Grasso, M., Hannon, B., Limburg, K., Naeem, S., O'Neill, R. V., Paruelo, J., Raskin, G. R., Sutton, P. and van der Belt, M. 1997, 'The value of the world's ecosystem services and natural capital', *Nature*, **387** 251–60.

Counsell, S. 1999, *Trickery or truth? An examination of the effectiveness of the Forest Stewardship Council*, London: The Rainforest Foundation.

Counsell, S. and Terje Loraas, K. 2002, *Trading in credibility: The myth and reality of the Forest Stewardship Council*, London, Oslo: Rainforest Foundation

Courville, S. 2003, 'Social accountability audits: Challenging or defending democratic governance?', *Law and Policy*, **25** (3) 269–97.

Crowe, T. L. 2013, 'The potential of the CDM to deliver pro-poor benefits', *Climate Policy*, **13** (1) 58–79.

Curran, M., Hellweg, S. and Beck, J. 2014, 'Is there any empirical support for biodiversity offset policy?', *Ecological Applications*, **24** (4) 617–32.

Curtin, T. 2007, 'What constitutes illegal logging?', *Pacific Economic Bulletin*, **22** (1) 125–34.

Curtin, T. 2012, 'Ringbarking third world forestry', *Quadrant Online.* Viewed 3 July 2015, https://quadrant.org.au/opinion/doomed-planet/2012/09/ringbarking-third-world-forestry/.

Daily, G. C. 1997, *Nature's services: Societal dependence on natural ecosystems*, Washington, DC: Island Press.

Darragh, C., Streck, C. and Unger, M. v. 2014, 'REDD+ Finance in the European Union: Options for scaling-up near term support'. Viewed 3 July 2015, http://www.climatefocus.com/sites/default/files/redd_finance_in_the_european_union.pdf.

Davis, C., Daviet, F., Nakhooda, S. and Thuault, A. 2009, 'A Review of 25 readiness plan idea notes from the World Bank Forest Carbon Partnership facility'. Viewed 27 March 2013, http://www.wri.org/publication/world-bank-forest-carbon-partnership-facility-idea-note-review.

de Groot, R. S., Wilson, M. A. and Boumans, R. M. J. 2002, 'A typology for the classification, description and valuation of ecosystem functions, goods and services', *Ecological Economics*, **41** (3) 393–408.

de Leaniz, C. G. 2008, 'Weir removal in salmonid streams: implications, challenges and practicalities', *Hydrobiologia*, **609** (1) 83–96.

de Oliveira, J. P., Cadman, T., Ma, H. O., Maraseni, T., Koli, A., Jadhav, Y. D. and Prabowo, D. 2013, *Governing the forests: An institutional analysis of REDD+ and community forest management in Asia*, Yokohama: International Tropical Timber Organization (ITTO) and the United Nations University Institute of Advanced Studies (UNU-IAS).

Department of Economic and Social Affairs/Secretariat of the United Nations Forum on Forests and Department of Economic and Social Affairs/UNFF Secretariat 2004, 'United Nation forum on forests. Global partnership: For forests for people', *Fact Sheet 1*.

Depledge, J. 2006, 'The opposite of learning: Ossification in the climate change regime', *Global Environmental Politics*, **6** (1) 1–22.

Digital Democracy 2010, *Technologists and indigenous activists convene in the Peruvian Amazon*. Viewed 10 May 2015, http://www.hacktherainforest.org/new-blog-1/.

Dooley, K., Griffiths, T., Martone, F. and Ozinga, S. 2011, 'Smoke and mirrors: A critical assessment of the forest carbon partnership facility'. Viewed 3 July 2015, http://www.forestpeoples.org/sites/fpp/files/publication/2011/03/smokeandmirrorsinternet.pdf.

Doyle, T. and Chaturvedi, S. 2010, 'Climate territories: A global soul for the global south?', *Geopolitics*, **15** (3) 516–35.

Dryzek, J. S. 1994, *Discursive democracy: Politics, policy, and political science*, Cambridge: Cambridge University Press.

Eastwood, L. E. (ed.) 2013, *Gender and climate change: Stakeholder participation and conceptual currency in the climate negotiations regime*, Basingstoke, London: Palgrave Macmillan.

Eba'a Atyi, R., Assembe-Mvondo, S., Lescuyer, G. and Cerutti, P. 2013, 'Impacts of international timber procurement policies on Central

Africa's forestry sector: The case of Cameroon', *Forest Policy and Economics*, **32** 40–8.

ECOSOC 2000, *Report of the fourth session of the intergovernmental forum on forests*.

Elliott, C. 2000, *Forest certification: A policy perspective*, Bogor: Center for International Forestry Research.

Engel, S., Pagiola, S. and Wunder, S. 2008, 'Designing payments for environmental services in theory and practice: An overview of the issues', *Ecological Economics*, **65** (4) 663–74.

Equator Principles 2003, *Leading banks announce adoption of Equator Principles*. Viewed 14 April 2015, http://www.equator-principles.com/index.php/all-adoption/adoption-news-by-year/65-2003/167-leading-banks-announce-adoption-of-equator-principles.

Espach, R. 2006, 'When is sustainable forestry sustainable? The Forest Stewardship Council in Argentina and Brazil', *Global Environmental Politics*, **6** (2) 55–84.

EU FLEGT Facility 2015 'China–EU cooperation. Bilateral coordination mechanism'. Viewed 15 April 2015, http://www.euflegt.efi.int/china-eu.

EU FLEGT Facility 2015a, *Vietnam*. Viewed 14 April 2015, http://www.euflegt.efi.int/vietnam.

EU FLEGT Facility 2015b, *VPA countries*. Viewed 14 April 2015, http://www.euflegt.efi.int/vpa-countries.

European Commission 2003, 'Forest law enforcement, governance and trade (FLEGT). Proposal for an EU action plan', *Communication from the Commission to the Council and the European Parliament*. Viewed 12 April 2015, http://www.euflegt.efi.int/documents/10180/23398/FLEGT+Action+Plan/3c0cfca1-1503-458a-9d05-1717bf226e23.

European Commission 2007a, 'Control of the supply chain: Wood tracing systems and chain of custody', *FLEGT Briefing Note Number 04*. Viewed 14 April 2015, http://www.euflegt.efi.int/documents/10180/28299/FLEGT+Briefing+Notes+4+-+Control+of+the+supply+chain+-+Wood+tracing+systems+and+chain+of+custody/707452ca-4d0e-4fa1-b4c1-71d68888b51e.

European Commission 2007b, 'Guidelines for independent monitoring', *FLEGT Briefing Note Number 07*. Viewed 15 April 2015, http://www.euflegt.efi.int/documents/10180/28299/FLEGT+Briefing+Notes+7+-+Guidelines+for+independent+monitoring/8785cc01-fda3-46d3-ae2b-d9f79cfb57fa.

European Commission 2007c, 'Legality assurance systems: Requirements for verification', *FLEGT Briefing Note Number 05*. Viewed 14 April 2015, http://www.euflegt.efi.int/documents/10180/28299/FLEGT+

Briefing+Notes+5+-+Legality+assurance+systems+-+requirements+for
+verification/9f30f065-ff3d-41b0-9ea2-726e293e0231.

European Commission 2007d, 'What is FLEGT?' *FLEGT Briefing Note Number 01.* Viewed 13 April 2015, http://www.euflegt.efi.int/ documents/10180/28299/FLEGT+Briefing+Notes+1+-+What+is+ FLEGT/ 8e6155fe-6a0e-4606-98d1-2aaa74160e26.

European Commission 2007e, 'What is legal timber?' *FLEGT Briefing Note Number 02.* Viewed 5 May 2015, http://ec.europa.eu/europeaid/ sites/devco/files/publication-flegt-briefing-note-series-2007-2-200703_ en.pdf.

European Commission 2010, *Timber regulation.* Viewed 15 April 2015, http://ec.europa.eu/environment/forests/timber_regulation.htm.

European Commission 2015, *State of implementation of EU timber regulation in 28 member states.* Viewed 30 April 2015, http://ec. europa.eu/environment/forests/pdf/EUTR%20implementation%20score board.pdf.

European Forest Institute 2009, 'What is a voluntary partnership agreement?' *EFI Policy Brief 3.* Viewed 13 April 2015, http://www.euflegt. efi.int/documents/10180/23013/EFI+Policy+Brief+3+-+What+is+a+ Voluntary+Partnership+Agreement/076495d8-741e-49da-aeaf-b67e2 d3d2239.

European Forest Institute 2015, 'EU timber regulation and FLEGT action plan: Lessons learned and policy implications', *Think Forest.* Viewed 30 April 2015, http://www.efi.int/files/attachments/thinkforest/efi_think forest-brief_eutr.pdf.

European Union 2008, *Guidelines on a Common Understanding of Article 11b (6) of Directive 2003/87/EC as Amended by Directive 2004/101/EC (non-paper).* Viewed 14 May 2015, http://ec.europa.eu/ clima/policies/ets/linking/docs/art11b6_guide_en.pdf.

FAO 2004, 'Proceedings FAO Advisory Committee on Paper and Wood Products Forty-fifth Session', 16–17 April, Canberra, Australia.

FAO 2011, *Payment for ecosystem services and food security*, Rome: FAO. Viewed 12 May 2015, http://www.fao.org/docrep/014/i2100e/ i2100e.PDF.

FAO 2012, *Sustainable management of forests and REDD+: Negotiations need clear terminology.* Viewed 3 July 2015, http://www.un redd.net/ index.php?option=com_docman&task=doc_download&gid=1   148% Itemid=53.

FERN 2014, *Briefing note 3: Biodiversity offsetting in practice.* Viewed 17 May 2015, http://www.fern.org/sites/fern.org/files/Biodiversity3_ EN.pdf.

FERN, Greenpeace, Inter-African Forest Industry Association, Precious Woods, Swedish Society for Nature Conservation and Tropical Forest

Trust 2008, *Regaining credibility and rebuilding support: Changes the FSC needs to make*. Viewed 16 November 2014, http://www.fern.org/publications/ngo-statements/regaining-credibility-and-rebuilding-support-changes-fsc-needs-make.

Finnish Forest Industries Federation 1998a, 'Increased credibility for Finnish forest certification approach through European co-operation', *Media release.*

Finnish Forest Industries Federation 1998b, 'Industry fully supports the Finnish Forest Certification System (FFCS): FSC-labelling of products becomes available, too?', *Media release.*

Food and Agriculture Organization, United Nations Development Programme and United Nations Environment Programme 2008, 'UN collaborative programme on reducing emissions from deforestation and forest degradation in developing countries', *FAO, UNDP, UNEP Framework Document*. Viewed 20 February 2013, http://mptf.undp.org/document/download/1740.

Forest Carbon Partnership Facility 2010, *Demonstrating activities that reduce emissions from deforestation and forest degradation*. Viewed 18 February 2013, http://www.forestcarbonpartnership.org/sites/forest carbonpartnership.org/files/Documents/PDF/Sep2010/New%20FCPF%20brochure%20–%20low%20resolution%20051809_0.pdf.

Forest Carbon Partnership Facility 2012a, *2012 Annual Report*. Viewed 27 March 2013, http://www.forestcarbonpartnership.org/sites/fcp/files/2013/FCPF%20FY12%20Anual%20Report%20FINAL%20Oct8.pdf.

Forest Carbon Partnership Facility 2012b, *Common approach to environmental and social safeguards for multiple delivery partners*. Viewed 30 March 2013, https://www.forestcarbonpartnership.org/sites/forest carbonpartnership.org/files/Documents/PDF/Aug2012/FCPF%20Readiness%20Fund%20Common%20Approach%208-9-12.pdf.

Forest Carbon Partnership Facility 2012c, *Contributions to the FCPF Carbon Fund as of December 31, 2012 (US$m)*. Viewed 20 April 2015, http://www.forestcarbonpartnership.org/sites/fcp/files/2013/FCPF%20Readiness%20Fund%20Contributions%20as%20of%20Dec%2031_2012.pdf.

Forest Carbon Partnership Facility 2012d, *The FCPF carbon fund: Pioneering performance based payments for REDD+*. Viewed 26 April 2013, http://www.forestcarbonpartnership.org/sites/forestcarbonpartnership.org/files/Documents/PDF/June2012/FCPF%20Brouchure_June%2013_2012.pdf.

Forest Carbon Partnership Facility 2013a, 'Delivery partners'. Viewed 20 April 2013, http://www.forestcarbonpartnership.org/delivery-partners.

Forest Carbon Partnership Facility 2013b, *Readiness Fund*. Viewed 3 April 2013, http://www.forestcarbonpartnership.org/readiness-fund.

Forest Stewardship Council 2004, 'Annual review 2003', *FSC News and Notes*, **3** (1).

Forest Stewardship Council 2006a, 'FSC plantations review policy working group completes its task', *FSC News and Notes*, **4** (9) 1.

Forest Stewardship Council 2006b, *FSC plantations review policy working group final report*. Viewed 1 July 2015, http://plantations.fsc.org/.

Forest Stewardship Council 2007, *Plantations review*. Viewed 10 July 2007, http://plantations.fsc.org.

Forest Stewardship Council 2012, *FSC guidelines for the implementation of the right to free, prior and informed Consent (FPIC)*. Viewed 18 March 2013, http://www.unredd.net/index.php?option=com_docman &task=doc_download&gid=8973&Itemid=53.

Forest Stewardship Council 2014a, *FSC general assembly 2014 motion outcomes*. Viewed 16 November 2014, http://ga2014.fsc.org/motion-updates.

Forest Stewardship Council 2014b, *FSC principles and criteria international guidelines to forest management*. Viewed 8 December 2014, https://ic.fsc.org/principles-and-criteria.34.htm.

Forest Stewardship Council 2014c, *IGI International Generic Indicators background information*. Viewed 8 December 2014, http://igi.fsc.org/ background.5.htm.

Forest Stewardship Council n.d., 'Final motions and results from FSC general assembly 2002'.

Forest Stewardship Council, *Statutes (Version 1.3, Revised August 2000, November 2002 and June 2005)*. Viewed 1 July 2015, http://au.fsc.org/ download.fsc-ac-statutes.389.pdf.

Freemen, A. 2015, *Canada and Russia beat tropical countries to top global deforestation list*. Viewed 16 April 2015, http://mashable.com/ 2015/04/09/canada-russia-top-deforestation-list/.

Frydenberg, J. 2014, 'Time to cut down Labor's approach to logging control', *Australian Financial Review*, 11 December.

FSC Canada 2012, *FSC Guidelines for the implementation of the right to Free, Prior and Informed Consent released*. Viewed 10 April 2015, https://ca.fsc.org/newsroom.239.116.htm.

FSC International 2014, *Putting free, prior and informed consent into practice: FSC and indigenous peoples*. Viewed 10 April 2014, https:// ic.fsc.org/newsroom.9.791.htm.

FSC International 2015a, *Facts and figures*. Viewed 7 April 2015, https://ic.fsc.org/facts-figures.839.htm.

FSC International 2015b, *FSC Modular Approach Program (MAP)*. Viewed 7 April 2015, https://ic.fsc.org/map.656.htm.

Gale, F. 1998, *The tropical timber trade regime*, Basingstoke, London: Macmillan Press.

Gale, F. and Burda, C. (eds) 1999, *The pitfalls and potential of eco-certification as a market incentive for sustainable forest management*, Vancouver: UBC Press.

Gardner, T. A., Hase, A., Brownlie, S., Ekstrom, J. M. M., Pilgrim, J. D., Savy, C. E., Stephens, R. T. T., Treweek, J. O., Ussher, G. T., Ward, G. and Ten Kate, K. 2013, 'Biodiversity Offsets and the Challenge of Achieving No Net Loss', *Conservation Biology*, **27** (6) 1254–64.

Gehring, T. and Oberthur, S. 2006, 'Institutional interaction in global environmental governance: The case of the Cartagena protocol and the world trade organization', *Global Environmental Politics*, **6** (2) 1–31.

Gibbons, P. and Zeil, J. 2014, 'It's becoming harder to see the trees for the revenue', *The Age*. Viewed 16 May 2015, http://www.theage.com.au/comment/its-becoming-harder-to-see-the-trees-for-the-revenue-20140128-31l2b.html.

Gill, E. 2001, 'Unfounded criticism of Norway's forest owners federation by WWF', *PEFCC Newsletter*, **8** 3–4.

Global Environment Facility 2010, *The GEF incentive mechanism for forests a new REDD+ multilateral finance program*. Viewed 7 April 2015, https://www.thegef.org/gef/sites/thegef.org/files/publication/REDD English.pdf.

Global Forest Watch 2015, *Countries with greatest tree cover loss (2001–2013)*. Viewed 16 April 2015, http://www.globalforestwatch.org/countries/overview.

Global Sustainable Investment Alliance (GSIA) 2012, *Global sustainable investment review*. Viewed 16 May 2015, http://gsiareview2012.gsi-alliance.org/pubData/source/Global%20Sustainable%20Investement%20Alliance.pdf.

Global Witness 2009, *Understanding REDD+: The role of governance, enforcement and safeguards in reducing emissions from deforestation and forest degradation*. Viewed 15 March 2015, http://www.forest carbonpartnership.org/sites/forestcarbonpartnership.org/files/Documents/PDF/Apr2011/Understanding REDD+.pdf.

Global Witness 2013, *Three-quarters of Ghana's logging permits could break Europe's new timber law. Global Witness analysis of official Ghana logging permit lists*. Viewed 30 April 2015, https://www.globalwitness.org/sites/default/files/gw_ghana_logging_permits.pdf.

Goetzman, K. 2010, 'Ecological internet: Radical, green, and wired', *UTNE Wild Green*, Kansas, MI: Ogden Publications, Inc.

Gómez-Baggethun, E. and Ruiz-Perez, M. 2011, 'Economic valuation and the commodification of ecosystem services', *Progress in Physical Geography*, **35** (5) 613–28.

Goncalves, M., Panjer, M., Greenberg, T. and Magrath, W. 2012, 'Justice for forests. Improving criminal justice efforts to combat illegal logging', The World Bank. Viewed 12 April 2015, http://issuu.com/world.bank.publications/docs/9780821389782.

Green, P., Ward, T. and McConnachie, K. 2007, 'Logging and legality: Environmental crime, civil society and the state', *Social Justice*, **34** (2) 94–110.

Greenpeace 2004, *The untouchables: Rimbunan Hijau's world of forest crime and political patronage*, Amsterdam: Greenpeace International. Viewed 26 April 2015, http://www.greenpeace.org/australia/admin/image-library2/the-untouchables-report.

Greenpeace 2006, *Partners in crime: A Greenpeace investigation into Finland's illegal timber trade with Russia*. Viewed 9 May 2015, http://www.greenpeace.org/raw/content/international/press/reports/forest-crime-finland.pdf.

Greenpeace 2010, *How Sinar Mas is pulping the planet*, Greenpeace International. Viewed 7 May 2015, http://www.greenpeace.org/international/en/publications/reports/SinarMas-APP/.

Greenpeace 2013, *FSC at risk. A join 4-step action plan to strengthen and restore credibility*. Viewed 15 November 2014, http://www.greenpeace.org/international/en/campaigns/forests/solutions/alternatives-to-forest-destruc/FSC-at-Risk.

Greenpeace 2014a, *FSC progress report on Greenpeace's key issues of concern, and progress on its recommendations*. Viewed 15 November 2014, http://www.greenpeace.org/international/en/campaigns/forests/solutions/alternatives-to-forest-destruc/FSC-at-Risk/.

Greenpeace 2014b, *Licence to launder. How Herakles Farms' illegal timber trade threatens Cameroon's forests and VPA*. Viewed 30 April 2015, http://www.greenpeace.org/usa/Global/international/publications/forests/2014/Licence-to-Launder.pdf.

Greenpeace Australia Pacific 2010, *Papua New Guinea: Not ready for REDD*. Viewed 21 April 2013, http://www.greenpeace.org/australia/en/what-we-do/forests/resources/reports/papua-new-guinea-not-ready-fo/.

Griffiths, T. 2008, 'Seeing "REDD"? Forests, climate change mitigation and the rights of indigenous peoples and local communities'. Viewed 3 July 2015, http://www.forestpeoples.org/sites/fpp/files/publication/2010/08/seeingreddupdatedraft3dec08eng.pdf.

Groot, R. S. d., Brander, L., Ploeg, S. v. d., Costanza, R., Bernard, F., Braat, L. C., Christie, M., Crossman, N., Ghermandi, A., Hein, L. G., Hussain, S., Kumar, P., McVittie, A., Portela, R., Rodriguez, L. C., Brink, P. t. and Beukering, P. J. H. v. 2012, 'Global estimates of the value of ecosystems and their services in monetary units', *Ecosystem Services*, **1** (1).

Gulbrandsen, L. H. 2004, 'Overlapping public and private governance: Can forest certification fill the gaps in the global forest regime?', *Global Environmental Politics*, **4** (2) 75–99.

Gulbrandsen, L. H. 2005a, 'Explaining different approaches to voluntary standards: A study of forest certification choices in Norway and Sweden', *Journal of Environmental Policy and Planning*, **7** (1) 43–59.

Gulbrandsen, L. H. 2005b, 'Sustainable forestry in Sweden: The effect of competition among private certification schemes', *Journal of Environment and Development*, **14** (3) 338–55.

Gunnerberg, B. 2002a, 'General assembly synopsis', *PEFCC News Special*, **1**.

Gunnerberg, B. 2002b, 'PEFC forging ahead', *PEFCC Newsletter,* **11** 1.

Gunnerberg, B. 2010a, 'Letter to Andy Tait regarding Greenpeace report and letter'. Viewed 20 April 2015, http://www.pefc.org/news-a-media/general-sfm-news/534-statement-regarding-greenpeace-report-and-letter-to-pefc-and-pefc-stakeholders-7th-july-2010.

Gunnerberg, B. 2010b, 'Letter to Steve Baer, Chair of USGBC's Materials & Resources Technical Advisory Group'. Viewed 7 May 2015, http://www.pefc.org/news-a-media/general-sfm-news/302-usgbc-urged-to-support-forest-certification.

Gupta, M., Davey, S., Townsend, P. and Cunningham, D. 2012, 'Illegal logging regulations: Analysis of Australia's timber imports in 2007 and 2010', ABARES. Viewed 12 May 2015, http://www.daff.gov.au/SiteCollectionDocuments/abares/publications/clientreports/Illegal_logging.pdf.

Haas, P. M. 2004, 'Addressing the global governance deficit', *Global Environmental Politics*, **4** (4) 1–15.

Haigh, M. 2013, 'Stakeholders in climate policy instruments: What role for financial institutions?', in *Climate Change and Global Policy Regimes: Towards Institutional Legitimacy*, London: Palgrave Macmillan, 111.

Hain, H. and Ahas, R. 2007, 'Can forest certification improve forest management? Case study of the FSC certified Estonian State Forest Management Centre', *International Forestry Review*, **9** (3) 759–70.

Haites, E. 2011, 'Climate change finance', *Climate Policy*, **11** (3) 963–9.

Halsey, M. and White, R. 2006, *Crime, Ecophilosophy and Environmental Harm*, Aldershot: Ashgate Publishing.

Hance, J. 2012, 'Asia Pulp & Paper loses another customer: Danone', Mongabay. Viewed 9 May 2015, http://news.mongabay.com/2012/0402-hance_danone_app.html.

Harvey, D. 2005, *A brief history of neoliberalism*, New York: Oxford University Press.

Hauselmann, P. 1997, *ISO inside out: ISO and environmental manage-ment*, Godalming: WWF International.

Haya, B. 2007, 'How the CDM is subsidizing hydro developers and harming the Kyoto Protocol'. Viewed 14 May 2015, https://ideas.repec.org/p/ess/wpaper/id4822.html.

Heal, G. 2000, 'Valuing ecosystem services', *Ecosystems*, **3** (2000) 24–30.

Herendeen, R. A. 1998, 'Monetary-costing environmental services: Noth-ing is lost, something is gained', *Ecology Economics*, **25** (1) 29–30.

Herrera Izaguirre, J. A. 2008, 'The 1992 United Nations Convention on Biological Diversity', *Boletín Mexicano de Derecho Comparado*, **XLI** (122) 1023–40.

Herzog, G. 2001, 'PEFC Austria – totally compliant with Austrian law – issues first logo licenses', *PEFCC Newsletter*, **8** 5.

Hindle, T. 2008, *Guide to management ideas and gurus*, Hoboken, NJ: John Wiley & Sons.

Hoare, A. 2014, 'Europe's forest strategy in the next decade: options for the Voluntary Partnership Agreements', EER PP 2014/06 ed., London: Chatham House.

Hortensius, D. 1999, 'ISO 14000 and forestry management: ISO devel-ops "bridging" document'. Viewed 1 July 2015, http://infohouse.p2ric.org/ref/39/38678.pdf.

Howlett, M. and Rayner, J. 2006, 'Globalization and governance cap-acity: Explaining divergence in national forest programs as instances of "next generation" regulation in Canada and Europe', *Governance: An International Journal of Policy, Administration and Institutions*, **19** (2) 251–75.

Hudson, J. and Paul, C. 2011, 'FLEGT action plan. Progress report 2003-2010', European Commission. Viewed 30 April 2015, https://ec.europa.eu/europeaid/sites/devco/files/report-progess-2003-2010-flegt-20110126_en.pdf.

Humphreys, D. 1996, *Forest politics: The evolution of international cooperation,* London: Earthscan.

Humphreys, D. 2004, 'Redefining the issues: NGO influence on inter-national forest negotiations', *Global Environmental Politics*, **4** (2) 51–74.

Humphreys, D. 2005, 'The certification wars: Forest certification schemes as sites for trade-environment conflicts', *The privatizing environmental governance panel at the 46th annual convention of the International Studies Association.* Honolulu, Hawaii.

Humphreys, D. 2006, *Logjam: Deforestation and the crisis of global governance,* London: Earthscan.

IGES 2014, *Snapshots of selected REDD+ project designs.* Kanagawa, Japan: Institute for Global Environmental Strategies.

IMF 2015, *Factsheet: The IMF and the millennium development goals.* Viewed 27 March 2015, http://www.imf.org/external/np/exr/facts/mdg.htm.

International Rivers n.d., 'Spreadsheet of Hydro Projects in the CDM Project Pipeline'. Viewed 3 July 2015, http://www.international rivers.org/resources/spreadsheet-of-hydro-projects-in-the-cdm-project-pipeline-4039.

Interpol 2013a, 'Assessment of law enforcement capacity needs to tackle forest crime', *Interpol environmental crime programme.* Viewed 29 April 2015, http://www.interpol.int/Crime-areas/Environmental-crime/Resources.

Interpol 2013b, *Combating illegal logging key to saving our forests and preventing climate change.* Viewed 15 May 2015, http://www.interpol.int/en/layout/set/print/News-and-media/News/2013/N20130321.

Interpol 2014, 'Trade in illegal timber target of Interpol and WCO-supported operation in Peru'. Interpol. Viewed 29 April 2015, http://www.interpol.int/en/layout/set/print/News-and-media/News/2014/N20 14-139.

Interpol and World Bank 2009, 'The Chainsaw Project: An Interpol perspective on law enforcement in illegal logging'. Interpol General Secretariat. Viewed 12 April 2015, http://www.interpol.int/Public/EnvironmentalCrime/Manual/WorldBankChainsawIllegalLoggingReport.pdf.

IPBES 2015, *About IPBES.* Intergovernmental Platform on Biodiversity and Ecosystem Services. Viewed 10 July 2015, http://www.ipbes.net/about-ipbes.html.

ISO Technical Committee 207 1995a, 'Environment', *Articles and News*, 3.

ISO Technical Committee 207 1995b, 'Environment – ISO/TC 207 considers industry's needs', *Articles and News*, 3.

ISO Technical Committee 207 1998, *About ISO/TC 207.* Viewed 13 April 2015, https://web.archive.org/web/20000229103912/http://www.tc207.org/aboutTC207/index.html.

ISO Technical Committee 207 2003, 'Increasing the effectiveness of NGO participation in ISO TC 207', *N590 Rev/ISO/TC NGO TG N28.*

Jacobs, M. 2012, 'Green growth: Economic theory and political discourse', London, Inggris: Grantham Research Institute on Climate Change and the Environment, London School of Economics and Political Science (LSE). Viewed 15 April 2015, http://www.lse.ac.uk/GranthamInstitute/wp-content/uploads/2012/10/WP92-green-growth-economic-theory-political-discourse.pdf.

Janicke, M. 1992, 'Conditions for environmental policy success: An international comparison', *The Environmentalist*, **12** 47–58.

Jordan, A., Wurzel, R. K. W. and Zito, A. 2005, 'The rise of "New" policy instruments in comparative perspectives: Has governance eclipsed government?' *Political Studies*, **53** (3) 441–69.

Kaivola, A. 2002, 'Revision of forest certification requirements under way in Finland', *PEFCC Newsletter*, 11. Viewed 1 July 2015, http://pefc.org/index.php?option=com_sumointeractivecontent&view=item detail&id=577.

Kaivola, A. 2005, 'Ongoing debate about forestry and reindeer husbandry in Upper Lapland in Finland', *PEFC Newsletter*, 25. Viewed 1 July 2015, http://pefc.org/index.php?option=com_sumointeractivecontent& view=itemdetail&id=563.

Kanowski, P. J., McDermott, C. L. and Cashore, B. W. 2011, 'Implementing REDD+: lessons from analysis of forest governance', *Environmental Science and Policy*, **14** (2) 111–17.

Karani, P. and Gantsho, M. 2007, 'The role of Development Finance Institutions (DFIs) in promoting the Clean Development Mechanism (CDM) in Africa', *Environment, Development and Sustainability*, **9** (3) 203–28.

Kazi, W. B. and Sarker, T. 2012, 'Fiscal sustainability and the natural resource curse in resource-rich african countries: A case study of Uganda', *Bulletin for International Taxation*, **66** (8) 1–12.

Keck, M. E. and Sikkink, K. 1998, *Activists beyond borders: Advocacy networks in international politics*, New York: Cornell University Press.

Kersbergen, K. v. and Waarden, F. v. 2004, '"Governance" as a bridge between disciplines: Cross-disciplinary inspiration regarding shifts in governance and problems of governability, accountability and legitimacy', *European Journal of Political Research*, **43** (2) 143–71.

Kesperowicz, P. 2012, 'GOP plans vote to ease Lacey Act rules which led to raid on Gibson Guitar', *The Hill*. Viewed 10 May 2015, http://the hill.com/blogs/floor-action/house/238107-gop-plans-vote-to-ease-lacey-act-rules-on-imported-wood.

Khan, M. A. 2010, 'Timber mafia made floods worse', *Al Jazeera*. Viewed 24 April 2015, http://www.aljazeera.com/focus/floodofmisery/ 2010/08/201081614111704604.html.

Kölliker, A. 2006, *Conclusion 1: Governance and public goods theory*, Basingstoke, London: Palgrave Macmillan.

Kooiman, J. 1993, *Findings, speculations and recommendations in modern governance: New government society interactions*, London: Sage.

Kosoy, N. and Corbera, E. 2010, 'Payments for ecosystem services as commodity fetishism', *Ecological Economics*, **69** (6) 1228–36.

Koyuncu, C. and Yilmaz, R. 2009, 'The impact of corruption on deforestation: A cross-country evidence', *The Journal of Developing Areas*, **42** (2).

Kuehls, T. 1996, *Beyond Sovereign Territory: The Space of Ecopolitics*, Minneapolis, MN: University of Minnesota Press.

La Vina, A. G. M., Labre, L., Ang, L. and de Leon, A. 2014, 'The Road to Doha: The future of REDD-Plus, agriculture, and land-use change in the UNFCCC', Philippines: Foundation for International Environmental Law and Development.

Lammerts van Beuren, E. M. and Blom, E. M. 1997, *Hierarchical framework for the formulation of sustainable forest management standards*, Leiden: The Tropenbos Foundation.

Landell-Mills, N. and Porras, I. 2002, *Silver bullet or fools' gold: Developing markets for forest environmental services and the poor*, London, UK: IIED.

Lang, C. 2010, 'World Bank's FCPF in Indonesia fails to address civil society concern'. Viewed 21 April 2013, http://www.redd-monitor.org/2010/05/25/world-banks-fcpf-in-indonesia-fails-to-address-civil-society-concerns/.

Lang, C. 2013, 'COONAPIP, Panama's Indigenous Peoples Coordinating Body, withdraws from UN-REDD'. Viewed 18 March 2013, http://www.redd-monitor.org/2013/03/06/coonapip-panamas-indigenous-peoples-coordinating-body-withdraws-from-un-redd/.

Lawson, S. and MacFaul, L. 2010, *Illegal Logging and Related Trade. Indicators of the Global Response*, London: Chatham House.

Lecocq, F. and Ambrosi, P. 2007, 'The clean development mechanism: History, status, and prospects', *Review of Environmental Economics and Policy*, **1** (1) 134–51.

Lesniewska, F. and McDermott, C. L. 2014, 'FLEGT VPAs: Laying a pathway to sustainability via legality lessons from Ghana and Indonesia', *Forest Policy and Economics*. Viewed 24 April 2015, http://www.sciencedirect.com/science/article/pii/S1389934114000185.

Liimatainen, M. and Harkki, S. 2001, *Anything goes? Report on PEFC certified forestry*, Helsinki: Greenpeace Nordic and the Finnish Nature League.

Lohmann, L. (ed.) 2003, *Certifying the uncertifiable: FSC certification of tree plantations in Thailand and Brazil*, Montevideo and Moreton-in-Marsh: World Rainforest Movement.

Lovell, H. C. 2010, 'Governing the carbon offset market', *Wiley Interdisciplinary Reviews: Climate Change*, **1** (3) 353–62.

Lubis, A. M. 2013, 'APEC agrees to isolate the US, Australia over forestry trade bans', *Jakarta Post*. Viewed 10 May 2015, http://www.

thejakartapost.com/news/2013/08/19/apec-agrees-isolate-us-australia-over-forestry-trade-bans.html.

MacDonald, K. I. and Corson, C. 2012, '"TEEB begins now": A virtual moment in the production of natural capital', *Development and Change*, **43** (1) 159–84.

Mackendrick, N. A. 2005, 'The role of the state in voluntary environmental reform: A case study of public land', *Policy Sciences*, **38** (1) 21–44.

Mann, M. L., Kaufmann, R. K., Bauer, D. M., Gopal, S., Baldwin, J. G. and Del Carmen Vera-Diaz, M. 2012, 'Ecosystem service value and agricultural conversion in the Amazon: implications for policy intervention', *Environmental and Resource Economics*, **53** (2) 279–95.

Mantyranta, H. 2002, *Forest certification – an ideal that became an absolute, translation by Heli Mantyranta*, Helsinki: Metsalehti Kustannus.

Marais, G. 2011, 'Letter from SGS to PEFC International regarding results of investigation into APP'. Viewed 30 April 2015, www.pefc.org/news-a-media/general-sfm-news/1166.

Maraseni, T. (ed.) 2013, *Evaluating the Clean Development Mechanism*, Basingstoke, London: Palgrave Macmillan.

Martin, C. 2013, 'Protecting climate finance: An anti-corruption assessment of the UN-REDD programme'. Berlin: Transparency International, viewed 10 April 2015, http://files.transparency.org/content/download/723/3100/file/2013_ProtectingClimateFinance_UNREDD_EN.pdf.

Martin, C. and Elges, E. 2013, 'Protecting climate finance: an anti-corruption assessment of the Forest Carbon Partnership Facility'. Berlin: Transparency International, viewed 10 April 2015, http://files.transparency.org/content/download/1442/10766/file/2013_ProtectingClimateFinance_FCPF_EN.pdf.

Mason, C. 2012, 'PNG investigator claims Australia "Cayman Islands" of Pacific money-laundering', *Pacific Scoop*. Viewed 12 April 2015, http://pacific.scoop.co.nz/2012/11/png-investigator-claims-Australia-cayman-is-of-pacific-money-laundering/print/.

Matulis, B. S. 2014, 'The economic valuation of nature: A question of justice?' *Ecological Economics*, **104** 155–7.

McAfee, K. 2012, 'The contradictory logic of global ecosystem services markets', *Development and Change*, **43** (1) 105–31.

McElwee, P. 2004, *You say illegal, I say legal: The relationship between 'illegal' logging and land tenure, poverty, and forest use rights in Vietnam*, Binghamton, NY: Haworth Press.

McIntyre, M., DeSantis, A. and Quealy, K. 2011, 'A hidden lobby for Indonesian paper', *The New York Times.* Viewed 8 May 2015, http://www.nytimes.com/interactive/2011/03/29/us/liberty-graphic.html?_r=0.

McKenney, B. A. and Kiesecker, J. M. 2010, 'Policy Development for Biodiversity Offsets: A Review of Offset Frameworks', *Environmental Management*, **45** (1) 165–76.

MCPFE 1998, 'Sustainable forest management in Europe, special report on the follow-up on the implementation of resolutions H1 and H2 of the Helsinki ministerial conference', in Liaison Unit in Lisbon (ed.) *Follow-up Reports on the Ministerial Conferences on the Protection of Forests in Europe*, Lisbon: Ministry of Agriculture, Rural Development and Fisheries of Portugal.

Michaelowa, A. and Michaelowa, K. 2011, 'Climate business for poverty reduction? The role of the World Bank', The Review of International Organizations, **6** (3–4), 259–86.

Millennium Ecosystem Assessment 2005, *Ecosystems and human well-being: Synthesis*, Washington, DC: Island Press.

Miller, D. C., Agrawal, A. and Roberts, J. T. 2013, 'Biodiversity, governance, and the allocation of international aid for conservation', *Conservation Letters*, **6** (1) 12–20.

Milliken, R. 2013, 'Hug those trees', *Anne Summers Reports.* Viewed 4 May 2015, http://annesummers.com.au/wp-content/uploads/2014/11/hugthosetrees.pdf.

Minichiello, V., Aroni, R., Timewell, E. and Alexander, L. 1995, *In-depth interviewing: Principles, techniques, analysis*, Sydney: Addison Wesley Longman.

Miteva, D. A. and Pattanayak, S. K. 2012, 'Evaluation of biodiversity policy instruments: what works and what doesn't?' *Oxford Review of Economic Policy*, **28** (1) 69–92.

Mohammadi, A., Abbaspour, M., Soltanieh, M., Atabi, F. and Rahmatian, M. 2013, 'Post-2012 CDM multi-criteria analysis of industries in six Asian countries: Iranian case study', *Climate Policy*, **13** (2) 210–39.

Multipartner Trust Fund Office (MTFO) 2013, 'UN-REDD Programme Fund', *Trust Fund Factsheet.* Viewed 20 February 2013, http://mptf.undp.org/factsheet/fund/CCF00.

Muradian, R., Corbera, E., Pascual, U., Kosoy, N. and May, P. H. 2010, 'Reconciling theory and practice: An alternative conceptual framework for understanding payments for environmental services', *Ecological Economics*, **69** (6) 1202–8.

Narayanasamy, S. 2014, 'Banking on shaky ground: Australia's big four banks and land grabs', OXFAM Australia. Viewed 26 April 2015, www.oxfam.org.au.

Nellemann, C. and Interpol Environmental Crime Programme (eds) 2012, 'Green carbon, black trade', *United Nations Environment Programme*, Arendal: CRID. Viewed 6 May 2015, www.grida.no.

Neuman, W. and Zarate, A. 2013, 'Corruption in Peru aids cutting of rain forest', *The New York Times*. Viewed 8 May 2015, http://www.nytimes.com/2013/10/19/world/americas/corrruption-in-peru-aids-cutting-of-rain forest.html?r=0.

Newell, P. 2009, 'Varieties of CDM governance: some reflections', *The Journal of Environment and Development*, **18** (4) 425–35.

Nilsson, C., Reidy, C. A., Dynesius, M. and Revenga, C. 2005, 'Fragmentation and flow regulation of the world's large river systems', *Science*, **308** (5720) 405–8.

Ochieng, R. M., Visseren-Hamakers, I. J. and Nketiah, K. S. 2013, 'Interaction between the FLEGT-VPA and REDD+ in Ghana: Recommendations for interaction management', *Forest Policy and Economics*, **32** 32–9.

Office of the Secretary 2014, *U.S.– China joint announcement on climate change*, Washington DC: Whitehouse. Viewed 16 May 2015, https://www.whitehouse.gov/the-press-office/2014/11/11/us-china-joint-announce ment-climate-change.

Okereke, C. 2010, 'Climate justice and the international regime', *Wiley Interdisciplinary Reviews: Climate Change*, **1** (3) 462–74.

Olsen, T. 2004, 'PEFC certification Denmark', *PEFC News*, **23** 5.

Orr, C. 2001, 'Dams and development: A new framework for decision-making', *The report of the World Commission on Dams 2000*. London: Earthscan.

Overdevest, C. 2004, 'Codes of conduct and standard setting in the forest sector constructing markets for democracy?' *Relations Industrielles/Industrial Relations*, **59** (1) 172–97.

Overdevest, C. and Zeitlin, J. 2014a, 'Assembling an experimentalist regime: Transnational governance interactions in the forest sector', *Regulation and Governance*, **8** (1) 22–48.

Overdevest, C. and Zeitlin, J. 2014b, 'Constructing a transnational timber legality assurance regime: Architecture, accomplishments, challenges', *Forest Policy and Economics*, **48** 6–15.

Overton, J. M., Stephens, R. T. T. and Ferrier, S. 2013, 'Net present biodiversity value and the design of biodiversity offsets', *Ambio*, **42** (1) 100–10.

Oxley, A. 2013, 'A contender for Australia's worst law', *Quadrant*. Viewed 6 May 2015, https://quadrant.org.au/magazine/2013/10/contender-worst-law-australia/.

Ozinga, S. 2001, 'Behind the logo: An environmental and social assessment of forest certification schemes'. Moreton-in-Marsh: FERN.

Ozinga, S. 2004, *Footprints in the forest: Current practice and future challenges in forest certification*, Moreton-in-Marsh: FERN.

Ozinga, S. and Gerard, N. 2005, *Strategies to prevent illegal logging*, Cornwall: MPG Books.

Pachauri, R. 2014, 'Chairperson of the intergovernmental panel on climate change, presentation to the sixth international forum for sustainable Asia and the Pacific (ISAP)', Yokohama: ISAP, 23 July.

Pagiola, S. 2008, 'Can payments for environmental services help protect coastal and marine areas?' Viewed 12 May 2015, http://siteresources. worldbank.org/INTENVMAT/Resources/3011340-1238620444756/598 0735-1238620476358/8CanPayments.pdf.

Pagiola, S., Arcenas, A. and Platais, G. 2005a, 'Can payment for environmental services help reduce poverty?', *World Development*, **33** (2) 237–53.

Pagiola, S., Arcenas, A. and Platais, G. 2005b, 'Can payments for environmental services help reduce poverty? An exploration of the issues and the evidence to date from Latin America', *World Development*, **33** (2) 237–53.

Pagiola, S., Bishop, J. and Landell-Mills, N. 2002, *Selling forest environmental services: Market-based mechanisms for conservation and development*, Sterling, VA: Earthscan.

Panayotou, T. 2013, *Instruments of change: Motivating and financing sustainable development*, London: Routledge.

Paolini, A. J., Jarvis, A. P. and Reus-Smit, C. 1998, *Between sovereignty and global governance: The United Nations, the state and civil society*, Basingstoke, London: Macmillan.

Parks, B. C. and Roberts, J. T. 2008, 'Inequality and the global climate regime: breaking the north-south impasse', *Cambridge Review of International Affairs*, **21** (4) 621–48.

Parto, S. 1999, *Aiming low*, Peterborough: Broadview Press.

Paterson, M. and Stripple, J. (eds) 2007, *Singing climate change into existence: On the territorialization of climate policymaking*, Aldershot and Burlington: Ashgate.

Pattberg, P. H. 2005, 'The Forest Stewardship Council: Risk and potential of private forest governance', *Journal of Environment and Development*, **14** (3) 356–74.

Pearce, D. (ed.) 1991, *New environmental policies: The recent experience of OECD countries and its relevance to developing countries*.

PEFC 2003, 'Summary of presentation by Mr Pekka Patosaari, UNFF coordinator and head of secretariat', *PEFC News*, 17.

PEFC 2007a, *About PEFC*. Viewed 14 June 2007, http://www.pefc.org/ internet/html/about_PEFC/4_1137_498.htm.

PEFC 2007b, *A short history*. Viewed 14 June 2007, http://www.pefc.org/internet/html/about_PEFC/4_1137_498.htm.

PEFC and FSC 2010, *Joint statement by the Forest Stewardship Council (FSC) and the Programme for the Endorsement of Forest Certification (PEFC) recommending ISO members to vote against the new work item proposal chain of custody of forest based products – requirements.* Viewed 8 May 2015, http://www.pefc.org/images/documents/external/Joint_Statement_FSC_PEFC_July_8_2013.pdf.

PEFC Council 2014, *Chain of custody of forest-based products – Guidance for use*, Geneva, Switzerland: PEFC Council. Viewed 28 April 2015, http://pefc.org/images/documents/guides/PEFC_GD_2001-2014_Guidance_for_use_of_Chain_of_Custody_2014-06-23.pdf.

PEFC Council 2015, 'Chain of custody of forest-based products – Social requirements: Guidance for use (Enquiry draft)', *PEFC Guides*, Geneva: PEFC. Viewed 8 May 2015, http://www.pefc.org/news-a-media/general-sfm-news/1832-public-consultation-on-guidance-on-social-requirements-in-chain-of-custody-certification.

PEFC News 2003, 'Alteration to the PEFC name', **17** 4.

PEFC News 2005, 'EU parliament regards PEFC and FSC as equally suitable', **30** 1.

PEFC News 2006a, 'Belgian public procurement policy includes PEFC', **31** 2.

PEFC News 2006b, 'Key note speech by Peter Seligmann from Conservation International', **34** 2.

PEFC News 2006c, 'PEFC – World's largest resource of certified wood', *PEFC Newsletter* 29. Viewed 1 July 2015, http://pefc.org/index.php?option=com_sumointeractivecontent&view=itemdetail&id=559.

PEFC News 2007a, 'Assessment of forest certification systems', *PEFC Newsletter* 37. Viewed 1 July 2015, http://pefc.org/index.php?option=com_sumointeractivecontent&view=itemdetail&id=551.

PEFC News 2007b, 'PEFC Council global statistics', **37** 3.

PEFC News 2007c, 'PEFC: Only European? Based on merely a handful of criteria? Not for indigenous people? No social dialogue …?' **37** 2.

PEFC News 2009, *Who gains from FSC's latest effort to undermine other forest certification systems?* Viewed 17 April 2015, http://www.pefc.org/news-a-media/general-sfm-news/617-who-gains-from-fsc.

PEFC News 2010a, *Indigenous peoples representative joins PEFC board of directors*. Viewed 21 April 2015, http://www.pefc.org/news-a-media/general-sfm-news/659-pefc-adds-three-new-board-members.

PEFC News 2010b, *Pressure mounts for USGBC to accept multiple forest certification programmes*. Viewed 20 April 2015, http://www.pefc.org/news-a-media/general-sfm-news/589-pressure-mounts-for-usgbc-to-accept-multiple-forest-certification-programmes.

PEFC News 2011, *Developing country representative elected as vice chair to PEFC board of directors*. Viewed 27 April 2015, http://www.pefc.org/news-a-media/general-sfm-news/662-developing-country-representative-elected-as-vice-chair-to-pefc-board-of-directors.

PEFC News 2012, *USGBC LEED: A never-ending story?* Viewed 27 April 2015, http://www.pefc.org/news-a-media/general-sfm-news/1085-usgbc-leed-a-never-ending-story.

PEFC News 2013, 'Indigenous Leader Joins PEFC Board of Directors'. Viewed 27 April 2015, http://www.pefc.org/news-a-media/general-sfm-news/1165-indigenous-leader-joins-pefc-board-of-directors.

PEFCC News Special 2002, 'Continuing globalisation of the PEFC council', 2.

PEFCC Newsletter 2001, 'Statistics on main forest certification schemes', *PEFCC Newsletter*, **7** 1.

PEFCC Newsletter 2002, 'PEFC chairman to visit Gabon to discuss feasibility of pan African forest certification system', December, 3.

PEFCC Newsletter 2003, 'Globalisation', *PEFCC Newsletter*, **14** 1.

Peluso, N. 2012, 'What's nature got to do with it? A situated historical perspective on socio-natural commodities', *Development Change*, **43** (1) 79–104.

Person, B. 2002, 'The Plantar CDM project: Why it must be rejected by the CDM Board and PCF investors'. Viewed 20 April 2015, https://web.archive.org/web/20030128020205/http://www.cdmwatch.org/plantar.html.

Pilgrim, J. D. and Bennun, L. 2014, 'Will biodiversity offsets save or sink protected areas?' *Conservation Letters*, **7** (5) 423–4.

Pirard, R. 2011, 'Luca Tacconi, Sango Mahanty and Helen Suich (eds): Payments for environmental services, forest conservation and climate change: livelihoods in the REDD?' *International Environmental Agreements: Politics, Law and Economics*, **11** (4) 381.

Pittock, J. 2010, 'A pale reflection of political reality: Integration of global climate, wetland, and biodiversity agreements', *Climate Law*, **1** (3) 343–73.

Pittock, J. 2011, 'National climate change policies and sustainable water management: conflicts and synergies', *Ecology and Society*, **13** (2) 25.

Pittock, J. 2013, Climate change and sustainable water management, in Cadman, T. (ed.) *Climate Change and Global Policy Regimes: Towards Institutional Legitimacy*, London: Palgrave Macmillan.

PNGFIA 2011, *Harming PNG: Australia's illegal logging prohibition bill*, Papua New Guinea: Papua New Guinea Forest Industries Association, viewed 27 April 2015, www.fiapng.com.

Pottinger, L. 2008, 'Bad deal for the planet: Why carbon offsets aren't working. And how to create a fair global climate accord'. Viewed 14

May 2015, http://www.internationalrivers.org/resources/bad-deal-for-the-planet-why-carbon-offsets-aren-t-working-and-how-to-create-a-fair-global.

Poynton, S. 2013, 'Chain of custody nonsense from FSC & PEFC: Protecting income streams rather than the world's forests'. Viewed 23 November 2013, http://news.mongabay.com/2013/0710-poynton-fsc-pefc-coc-commentary.html-LyGruZuAyDl91J3g.99.

Quigley, J. T. and Harper, D. J. 2006, 'Compliance with Canada's Fisheries Act: A field audit of habitat compensation projects', *Environmental Management*, **37** (3) 334–50.

Quintero, J. D. and Mathur, A. 2011, 'Biodiversity offsets and infrastructure', *Conservation Biology*, **25** (6) 1121–3.

Raines, S. S. 2006, 'Judicious incentives: International public policy responses to the globalization of environmental management', *Review of Policy Research*, **23** (2) 473–90.

REDD Monitor 2008, *The World Bank forest carbon partnership facility: REDDy or not, here it comes!* Viewed 23 March 2013, http://www.redd-monitor.org/2008/11/10/the-world-bank-forest-carbon-partnership-facility-reddy-or-not-here-it-comes/.

Resanond, A., Jittsanguan, T. and Sriphraram, D. 2011, 'Company's Competitiveness Enhancement for Thai Agribusiness through the Clean Development Mechanism (CDM) under the Kyoto Protocol', *Journal of Sustainable Development*, **4** (2) 80.

Rey, D. and Swan, S. 2014, *A Country-Led Safeguards Approach: Guidelines for National REDD+ Programmes*. Ho Chi Minh City, Vietnam: The Netherlands Development Organisation, REDD+ Programme.

Richards, M. and Swan, S. 2014, *Participatory Subnational Planning for REDD+ and other Land Use Programmes: Methodology and Step-by-Step Guidance*, Ho Chi Minh City, Vietnam: SNV Netherlands Development Organisation, REDD+ Programme.

Rickenbach, M. and Overdevest, C. 2006, 'More than markets: Assessing Forest Stewardship Council (FSC) Certification as a policy tool', *Journal of Forestry*, **104** (3) 143.

Riddell, R. C. 2007, *Does foreign aid really work?* Oxford: Oxford University Press.

Ritchie, J. and Lewis, J. 2003, *Qualitative research practice*, London: Sage Publications.

Robertson, M. 2006, 'The nature that capital can see: Science, state, and market in the commodification of ecosystem services', *Environment and Planning D: Society and Space*, **24** (3) 367–87.

Romeijn, P. and Wageningen, L. 1999, *Green Gold: On Variations of Truth in Plantation Forestry*, Hedsum, Netherlands: Treemail Publishers.

Royal Forest and Bird Protection Society (RFBPS), Greenpeace NZ, World Wide Fund For Nature NZ, Environment and Conservation Organisations of NZ, Native Forest Action, F. o. t. E. N., Native Forest Network – Southern Hemisphere & Federated Mountain Clubs of NZ 2001, 'Letter to FSC accredited forest management certifiers'.

Rubin, J. 2012, *The End of Growth*, Toronto, Canada: Random House.

Ruggiero, V. and South, N. 2013, 'Green criminology and crimes of the economy: Theory, research and praxis', *Critical Criminology*, **21** 359–73.

Sachs, J. 2015, *The age of sustainable development*, New York: Columbia University Press.

Sample, V. A., Price, W. and Mater, C. M. 2003, 'Certification on public and university lands: Evaluations of FSC and SFI by the forest managers', *Journal of Forestry*, **101** (8) 21.

Sarker, T. 2013, 'Taxing for the future: an intergenerational perspective', *The Asian Century, Sustainable Growth and Climate Change*, Cheltenham: Edward Elgar, 85.

Scharpf, F. W. 1997, *Games real actors play: Actor-centered institutionalism in policy research*, Boulder, CO: Westview Press.

Scheyvens, H. and López-Casero, F. 2010, 'Enhancing customs collaboration to combat the trade in illegal timber', *Policy Report*, Kanagawa, Japan: IGES.

Schloenhardt, A. 2008, 'The illegal trade in timber and timber products in the Asia-Pacific region', Canberra, ACT: Australian Institute of Criminology. Viewed 20 April 2015, http://aic.gov.au/crime_types/environmental/illegal%20logging.html.

Setiono, B. 2007, *Fighting illegal logging and forest-related financial crimes: The anti-money laundering approach*, Canberra, ACT: Department of International Relations, Australian National University.

Setiono, B. and Husein, Y. 2005, *Fighting forest crime and promoting prudent banking for sustainable forest management: The anti-money laundering approach*. Bogor, Indonesia: Centre for International Forestry Research.

Shrestha, R. M. and Timilsina, G. R. 2002, 'The additionality criterion for identifying clean development mechanism projects under the Kyoto Protocol', *Energy Policy*, **30** (1) 73–9.

SinksWatch 2003, *Background information: Plantar project*. Viewed 15 May 2015, http://www.sinkswatch.org/node/4554.

Sirohi, S. 2007, 'CDM: Is it a "win–win" strategy for rural poverty alleviation in India?' *Climatic Change*, **84** (1) 91–110.

Smismans, S. 2004, *Law, legitimacy, and European governance: Functional participation in social regulation*, Oxford: Oxford University Press.

Somorin, O. A., Smit, B., Brown, H. C. P., Sonwa, D. J. and Nkem, J. 2011, 'Institutional perceptions of opportunities and challenges of REDD+ in the Congo Basin', *The Journal of Environment and Development*, **20** (4) 381–404.

Statista n.d., 'Global assets under management from 2007 to 2013, by region (in trillion U.S. dollars)'. Viewed 16 May 2015, http://www.statista.com/statistics/264907/asset-under-management-worldwide-by-region/.

Stavins, R. N. 1988, *Project 88: Harnessing market forces to protect our environment*, sponsored by Senator Timothy E. Wirth, Colorado, and Senator John Heinz, Pennsylvania, Washington, DC: Environmental Policy Institute.

Stiglitz, J. E. 2003, 'Globalization and development', in Held, D. and Koenig-Archibugi, M. (eds) *Taming globalisation: Frontiers of governance*, Cambridge: Polity Press.

Stirling, R. 2005, 'Rival groups slam PEFC endorsement (Programme for the Endorsement of Forest Certification Schemes)', *Contract Journal*, **429** (6530) 13.

Strauss, S. H., Campbell, M. M., Pryor, S. N., Coventry, P. and Burley, J. 2001, 'Plantation certification and genetic engineering: FSC's ban on research is counterproductive', *Journal of Forestry*, **99** (12) 4.

Stringer, C. 2006, 'Forest certification and changing global commodity chains', *Journal of Economic Geography*, **6** (5) 701–22.

Suiseeya, K. R. M. 2014, 'Negotiating the Nagoya protocol: Indigenous demands for justice', *Global Environmental Politics*, **14** (3) 102–24.

Susskind, L. 1994, *Environmental diplomacy: Negotiating more effective global agreements*, New York, Oxford: Oxford University Press.

Tacconi, L. 2007, *Illegal logging: Law enforcement, livelihoods and the timber trade*, Sterling: Earthscan.

Tacconi, L., Mahanty, S. and Suich, H. 2010, *Payments for environmental services, forest conservation and climate change: Livelihoods in the REDD*, Cheltenham, UK: Edward Elgar Publishing.

Tait, A. 2010, 'Letter from Greenpeace to PEFC International regarding APP controversy'. Viewed 30 April 2015, http://www.pefc.org/news-a-media/general-sfm-news/672.

Tanwar, N. 2007, 'Clean development mechanism and off-grid small-scale hydropower projects: Evaluation of additionality', *Energy Policy*, **35** (1) 714–21.

Tas, A. and Rodrigues, J. 2009, *Under the cover of forest certification*, Sweden: Greenpeace Nordic.

Taylor, P. L. 2005, 'In the market but not of it: fair trade coffee and Forest Stewardship Council certification as market-based social change', *World Development*, **33** (1) 129–47.

TEEB 2010, *The economics of ecosystems and biodiversity: Ecological and economic foundations*, London: Earthscan.

Teegelbekkers, D. 2001a, 'ENGOs invited to witness the auditing process in Germany', *PEFCC Newsletter*, **7** 5–6.

Teegelbekkers, D. 2001b, 'Germany – Over 5 million hectares already certified', *PEFCC Newsletter*, **9** 5.

Teegelbekkers, D. 2003a, 'Chain-of-Custody certificates increasing in Germany', *PEFCC Newsletter*, **14** 6.

Teegelbekkers, D. 2003b, 'Germany: Chain-of-Custody', *PEFC News*, **16** 5.

The Forest Peoples Programme (FPP) 2008, *The Forest Carbon Partnership Facility: Facilitating the weakening of indigenous peoples' rights to lands and resources*. Viewed 1 April 2013, http://www.forest peoples.org/sites/fpp/files/publication/2010/08/fcpffppbriefingfeb08eng.pdf.

The Guardian n.d., 'Lost in a Forest of Acronyms', *Environment Blog* (online). Viewed 21 May 2010, http://www.guardian.co.uk/environment/blog/2009/oct/08/bangkok-climate-change-talks.

The World Bank 2011, 'Uganda country brief', Washington: World Bank.

Thinnes, M. 2006, 'ENGOs join PEFC', *PEFC News*, **33** 4.

Thompson, M. C., Baruah, M. and Carr, E. R. 2011, 'Seeing REDD+ as a project of environmental governance', *Environmental Science and Policy*, **14** (2) 100–10.

Tollefson, C., Gale, F. and Haley, D. 2008, *Setting the standard: Certification, governance and the forest stewardship council*, Vancouver: UBC Press.

Torvanger, A., Shrivastava, M. K., Pandey, N. and Tornblad, S. H. 2013, 'A two-track CDM: improved incentives for sustainable development and offset production', *Climate Policy*, **13** (4) 471–89.

UN 1987, *Report of the World Commission on Environment and Development: Our common future*, New York: United Nations Publications Department of Public Information. Viewed 15 July 2015, http://www.un-documents.net/wced-ocf.htm.

UN 1993, *Agenda 21: Programme of action for sustainable development, Rio declaration on environment and development, statement of forest principles*, New York: United Nations Publications Department of Public Information.

UN 2006, *Delivering as one*. Viewed 4 March 2013, http://www.undg.org/docs/6879/coh_10_waysE.pdf.

UN 2007, *UN Resolution 62/98, establishing the Non-Legally binding instrument on all types of forests*. http://daccess-dds-ny.un.org/doc/ UNDOC/GEN/N07/469/65/PDF/N0746965.pdf?OpenElement.

UNECE 2012, *Forest products: annual market review 2011–2012*. Viewed 16 May 2015, http://www.unece.org/fileadmin/DAM/timber/ publications/FPAMR_2012.pdf.

UNEP 2008, 'Payments for Ecosystem Services: Getting Started. A Primer'. Viewed 10 July 2015, http://www.unep.org/pdf/Payments ForEcosystemServices_en.pdf.

UNEP 2014, 'Forests in a Changing Climate: A Sourcebook for Integrating REDD+ into Academic Programmes'. Nairobi, Kenya. Viewed 15 July 2015, http://www.unep.org/Training/docs/Forest_in_a_Changing_ Climate.pdf.

UNFCCC 1992, *United Nations framework on climate change*. Viewed 25 January 2015, https://unfccc.int/files/essential_background/ background_publications_htmlpdf/application/pdf/conveng.pdf.

UNFCCC 2011, *Report of the conference of the parties on its sixteenth session, held in Cancun from 29 November to 10 December 2010. Addendum part two: Action taken by the conference of the parties at its sixteenth session*. Viewed 18 February 2013, http://unfccc.int/resource/ docs/2010/cop16/eng/07a01.pdf.

UNFCCC 2012a, *News release: Kyoto protocol's clean development mechanism reaches milestone*. Viewed 9 April 2015, http://unfccc.int/ files/press/press_releases_advisories/application/pdf/pr20121304_cdm_ 4000.pdf.

UNFCCC 2012b, *Report of the Conference of the Parties on its Seventeenth Session, held in Durban from 28 November to 11 December 2011. Addendum. Part two: Action taken by the Conference of the Parties at its Seventeenth Session*. Viewed 23 January 2015, http:// unfccc.int/resource/docs/2011/cop17/eng/09a01.pdf#page=2.

UNFCCC 2014a, *New market-based mechanism*. Viewed 28 December 2014, http://unfccc.int/cooperation_support/market_and_non-market_ mechanisms/items/7710.php.

UNFCCC 2014b, *Status of the Doha amendment*. Viewed 15 May 2015, http://unfccc.int/kyoto_protocol/doha_amendment/items/7362.php.

United Nations Development Group Viet Nam, n.d., *Joint programmes*. Viewed 3 July 2015, http://www.un.org.vn/en/what-we-do-mainmenu-203/joint-programmes-a-teams-mainmenu-208.html.

UNODC 2010, *The globalisation of crime, a transnational organized crime threat assessment*. Viewed 5 March 2015, http://www.unodc.org/ unodc/en/data-and-analysis/tocta-2010.html.

UN-REDD 2009, *Report of the Third Policy Board Meeting Washington D.C., U.S.* Viewed 18 February 2013, http://www.unredd.net/index.php?option=com_docman&task=doc_details&gid=1234&Itemid=53.

UN-REDD 2011a, 'REDD+ participatory governance assessments piloted in Indonesia and Nigeria', *UN-REDD Newsletter*. Viewed 28 April 2015, http://www.un-redd.org/Newsletter20/ParticipatoryGovernance Assessments/tabid/54365/Default.aspx.

UN-REDD 2011b, *The UN-REDD programme strategy 2011–2015*. Viewed 20 February 2013, http://mptf.undp.org/document/download/5623.

UN-REDD 2012, *Programme handbook for national programmes and other national-level activities*. Viewed 4 March 2013, http://www.unredd.net/index.php?option=com_docman&task=doc_download&gid=8148&Itemid=53.

UN-REDD 2013, *Guidelines on free, prior and informed consent*. Viewed 18 March 2013, http://www.unredd.net/index.php?option=com_docman&task=doc_download&gid=8717&Itemid=53.

UN-REDD n.d., 'Putting REDD+ safeguards and safeguard information systems into practice', *Policy Brief #3*. Viewed 20 March 2013, http://www.unredd.net/index.php?option=com_docman&task=doc_view&gid=9167&tmpl=component&format=raw&Itemid=53.

USAID 2013, *Emerging compliance markets for REDD+: An assessment of supply and demand*, San Francisco, CA: USAID.

Vatn, A. 2000, 'The environment as a commodity', *Environmental Values*, **9** 493–509.

Victor, D. G. and Keohane, R. O., 2010, *The Regime Complex for Climate Change*, Cambridge, MA: The Harvard Project on International Climate Agreements.

Villarroya, A., Barros, A. C. and Kiesecker, J. 2014, 'Policy development for environmental licensing and biodiversity offsets in Latin America', PLOS. Viewed 18 May 2015, http://journals.plos.org/plosone/article?id=10.1371/journal.pone.0107144.

Voldovici, V. and Lauder, D. 2014, 'Republicans vow EPA fight as Obama touts China climate deal'. Viewed 16 May 2015, http://www.reuters.com/article/2014/11/12/us-china-usa-climatechange-mcconnell-idUSKCN0IW1TZ20141112.

Watson, A. 2006, *The proposed New Zealand approach towards addressing illegal logging and associated trade activities*, Ministry of Agriculture and Forestry Wellington. Viewed 2 April 2015, http://maxa.maf.govt.nz/forestry/illegal-logging/illegal-logging-discussion-paper/index.htm.

Wettestad, J. 2001, 'Designing effective environmental regimes: The conditional keys', *Global Governance*, **7** (3) 317–41.

Wilson, C. 2014, 'Illegal logging wreaking havoc on impoverished rural communities', *Inter Press Service News Agency*. Viewed 10 April 2015, http://www.ipsnews.net/2014/12/illegal-loggin-wreaking-havoc-on-impoverished-rural-communities/.

Wold, C. 1998, 'The futility, utility, and future of the biodiversity convention', *Colorado Journal of International Environmental Law and Policy*, **9** (1) 1–42.

Woods, K. and Canby, K. 2011, 'Baseline study 4, Myanmar: Overview of forest law enforcement, governance and trade', EU FLEGT. Viewed 10 July 2015, http://www.forest-trends.org/documents/files/doc_3159.pdf.

World Bank 2015, *Prototype carbon fund*. Viewed 20 April 2015, http://wbcarbonfinance.org/PCF.

World Commission on Dams 2002, *The report of the World Commission on Dams (WCD) and its relevance to the Ramsar Convention*. WCD, viewed 14 May 2015, http://archive.ramsar.org/pdf/res/key_res_viii_02_e.pdf.

World Rainforest Movement (WRM) 2010, *Brazil: Once again opposing Plantar's CDM project'*. Viewed 20 April 2015, http://www.wrm.org.uy/oldsite/bulletin/151/Brazil.html.

Wunder, S. 2005, 'Payments for environmental services: Some nuts and bolts. CIFOR Occasional Paper'. Bogor, Indonesia: CIFOR. Viewed 15 May 2015, http://www.cifor.org/publications/pdf_files/OccPapers/OP-42.pdf.

WWF 2006, 'Payments for Environmental Services – An Equitable Approach for Reducing Poverty and Conserving Nature', Gland, Switzerland: WWF. Viewed November 2008, http://assets.panda.org/downloads/pes_report_2006.pdf.

WWF 2015a, *Deforestation*. Viewed 18 April 2015, http://wwf.panda.org/about_our_earth/about_forests/deforestation/forest_illegal_logging.

WWF 2015b, *Review of the European Union Timber Regulation*. Viewed 30 April 2015, http://assets.wwf.org.uk/downloads/eutr_briefing_march_2015.pdf.

Young, O. R. (ed.) 1999, *Hitting the mark: Why are some environmental agreements more effective than others? Environment* **20** 189–91.

Young, O. R. 2010, *Institutional dynamics: Emergent patterns in international environmental governance*, Cambridge, MA: MIT Press.

Yrjo-Koskinen, E., Liimatainen, M. and Ruokanen, L. 2004, *Certifying extinction? An assessment of the revised standards of the Finnish forest certification system,* Helsinki: Greenpeace Finland, Finnish Association for Nature Conservation, Finnish Nature League.

Zarin, D., Angelsen, A., Brown, S., Loisel, C., Peskett, L. and Streck, C. 2009, 'Reducing Emissions from Deforestation and Forest Degradation (REDD): An options assessment report'. Meridian Institute, viewed 20 April 2015, http://redd-oar.org/links/REDD-OAR_en.pdf.

Zurn, M. and Koenig-Archibugi, M. 2006, 'Conclusion II: Modes and dynamics of global governance', in Koenig-Archibugi, M. and Zurn, M. (eds) *New Modes of Governance in the International System: Exploring Publicness, Delegation and Inclusion*, Basingstoke, London: Palgrave Macmillan.

References

Index